GOD

Eight Enduring Questions

DISCARDED

Cary Area Public Library
1606 Three Oaks Road
Cary, IL 60013

GOD

Eight Enduring Questions

DISCARDED

C. STEPHEN LAYMAN

University of Notre Dame Press
Notre Dame, Indiana

Cary Area Public Library
1606 Three Oaks Road
Cary, IL 60013

Copyright © 2022 by the University of Notre Dame
Notre Dame, Indiana 46556
undpress.nd.edu
All Rights Reserved

Published in the United States of America

All Scripture quotations are from the *New Revised Standard Version Bible*,
copyright 1989, the Division of Christian Education of the
National Council of Churches of Christ in the United States of America.

Library of Congress Control Number: 2021948506

ISBN: 978-0-268-20205-7 (Hardback)
ISBN: 978-0-268-20206-4 (Paperback)
ISBN: 978-0-268-20207-1 (WebPDF)
ISBN: 978-0-268-20204-0 (Epub)

For Maverick, Kallum, and Bellamy

CONTENTS

This book asks—and offers answers to—a series of enduring questions about God, where "God" is defined (roughly) as the almighty, perfectly good, Creator of the universe:

1. Does God exist?
2. Why does God permit evil?
3. Why think God is good?
4. Why is God hidden?
5. How is God related to ethics?
6. Is divine foreknowledge compatible with human free will?
7. Do humans have souls?
8. Does reincarnation provide the best explanation of suffering?

Among those who are thoughtful about the belief in God, these questions come up again and again. (Obviously, the last two questions aren't *directly* about God, but I think it will become clear that answers to them have important links with *theism*—the belief that God exists.) Of course, the eight questions listed above aren't the only enduring questions about God, but they are among the most important questions for believers and non-believers alike.

The plan of the book is as follows. Chapters 1 and 2 set forth a case—an extended argument—for theism, thus providing one way of answering the question "Does God exist?" Chapter 3 attempts to answer the question "Why does God permit evil?" The presence of evil and suffering in the world have proven to be difficult for theists to explain, and thus the "problem of evil" is generally considered the strongest objection to theism.

Chapter 4 ("Why Think God Is Good?") takes up another challenge to theism, namely, the idea that the postulate of an evil God explains a full range of phenomena (suffering, pleasure, evil, good, beauty, ugliness, an orderly universe, religious experience, etc.) at least as well as theism does. Chapters 5 and 6 discuss yet another important objection to theism, "Why is God hidden?" In other words, if indeed there is a God of love, why doesn't God make his existence known to everyone? (Think, for example, of people brought up in non-theistic religions, both down through the ages and still today.)

Chapter 7 raises the question "How is God related to ethics?" The answer to this question forms a crucial part of any complete theistic worldview. (A worldview is a comprehensive philosophical position, one that provides a fundamental outlook on the world and on human existence.) As we shall see, theists disagree among themselves about God's relation to ethics, and some of the theistic views seem much more plausible than others.

Chapters 8 and 9 take on the classic question "Is divine foreknowledge compatible with human free will?" These chapters underscore the importance of the issue of free will. They also explore four very different answers to the question about God's knowledge of the future. An answer to this question is, once again, a necessary component of any complete theistic worldview.

Chapters 10 and 11 take up the question "Do humans have souls?" This question has taken on new urgency given the advances in neuroscience in recent years. What are the strengths and weaknesses of the main physicalist views of the mind or person, according to which there is no (non-physical) soul? Are there any good reasons to think that humans have (non-physical) souls? Are physicalist views of the mind or person consistent with theism? Here again we have an issue that theists must sort out in order to have a comprehensive worldview.

Finally, chapter 12 considers theism in relation to a view involving reincarnation and the law of karma. Does a worldview involving an impersonal law of karma (together with reincarnation) provide a better explanation of suffering than theism can? If theism were combined with the ideas of karma and reincarnation, would it have a better explanation of evil and suffering? These questions may be seen partly as a challenge to theism but also as an invitation to further develop a theistic worldview.

Nowadays many are quick to downplay the value of rational argument about religious and theological issues. This, I believe, is unfortunate. It is true that rational argument is quite limited in what it can do, either in persuading others or in clearly establishing the truth. Nevertheless, in the contemporary scene multiple worldviews are vying for our attention and our adherence. Any thoughtful person naturally wants to understand what the basic worldview options are and also what their strengths and weaknesses are. Knowing such things helps one navigate the confusing waters of the contemporary world of thought. In addition, rational argument can give us *some* measure of objectivity in our thinking. No human being, I assume, can be entirely free of non-rational influences of various kinds, but it is surely good to strive to have beliefs that hold up well in terms of the available evidence.[1] Furthermore, given that many believers have neither the time nor the inclination to sort through the various worldview options, they are apt to rely on the authority of a religious tradition. This reliance on authority can be legitimate, in my view, if the tradition carries within it adequate evidence or grounds for its teachings. But such a tradition can function well as an authority only if many who are part of it are well acquainted with the evidence or grounds in question.[2]

Two of the most important worldviews are theism (roughly, the belief that God exists and is the Creator of the universe) and naturalism (roughly, the view that there is no God and that reality is a vast physical process). (More precise definitions of these worldviews will be provided in chapter 1; here I'm merely giving the basic idea.) Most of the chapters of this book bring out strengths and weaknesses of theism and naturalism. The last chapter considers theism in relation to an alternative worldview in which reincarnation and karma are the fundamental metaphysical postulates.

Philosophy is inherently a comparative enterprise. Very often, the best objection to one view is the availability of another view that arguably has fewer problems or provides more plausible explanations. That is why the comparison between theism and naturalism (and occasionally other views) comes up again and again in the chapters of this book. I should add that most philosophers would agree that there are few if any problem-free views in philosophy; virtually every view faces significant objections from some quarter. Therefore, in assessing philosophical views, we nearly always find ourselves in the very difficult business of trying to identify the view with the fewest or least severe difficulties.

There are plenty of philosophical works that take up questions about God; why read this one? What sets it apart? At least the following:

a. The chapters of this book will plunge you very quickly into the arguments, pro and con, per question. Preliminary considerations of any sort are kept to a minimum.

b. Every attempt is made to present the arguments clearly and simply, yet *without oversimplifying the issues*. This means, in part, that the discussions go more deeply into the philosophical issues than do most works not written for an audience of professional philosophers.

c. The chapters of this book "factor in" the most important developments in contemporary philosophical debates. These developments often complicate the discussion, but to leave them out is to avoid questions and arguments that must be faced in the interest of intellectual honesty. I believe the reader will find that each chapter of this book is replete with interesting ideas and arguments.

d. This book was written with the conviction that one seldom (if ever) gets "knockdown" arguments on major philosophical issues. Some religious thinkers claim or suggest that the evidence clearly and overwhelmingly favors their conclusions. While the chapters of this work move toward definite conclusions, I hope they do so in a modest way. It seems fairly obvious to me that two people with differing philosophical views can usually *both* hold their views rationally.

e. While most of the ideas and arguments in this book are borrowed—I am, after all, trying to put the reader in touch with the best arguments available—most of the chapters contain a novel argument or a novel way of approaching an issue. And where I am sorting through borrowed ideas and arguments, I hope that I provide the reader with an insightful and thought-provoking path through the complex issues.

What can you hope to gain by reading this book? (1) A clearer understanding of theism and naturalism and of their sometimes surprising implications; (2) an understanding of many of the strengths and weaknesses of theism and naturalism; (3) an ability to see why some arguments that theists often employ are in fact weak; (4) an ability to see why some arguments that naturalists often employ are in fact weak; (5) an understanding of some of the strengths and weaknesses of reincarnation (together with karma) as an alternative to traditional theism; and (6) a grasp of many of the most important ideas and arguments in the philosophy of religion.

The chapters of this book, taken together, provide the tools for developing a comprehensive theistic view of the world, but I have written the chapters so that they can be understood independently—except where the same question is addressed in two parts (chapters). That way, if one is interested in some of the enduring questions but not others, one can easily see which parts of the book to read. Making the chapters readable independently of one another requires that some arguments be repeated in a few places, but I think this makes the book more convenient for the reader.

I wish to thank the editors of the University of Notre Dame Press for their advice and support throughout the project: Matthew Dowd, Stephen Little, Rachel Kindler, and Marilyn Martin. I also wish to thank the anonymous reviewers for many helpful suggestions for improving the manuscript. It remains for me to thank friends and colleagues who have read one or more chapters of this book as I drafted them and who have provided me with constructive criticism. Their insightful comments and questions have helped me to make the book much better than it would otherwise be. Naturally, I'm responsible for any mistakes or problems that remain. Special thanks are due to Matthew Benton, Andrew Carson, Samuel Filby, Samuel Fullhart, Patrick McDonald, Rebekah Rice, Leland Saunders, and Kelly Weirich.

ONE

Does God Exist?

Part I

A worldview is a comprehensive philosophical position, one that provides a fundamental outlook on the world and on human existence. In this chapter I'll outline two contrasting worldviews, theism and naturalism. I will summarize some of the main arguments for naturalism and then take the first steps in developing a case (an extended argument) for theism.

Theism can be formulated as follows: (1) *There is exactly one Being that* (2) *is perfectly morally good and* (3) *almighty and that* (4) *exists of necessity*. Let me comment briefly on each of these clauses.

(1) By "theism" I refer to a view of God found in the great monotheistic religions, Judaism, Christianity, and Islam. On this view, there is exactly one God; both polytheism and atheism are false.

(2) Theists believe that God is perfectly morally good. Thus, God is perfectly loving, perfectly just, and perfectly wise.

(3) "God is almighty" means roughly that God is maximally powerful. More precisely, there is no state of affairs that God is unable to bring about due to a lack of power.[1] It needs to be noted, however, that there is wide agreement among theologians and theistic philosophers that God cannot do or bring about certain things. For example, God cannot bring it about that God both exists and does not exist (at the same time). Such a scenario is logically impossible, that is, its description is explicitly or implicitly logically inconsistent. And there is no such thing as a power to make logical contradictions true—talk about such a power

would simply be nonsense. Similarly, God cannot force a person to perform an act freely; if God forces a person to perform an act, the act is not freely undertaken. It is a *necessary truth* that no forced act is freely performed. (A necessary truth is one that cannot be false under *any* circumstances.) And there is no such thing as a power to make necessary truths false—the very idea is incoherent. Hence, these examples are not examples of things God is unable to bring about *due to a lack of power*; they are simply impossibilities. It would make no sense to say that if only God had more power, he could bring about logical impossibilities; that would be rather like saying, "If only Hercules were stronger, he could lift a thousand-pound *spherical cube*." On the other hand, of course, theists insist that God has the power to bring about quite amazing states of affairs. For example, God can create the entire physical universe ex nihilo (out of nothing), bring a dead person back to life, or still a raging storm.

An almighty being would be non-physical, since an entity counts as physical only if it is governed by laws of nature (such as the law of gravity), and an almighty being is not governed by laws of nature.[2] If a being were governed by laws of nature, it would be unable to do miracles, and clearly, in the traditional conception, God can do miracles. In addition, if God were a physical entity, God would be located in space.[3] But if God is the Creator of physical reality—as traditional theists claim—there simply were no physical locations prior to God's creation of the physical universe. Also, if God is a physical entity located somewhere (or everywhere), God's location must be (at least in principle) detectible—directly or indirectly—through the five senses.[4] Is there some tactile, olfactory, gustatory, or visual indication of God's location in space? Some color, shape, taste, or electrical charge that signals God's location? Surely not.[5] Finally, if God were a physical being, God could create only *part* of physical reality, specifically, the part outside of himself. But on the traditional conception of God, God creates the whole of physical reality, not just a part.

If knowledge is a form of power, then if God is almighty, God has as much knowledge as it is logically possible to have, that is, God is all-knowing or omniscient. And it is plausible to suppose that knowledge is a form of power. Imagine a true-false exam on *all* the knowable propositions. Among the powers an almighty being would have, surely, would be the power to answer all the items on the exam correctly. But then, clearly, an almighty being is also an all-knowing being.

(4) Many theologians have insisted that God exists of necessity. A necessary being is one that cannot fail to exist. By contrast, a contingent being is one that does exist but would not exist under different circumstances. For example, human beings exist contingently. Presumably I would never have existed if my parents had never met and had sex. Yet it is logically possible that one of my parents died at birth—that could have happened, though it did not. So I am a contingent being.

Why do many theologians claim that God exists of necessity? For at least two reasons. First, theists generally think of God as the most perfect being possible. And many theists believe that necessary existence is a more perfect form of existence than contingent existence. Second, God is the creator of *all* contingent beings, according to theists, but God is uncreated. So God must exist not contingently, but of necessity.

Naturalism can be formulated as follows: (1) *There is a physical reality that is by its very nature organized (i.e., the organization is not imposed by a god or any other force or agent); (2) physical reality exists eternally or by chance; and (3) leaving aside possible special cases (such as numbers or other abstract entities), all entities are physical.* Let me comment briefly on each of these clauses. (1) Physical reality doesn't need to be designed or organized by an intelligent being; it is *inherently* organized. Scientists can describe this organization in terms of the laws of nature, for example, the laws of physics, chemistry, and biology. (2) If physical reality wasn't created, how did it "get here"? Naturalists will say either that physical reality has always been in existence or that it came into existence purely by chance. Now, the idea that physical reality "popped" into existence out of nothing (and without any cause) is not very plausible.[6] So naturalists typically hold that physical reality in some form or other has always been in existence. Notice: They do not say that the physical universe of our acquaintance has always existed. According to contemporary science, our physical universe has existed for about 13.7 billion years. That's a long time, but it's not an infinitely long time. So naturalists usually claim that our universe was preceded by some other *physical* state or situation.

(3) Physical reality is the ultimate reality, according to naturalists. There is no God (or anything like God) and no angels, no demons, no

non-physical souls, and so on. Now, some naturalists allow for the existence of abstract entities, which are not physical. An abstract entity is one that cannot enter into causal relations. For example, take the number seventeen. You cannot bump into it; you cannot strike someone with the number seventeen; you cannot make it vanish. (Yes, you can erase *numerals* from a chalkboard, but that has no effect whatsoever on the *number* seventeen. And humans might conceivably destroy themselves in a nuclear holocaust, but if they did, surely there would still be some *number* of planets, stars, etc., even if there was no one around who could count them.) So some naturalists do allow for the existence of non-physical abstract entities, but these entities can play no causal role. *The only entities that can cause anything to happen are physical entities.*

It seems to me that theism and naturalism are the two greatest metaphysical alternatives in the contemporary marketplace of ideas. There are other alternatives, of course. Polytheism, for example. And we shall take up a combination of reincarnation and karma (minus the belief in a personal God) in chapter 12. But for the time being, let's consider the strengths and weaknesses of theism and naturalism.

Arguments for Naturalism

The Appeal to Simplicity and Science. Suppose someone is explaining how a combustion engine works. He explains in detail how the pistons, cylinders, valves, spark plugs, crankshaft, and so on operate together to make the engine run. He then adds, "Of course, each combustion engine is inhabited by an engine-angel, without which the engine won't work at all." No doubt you would reject this claim regarding engine-angels. Why? Basically, for two reasons. First, there is no direct evidence for engine-angels; no one has ever seen an engine-angel. But no one has ever seen subatomic particles such as quarks, either, yet scientists believe that quarks exist. So science isn't *necessarily* opposed to hypotheses involving unobservable entities. Why do scientists believe that quarks exist? Simply put, because, by postulating quarks, they get the best explanation of certain observable phenomena. But postulating engine-angels does not yield a similar benefit. The explanation in terms of pistons, cylinders, spark plugs, and so on, is fully adequate. We do not improve on that explanation by postulating engine-angels. The engine-angel idea unnecessarily complicates our explanation.

The general principle here is one that most people find plausible and acceptable. It is called the principle of simplicity: *If a hypothesis is unnecessarily complicated, it is probably false (and so should be rejected).* In practice, both theists and naturalists generally seem to presuppose a principle of this type.

From the naturalist's point of view, theism may have made sense before the rise of science. Faced with mystery upon mystery in the physical world, an appeal to God (or the gods) may have been the best explanation available to humans in many cases. But the situation has changed dramatically since the rise of science. For example, whereas lightning and thunder were seen by the ancient Greeks as the work of Zeus, nowadays we can explain such phenomena in terms of the laws of nature. And whereas the rich diversity of life forms on earth was perhaps once best explained by appeal to a Creator, this phenomenon can now be explained in terms of Darwin's theory of evolution. Furthermore, whereas human thoughts and feelings may once have been best explained by appeal to a non-physical soul, these phenomena are now best explained via neuroscience in terms of brain processes.

To sum up the naturalist's appeal to simplicity, it runs as follows: There is no direct evidence for God's existence. Indeed, it's obviously impossible to see or touch a non-physical entity. Furthermore, the "God hypothesis" is not the best explanation of any phenomenon; rather, the appeal to God is like the appeal to an engine-angel. Take any phenomenon: Either science can already explain it or probably will someday, and in any case the appeal to God seems unhelpful. For example, suppose scientists cannot *currently* explain how a certain type of bird migrates to the same location every year. Nevertheless, this seems to be the kind of thing that science will someday be able to explain, and furthermore, "God makes it happen" is not an illuminating explanation. It seems, then, that the belief that God exists is no more credible than the belief that engine-angels exist.

The Problem of Evil and Suffering. Naturalists argue that they can explain the amounts and kinds of evil and suffering in the world better than theists can. Consider: If God is perfectly morally good, God is perfectly loving and just. And if God is perfectly loving, God doesn't want people to suffer unless there is a good (adequate) reason to let them suffer. Now, theists have offered various reasons God might have for allowing suffering. And some of the reasons may explain *some* suffering. The problem is that the reasons don't come close to explaining either the total amount of suffering in the world or the more intense kinds of suffering. For example, if God gives us free will so that we can choose between good and evil, this might explain some suffering that results from the abuse of free will, as when one person tells a lie and someone else suffers as a result. But the appeal to free will explains none of the suffering that results from non-human causes, such as diseases, birth defects, earthquakes, hurricanes, tornadoes, droughts, floods, mudslides, extreme temperatures, and animal attacks. Furthermore, even if the appeal to free will explains some suffering due to the abuse of free will, it doesn't clearly justify the extreme suffering that results from genocide or torture. A loving parent would not allow such things to occur—he or she would interfere to stop them (if able to do so). Similarly, if God really is "our Father in heaven," God would surely interfere to stop such horrors. But since such horrors often occur, there is, or at least probably is, no God who is *both* perfectly loving and almighty.

Naturalists, on the other hand, have no need to square the facts about suffering and evil with a supposedly good God who allegedly governs the world. Much suffering results from the operation of laws of nature, for example, extremes of temperature, hurricanes, floods, earthquakes, diseases, and so on. Well, that is just a fact about the challenging environment we humans live in. The naturalist has no difficulty explaining why such unfortunate things occur.

Some theists think that naturalism makes no room for morality, but the main philosophical ethical theories make no reference to God. For example, utilitarianism is (very roughly) the view that we should always act so as to maximize the happiness of those affected by our actions.[7] And what we call wrong or evil acts very typically harm others in some way, thus making them unhappy or less happy. So the naturalist has no difficulty accounting for moral evil, either.

To sum up, it is widely acknowledged that theism seems unable to explain much of the suffering and evil in the world, while naturalism has no such difficulty. And according to naturalists, this gives us a very strong reason to think that naturalism is more likely to be true than theism is.

The Problem of Divine Hiddenness. John Schellenberg's "hiddenness argument" provides naturalists with another way of arguing that their view is superior to theism.[8]

1. If a God of love exists, reasonable non-belief (that is, not believing that God exits) does not occur.
2. But reasonable non-belief does occur.
3. So a God of love does not exist.

Assuming that there is *at most* one God, the hiddenness argument, if sound, supports atheism. "Non-belief" here includes atheism, agnosticism, never having conceived of God, believing in an unloving God, and so on. And a person's non-belief is reasonable if he or she cannot be faulted for lacking the belief that God exists.

The support for premise 2 would include claims such as the following: Some people are brought up in non-theistic religions, such as Theravada Buddhism or Advaita Vedanta (a non-theistic form of Hinduism). And, historically speaking, many cultures have believed in gods of a sort that do not engage in personal relationships with humans—for example, gods who are not loving and who keep their distance from humans. Furthermore, some people are brought up by parents who teach them that theology is simply superstition. Finally, some people are brought up to believe in God, but as adults, when they examine the evidence for God's existence, they honestly find it lacking, and—in spite of being predisposed to believe—their belief fades away. It is plausible to suppose that people in these types of situations are reasonable in their non-belief; they are not at fault for lacking the belief that God exists.[9]

The support for premise 1 runs as follows: A loving God would want a personal relationship with every human, for such a relationship would be a blessing for each human. But humans cannot have a personal relationship with God if they do not believe that God exists. Hence, God would make his existence clear to each human—except perhaps in the case of humans who may not want to relate to God (e.g., because they are devoted to a way of life that runs contrary to loving their neighbors).

To sum up, an almighty God would be able to make his presence known to human beings. A loving God would want to make his presence known to them. Yet a great many people, past and present, do not believe that a loving God exists. And it is implausible to suppose that this lack of belief is always the fault of the human individuals. A loving God would not leave people in ignorance of his existence, so there must be no such God. This is the problem of divine hiddenness, a well-known difficulty for theism.

Naturalists, on the other hand, have no difficulty explaining the fact that many people do not believe that God exists (through no fault of their own). There is no God, and so, not surprisingly, there is no good evidence that God exists. Thus, from the naturalistic perspective, there is no mystery whatsoever in regard to the fact that so many people do not believe that God exists (through no fault of their own). And once again, according to the naturalist, this gives us a strong reason to think naturalism is more likely to be true than theism is.

The Evidential Standard. Naturalists in general tend to regard the natural sciences (e.g., physics, chemistry, and biology) as the primary standard for good evidence. In effect, naturalists think we should believe only what can be established on the basis of solid empirical evidence and sound reasoning. Because theism involves belief in a *non-physical* entity (God), it cannot be supported with empirical evidence. Moreover, naturalists deny that theism can be supported by sound reasoning. And, according to naturalists, this gives us a further reason to think naturalism is more likely to be true than theism is.

We now have before us, in summary form, a series of arguments for naturalism. Taken together, they constitute a very strong challenge for theism. The best way to evaluate the case for naturalism is to consider what can be said in favor of theism. So let us now turn to a series of arguments for theism.

A Cumulative Case for Theism

It is widely agreed that the best case for theism involves a combination of different arguments. This might be compared to the combination of lines of evidence in a murder trial, for instance, eyewitness testimony, forensic evidence (e.g., fingerprints on the murder weapon), and the defendant's confession. While none of these lines of evidence may be adequate all by itself, together they may form a strong body of evidence.

Religious Experience. We will begin our cumulative case for theism with an appeal to religious experience. It makes sense to start with religious experience because this will connect the case for God's existence with the religious life. Also, the appeal to religious experience is relatively concrete compared to more abstract arguments we'll consider subsequently, specifically, a cosmological argument, a design argument, an argument from free will, and a type of moral argument.

The phrase "religious experience" can refer to many different types of experience, for instance, the experience of prayer, a feeling of peace while meditating, a conviction of guilt over sin, or an emotional "high" while singing a hymn. But for the present let's focus on *theistic mystical experience*, the apparent *direct awareness* of the presence of God. Here are some examples of theistic mystical experience:

- William James cites this example: "I was in perfect health: We were on our sixth day of tramping, and in good training. . . . I can best describe the condition in which I was by calling it a state of equilibrium. When all at once I experienced a feeling of being raised above myself. I felt the presence of God—I tell of the thing just as I was conscious of it—as if his goodness and his power were penetrating me altogether. The throb of emotion was so violent that I could barely tell the boys to pass on and not wait for me. I then sat down on a stone. . . . I thanked God that in the course of my life he had taught me to know him. . . . Then, slowly, the ecstasy left my heart; that is, I felt that God had withdrawn the communion which he had granted, and I was able to walk on, but slowly, so strongly was I still possessed by the interior emotion."[10]
- The French Carmelite Brother Lawrence once remarked that he "felt much closer to God in his day-to-day activities than most people ever believed to be possible. The worst trial he could imagine was losing his sense of God's presence, which had been with him for so long a time."[11]

- Here is another example cited by Timothy Beardsworth: "Then, just as I was exhausted and despairing—I had the most wonderful sense of the presence of God. . . . It was a feeling of an all-embracing love which called forth every ounce of love I had in me. It was the tenderest love I have ever encountered."[12]

- St. Teresa of Avila wrote: "In the beginning. . . . I was ignorant of one thing—I did not know that God is in all things: and when He seemed to me to be so near, I thought it impossible. [But] not to believe that He was present was not in my power; for it seemed to me, as it were, evident that I felt there His very presence."[13]

- From another example cited by James: "I remember the night, and almost the very spot on the hilltop, where my soul opened out, as it were, into the infinite. . . . I stood alone with Him who had made me, and all the beauty of the world, ... I did not seek Him, but felt the perfect unison of my spirit with His. The ordinary sense of things around me faded. . . . The darkness held a presence that was all the more felt because it was not seen. I could not any more have doubted that *He* was there than that I was. Indeed, I felt myself to be, if possible, the less real of the two."[14]

- The English mystic Walter Hilton said: "How that presence is felt, it may be better known by experience than by any writing, for it is the life and the love, the might and the light, the joy and the rest of a chosen soul. . . . He [God] cometh privily sometimes when thou art least aware of Him, but thou shalt well know Him; . . . for wonderfully He stirreth and mightily He turneth thy heart into beholding of His goodness, and doth thine heart melt delectably as wax against the fire into softness of His love."[15]

- Simone Weil had numerous experiences she described as follows: "In a moment of intense suffering, . . . I felt, without being in any way prepared for it (for I had never read the mystical writers) a presence more personal, more certain, more real than that of any human being, though inaccessible to the senses and the imagination."[16] Commenting on these experiences, Weil wrote: "In my arguments about the insolubility of the problem of God I had never foreseen the possibility of that, of a real contact, person to person, here below, between a human being and God."[17]

The appeal to religious experience can be formulated as an argument:

1. Any apparent experience of something is to be regarded as veridical unless we have sufficient reasons to the contrary (the principle of credulity).[18]
2. Experiences occur that seem to their subjects to be experiences of God.
3. There are no good reasons for thinking that all or most experiences that seem to their subjects to be of God are non-veridical (delusive).
4. So some experiences of God should be regarded as veridical.

Let me comment briefly on the premises of this argument. A *veridical* experience is one that is really of the object it appears to be of—as opposed to, say, a hallucination or a mirage. So the first premise, the principle of credulity, says, in effect, that any experience should be given the benefit of the doubt. In other words, in general, we don't have to prove that an experience is veridical; on the contrary, we need good reasons to *deny* that an experience is veridical before rejecting it. The principle of credulity is defended by claiming that, unless we accept it, we will fall into radical skepticism. For example, we have no way of proving that our sense experiences are veridical. Descartes pointed out that all our sense experiences could conceivably be caused by a very powerful evil demon intent on systematically deceiving us. And obviously, we cannot disprove such a possibility by appealing to our sense experiences. Instead, we must proceed by assuming that our sense experiences are veridical, rejecting only experiences that are problematic in some specific way. To illustrate: A pencil placed in a glass of water looks bent but feels straight. This conflict between visual experience and tactile experience forces us to discount one or the other experience *in these circumstances.*

Arguably, any appeal to experience depends *ultimately* on the principle of credulity. Consider, for example, my experience of trees. If this experience is challenged, how might I defend it? Of course, I might claim that others tell me they have experiences of trees. But this claim is based on further sense experiences, for example, that I seem to see other people and to hear what they tell me. (I would also be assuming that they are being sincere in what they tell me.) At some point I am surely forced simply to assume that my sense experiences should be regarded as veridical unless I have sufficient reasons to the contrary—otherwise I'll wind up in radical doubt. Thus, one might respond to a "tree skeptic" along these lines:

a. Any apparent experience of something is to be regarded as veridical unless we have sufficient reasons to the contrary (the principle of credulity).
b. Experiences occur that seem to their subjects to be experiences of trees.
c. There are no good reasons for thinking that all or most experiences that seem to their subjects to be of trees are non-veridical.
d. So some experiences of trees should be regarded as veridical.

Now, if our belief in trees can be justified by this type of argument, can the belief in God be justified by a similar argument? That's the question.[19]

The most controversial premise in the appeal to religious experience is premise 3. Various reasons have been proposed for thinking that all theistic mystical experiences are non-veridical, including these:

A. It is impossible for a merely finite human to experience the presence of a being that is infinite in power and knowledge.
B. Most people have never had experiences (in the sense of a direct awareness) of the presence of God.
C. People interpret experiences in terms of their prior beliefs. For example, while Roman Catholics occasionally have visions of the Blessed Virgin Mary, Protestants do not.
D. Religious experience cannot be tested as sense experience can. For example, I can confirm my visual experience of some object (such as a tree) by asking you if you see it. Or I can confirm my visual experience of, say, a tree or a table, by reaching out and touching it.
E. Religious experience can be caused by factors other than God, such as psychological or neurological factors. For example, some have suggested that religious experience may be caused by a brain abnormality.

F.   People in different religions have different experiences. For example, while Jews, Christians, and Muslims may have experiences of the presence of a personal God, for Buddhists and Hindus the object of religious experience may be "some fact or feature of reality, rather than some entity separate from the universe."[20] Thus, a Hindu may have an experience of "Brahman [ultimate reality], and its identity with the self"; a Zen Buddhist may have an experience revealing that "reality contains no distinctions or dualities."[21]

Defenders of religious experience reply in various ways. For example, regarding A, the issue of *what can be experienced* cannot be settled simply by armchair theorizing. And many people claim to have experienced the presence of a being that is all-powerful and perfectly good. Think about it like this. How do we experience the presence of other people? We see their bodies, of course, but when we say we see a person, we are claiming that we see something that has mental states—feelings, thoughts, beliefs, desires, intentions, and so on. And we cannot literally see such mental states. Nevertheless, we can rightly claim to experience the presence of other people. We simply seem to be "wired" to believe that a person is present when we detect the presence of a living human body. Similarly, perhaps we—or at least many people—are "wired" to believe that God is present under certain circumstances, such as when experiencing a profound sense of awe or when feeling guilty about something we've done wrong.

Regarding B, bear in mind that relatively few people can hear the subtle harmonies and disharmonies that the conductor of an orchestra can hear. And this is not a good reason to regard the conductor's auditory experiences as delusory. Similarly, a skilled tracker may be able to detect signs that the vast majority of people would overlook. So the mere fact that relatively few people have had experiences of a certain kind is not, by itself, a good reason to regard such experiences as delusory.[22]

Regarding C, it is true that most religious experiences conform to the subject's prior beliefs, and this admittedly limits the value of such experiences as evidence for God's existence. But some religious experiences do not conform to the subject's prior beliefs. One example, quoted above, is that of the French philosopher Simone Weil (1909–43), who had never believed in God and found the standard arguments for God's existence unconvincing. One day while she was reciting a poem, she had an experience of the presence of God, and as a result she became a believer.

Regarding D, the defenders of religious experience may suggest that it is wrong to assume that every veridical experience can be tested in the way sense experience can be tested. For example, through introspection I may know that I'm feeling a bit sad today, but if someone is skeptical about my introspective experience, what test can be applied? There doesn't seem to be any test, at least nothing similar to the kind of test we can use in the case of visual experience. (To test my visual experience of a tree, I might touch the tree or ask someone else if they see it.) And if we can trust introspection without having tests for it, perhaps it is reasonable to trust religious experience without tests.

As for E, defenders of religious experience will remind us of the need to distinguish between proximate causes and more remote causes. For example, the proximate cause of my visual experience of a tree may be a brain process; it doesn't follow that the tree itself is not a link in the causal chain that produced my experience. Similarly, even if the proximate cause of a religious experience is a brain process or a psychological factor, God could still be a more remote cause of the experience.

Regarding F, defenders of religious experience may make several observations. First, all experience is interpreted, and reports of sense experience often conflict—think of two eyewitnesses disagreeing in a court of law. We do not for these reasons conclude that sense experience in general is delusory. It is true, of course, that if experience-reports conflict logically, we need some reason to accept one report over another, or else we can only suspend judgment. But we need to make sure that the reports really do conflict logically, and in the case of religious experience, this is not always easy to discern. Second, many religious doctrines are not based on religious experience. For instance, the Christian belief that Jesus died on a cross is not based on religious experience; Christians take it to be based ultimately on eyewitness reports of his crucifixion. So, we should not automatically assume that, if the doctrines of two religions conflict, those doctrines are based on conflicting religious experience-reports. Third, in some cases the content of an experience-report is itself problematic. For example, some religious believers claim that God has told them to perform immoral acts.[23] Such alleged revelations seem highly dubious if we assume that God is loving and just. And consider the experience of some Hindu and Buddhist mystics that all apparent distinctions or differences are unreal. This experience contradicts the deliverances of our sense experience, which tell us that there are many distinct objects in the world and many distinct persons. And if the report of a religious experience conflicts with what sense experience tells us, doesn't that mean the report is highly problematic? It would seem so.

People react to the appeal to religious experience in various ways. Some dismiss it completely. Others enthusiastically endorse it. I would suggest that a middle course is more plausible: Religious experience can rightly lead us to take the possibility that God exists more seriously than we otherwise would, but by itself religious experience does not provide strong evidence for God's existence. The appeal to religious experience simply raises too many questions. Thus, theistic mystical experience needs support from some other quarter to give assurance that it is on the right track, especially as compared to religious experiences within non-theistic traditions. I do think, however, that given theistic mystical experience, "God exists" is in a very different category than, say, "Santa Claus exists" or "engine-angels exist," for there is a long tradition of apparently sincere reports of the experience of the presence of God, but nothing similar in the case of Santa and engine-angels.

A Cosmological Argument. Roughly speaking, cosmological arguments move from the existence of the world (cosmos) to the existence of a Being who causes (or caused) the world to exist. There are a variety of cosmological arguments, but we will consider just one here. This version depends on the distinction between contingent beings and necessary beings.

Recall that a necessary being is one that cannot fail to exist under any circumstances, while a contingent being is one that exists but could fail to exist under different circumstances. Most of the beings (or entities) of our acquaintance seem to be contingent. Animals are born, they die, and they cease to exist. Plants also come into being, then die and cease to exist. According to physicists, even subatomic particles did not always exist, but came into being at an early stage in the expansion of the universe. So all of these beings are apparently contingent.

And given that the universe itself began with a "Big Bang" about 13.7 billion years ago, it is plausible to suppose that the universe itself is a contingent being.[24]

Are there any necessary beings (entities)? That is a matter of controversy. But numbers are arguably necessary beings. Some people deny this because they think of numbers as existing in our minds. But suppose all human beings were annihilated in a nuclear war. Wouldn't there still be some number of planets and stars? Furthermore, there is no reason to think that one can destroy numbers by destroying physical objects. (If there were no physical objects, the number of physical objects would be zero, not one, not two, not three, and so on.) Thus, it is plausible to suppose that numbers exist of necessity; they cannot fail to exist under any circumstances. Now, theists think of God as the greatest being possible, so they think of God as having the greatest possible mode of existence. And necessary existence seems greater than merely contingent existence. So, if God exists, God exists of necessity. (Surely numbers do not have a greater mode of existence than God.) Furthermore, theists think of God as the creator of *all* contingent beings but not the creator of himself. So, again, from the perspective of traditional theism, if God exists, God exists of necessity.

The Scottish philosopher David Hume argued along these lines: If there is a necessary being—call it *Yahweh*, then "Yahweh exists" is a *necessary truth*, a truth that cannot be false under any circumstances. But a truth is necessary only if its denial is logically inconsistent (explicitly or by implication). For example, "All sisters are female" is a necessary truth. Its denial, "Not all sisters are female," implies "Some sisters are not female," which is equivalent to "Some female siblings are not female" (which is obviously logically inconsistent). But consider existential statements such as "Unicorns exist." Its denial, "Unicorns do not exist," is clearly not logically inconsistent. The same goes for "Odin exists" and presumably also for "Yahweh exists." So "Yahweh exists" is not a necessary truth, and Yahweh is not a necessary being.[25]

While Hume's argument has some initial plausibility, his reasoning rests on a false assumption about necessity. The denial of a necessary truth is a *necessary falsehood*, a statement that cannot be true in any circumstances. And it is now widely recognized among philosophers that not every necessary falsehood is logically inconsistent. Examples include these: "Red is not a color," "2 + 2 = 22," "Some blue objects have no size," "Abraham Lincoln is the number 13," and "Water is not H_2O." Statements such as these describe impossibilities, but one cannot derive a *logical* inconsistency ("A and not A") from them. Thus, Hume's argument rests on a misunderstanding about necessity.[26]

Now, consider all of the contingent beings—a vast number of entities. What explains their existence? Let's start with the *currently* living animals and plants. Naturally, we can explain their existence by appealing to biological reproduction. But the currently living animals and plants are preceded by a very long chain of causes. That chain of causes goes back beyond the time when life was first present on earth (roughly 3.5 billion years ago, according to contemporary science). Indeed, that chain of causes presumably goes all the way back to the so-called Big Bang about 13.7 billion years ago. Furthermore, as far as we can tell, all the entities in this chain of physical causes are contingent beings.

How does naturalism explain the presence of contingent beings— not this or that contingent being, but the very presence of contingent beings? In fact, naturalists typically offer no explanation. They typically claim that the existence of physical reality (and hence the existence of contingent beings) is a *brute fact*, that is, a fact that cannot be explained. They simply take the existence of physical reality for granted; they do not explain its presence. And notice that nothing would be gained by postulating (hypothesizing) the existence of additional contingent beings. We cannot explain the presence of a type of being simply by *postulating* that there are more beings of that type!

How does theism explain the presence of contingent beings? Theism explains their presence as ultimately due to God's choice. But to understand this explanation, we must think about a more fundamental issue: *Why would God create anything?* Here we must recall the content of the theistic hypothesis under consideration, which includes the idea that God is perfectly good—an idea with far-reaching implications. If God is perfectly good, God is perfectly loving. And a loving being is generous. A generous being wants to share good things with many others. And a powerful God could share many wonderful things, such as the experience of beauty, the delight in creative activity, the satisfaction of loving personal relationships, the joy of acquiring knowledge, and various pleasures—both physical and mental. But of course, to share these good things with many others, God must create many others. Thus, a loving, generous God would have good reason to create many intelligent conscious beings with whom to share good things, beings such as humans. Of course, God might also have reason to create non-physical intelligent beings, such as angels. But embodied, intelligent creatures could certainly be recipients of many good gifts from God. Moreover, embodied, intelligent creatures would plausibly be the most remarkable feature of a physical universe, its crowning feature. And God would have multiple reasons to create the physical universe. First, the universe is spectacularly beautiful—from the starry heavens to the intricate microscopic structures within a cell. Second, the stability of the universe makes it a suitable theater for the action of free agents. (Just consider how our actions presuppose the stability or regularity of our environment. For example, in a simple act such as handing a child a toy, we must take it for granted that the toy won't suddenly evaporate and that our arms and hands will do what we want them to do.) Third, the universe is, so to speak, an engineering marvel, fascinating in the way it works. To sum up, *theists can explain the presence of contingent beings in terms of reasons a generous God would have to create a physical reality that includes intelligent conscious creatures.*

Here's an outline of the cosmological argument:

1. There are contingent beings.
2. Theism explains the presence of contingent beings better than naturalism does. (The previous two paragraphs provide the support for this premise.)
3. In general, if hypothesis H1 explains the presence of some phenomenon better than a rival hypothesis H2 does, we have a reason to accept H1 over H2.
4. So the presence of contingent beings gives us a reason to accept theism over naturalism.

Notice that the conclusion is not that God exists. Rather, the point of the argument is that the presence of contingent beings gives us some reason to believe that God exists. (Recall that we are examining a *cumulative* case for God's existence. So this argument is meant to be combined with others.)

Now, you might be thinking: If naturalism can't explain the presence of contingent beings, theism can't explain the existence of God; so these hypotheses have a similar deficiency. But remember, according to our theistic hypothesis, if God exists, God is a necessary being. And a necessary being simply cannot fail to exist under any circumstances. So there is no need to find a cause or further explanation of the existence of a necessary being. By its very nature, it cannot fail to exist. Asking, "Why does God exist?" is like asking, "Why does 1 + 1 = 2? Or why is every object identical with itself?" Answer: It can't be otherwise.

One of the all-time great philosophical questions is "Why is there something rather than nothing?" Theism suggests, in effect, that we get the best answer to that question if we postulate a Creator who exists of necessity. Notice that it's important to the theistic argument that God is loving, for it is God's love (and hence God's generosity) that explains why God would want to create intelligent conscious beings and share good things with them. And it is God's *free* decision to create that explains the presence of *contingent* beings.

At this point a naturalist might observe that God's choice to create the world was not necessary but contingent. (It wouldn't be a choice if it were necessary.) So aren't theists explaining the presence of contingent beings by postulating another contingent being (which makes no sense)? In a word, no. A choice is not a being but an event or occurrence. And the cosmological argument, as stated here, is meant to address the question "Why is there some*thing* rather than nothing?" It is not an attempt to explain contingent events (or happenings). (Notice, however, that God's choice to create is based on intelligible reasons—basically, God creates in order to share good things with conscious creatures.)

A brief historical note may be in order here. Many versions of the cosmological argument have employed the principle of sufficient reason (PSR). This principle comes in more than one version, but here is a typical version of the PSR: *There is a sufficient reason for every positive fact.* ("Negative facts," such as "Unicorns do not exist," are not thought to require an explanation.) The PSR is open to question. First, a sufficient reason is typically regarded as one that necessitates the fact in question. With this in mind, the PSR would rule out free will (as it is ordinarily understood)—each "choice" would be a necessitated event; no other "choice" would be possible. Second, according to physicists, some subatomic events occur at random, for example, there is apparently no necessitating reason why certain atoms decay when they do. Third, what would necessitate the PSR itself? Is it supposed to be a necessary truth? Many philosophers doubt or deny that.[27]

The cosmological argument offered here does not rely on the PSR. It is a "best explanation" argument that simply claims we get the best explanation of the presence of contingent beings by postulating a necessarily existing Creator. Instead, of relying on the PSR, the best explanation version of the cosmological argument in effect proposes that we take our explanation of the presence of contingent *beings* as far as we *reasonably* can. *That point is reached when the attempt to go further yields no explanatory gain.*[28]

Some naturalists have suggested that physical reality is an infinite chain of contingent beings, without beginning, each contingent being caused to exist by a previously existing contingent being. This picture is questionable, of course, given Big Bang cosmology, according to which the physical universe began to exist about 13.7 billion years ago. But more importantly, postulating such a chain of contingent beings does not explain why there are *any* contingent beings. Here's an analogy. Suppose, just for the sake of illustration, that every human being is begotten by other human beings and that the history of the human race extends into an *infinite* past; even if this were true, it would not explain why there are any human beings in existence at all.[29]

But couldn't naturalists postulate that some part or aspect of physical reality is a necessary being? In principle they could, though they seldom do. First, since necessity is not testable in a scientific way, many naturalists reject the idea of a necessary being entirely.[30] Second, if naturalists attempt to explain the presence of contingent beings by postulating a necessary entity of some sort, they complicate their hypothesis in two very significant ways:

1. Many (if not most) physical entities are plainly contingent, so naturalists who claim that some physical entities are necessary would be committed to a dualism of physical entities, that is, there are two radically different kinds of physical entities, the contingent ones and the necessary ones. Such a dualism would be mysterious.

2. Naturalists would need to explain how the necessary part of physical reality generates contingent beings. Of course, naturalists are free to speculate, but they cannot do so without complicating their hypothesis.

In short, naturalism faces a dilemma. Either (a) it cannot explain the presence of contingent beings or (b) it must take on significant complications that sharply qualify its original "appeal to simplicity." The second horn of this dilemma, however, is arguably not open to the naturalist, for given that the physical universe had a beginning, it is hard to see a plausible physical candidate for necessary existence.

Some naturalists might reply that they simply accept the presence of contingent beings as a brute (inexplicable) fact. Why not? But consider how naturalists would be apt to respond to a theist who said, "I simply accept the presence of suffering as a brute fact. I feel no need to explain it." While no worldview can explain everything, the failure to explain some salient feature of the world is always a "demerit" for a worldview. A worldview is supposed to help us make sense of the world and of our place in it.

Here ends the first part of the cumulative case for theism. The rest of the positive case for theism is provided in the next chapter. Keep in mind that the cumulative case for theism is, in effect, an attempt to respond to the naturalist's appeal to simplicity. Is naturalism too simple, in the sense that it leaves some important things unexplained? Later chapters on the problem of evil and divine hiddenness provide theistic responses to the claim that naturalism explains suffering, evil, and divine hiddenness better than theism does.

TWO

Does God Exist?

Part II

Chapter 1 initiated a cumulated case argument for theism. In this chapter we complete that case. Recall that the cumulative case for theism is meant to be a response to the naturalist's appeal to simplicity. The question is "Is naturalism too simple in the sense that it leaves important things unexplained—things that theism explains well?"

A DESIGN ARGUMENT

Scientists tell us that if certain fundamental features of the physical universe had been only slightly different, it would not support life. To use the current idiom, the universe is "fine-tuned" for life. For example:

- If the force of the Big Bang explosion had been just a bit stronger or weaker, by as little as one part in 10^{60}, life would not be possible—stars could not have formed, and of course life depends on energy derived from stars such as our Sun.[1]
- There is an "almost unbelievable delicacy in the balance between gravity and electromagnetism within a star. Calculations show that changes in the strength of either force by only one part in 10^{40} would spell catastrophe for stars like the Sun."[2]
- If the weak nuclear force (which governs radioactive decay) had been just a little stronger or weaker, heavy elements such as carbon could not have formed. And heavy elements are necessary for life—

there can be no life if there are only gases such as hydrogen and helium.[3]

- If the strong nuclear force (which binds together such particles as protons and neutrons) had been just 2 percent stronger, all hydrogen would have been converted into helium, in which case there would be no hydrogen for stars to burn. If the strong nuclear force had been 5 percent weaker, there would be nothing but hydrogen. Either way, life would apparently be impossible.

- If the electromagnetic force were 4 percent weaker, there would be no hydrogen, and so no fuel for stars to burn.[4] If the electromagnetic force were a little stronger, there would be no planets.[5] Either way, there would be no life at all.

- To produce a universe such as the one we observe — almost 14 billion years after the Big Bang, "the earliest state of the universe must have had unimaginably low entropy [disorder] . . . ."[6] The odds of this state occurring are extremely small; one would have a better chance of randomly selecting "one particular particle from all of the protons, electrons, and neutrons in the observable universe."[7]

Thus it appears that a universe containing life must have foundational physical structures with values that fall within *highly* restricted ranges. Apparently there are in the vicinity of twenty such structures.[8]

To understand what "fine-tuned" means, imagine that you've received a "Universe Generator" in the mail. This device has about twenty dials on it and a start button. You set the dials and push the start button to create a universe. One of the dials is labeled "Force of the Big Bang." There are 10^{60} marks around the dial that are used to set it. Now 10^{60} is a big number:

$$10^{60} = 1,000,000,000,000,000,000,000,000,000,000,000,000,000,000,000,000,000,000,000,000$$

If you set the "Force of the Big Bang" dial but are off by one mark, you will get a universe that does not contain life. Similar remarks could be made about each of the dials.

Three further remarks may help to clarify what is meant by the phrase "fine-tuned universe." (1) A fine-tuned universe is one that produces the types of chemicals, such as carbon and nitrogen, that are necessary for life, and also the environments in which life is possible, such as the planet earth. (2) We are speaking of *basic* or *fundamental* aspects of physical reality, not derivative ones. For example, if our planet were much farther from the sun, it would be too cold to support life. But earth's distance from the sun can be explained in terms of more basic structures, such as the law of gravity. "Fine-tuning" refers to the *ultimate* or *most basic* structures of our universe. The fine-tuning consists of laws of nature (such as the law of gravity), constants (such as the speed of light), and initial conditions (such as the total amount of energy in the universe). (3) "Fine-tuned" does not mean "fine-tuned by God." Non-theists can and do accept the facts about fine-tuning, and there is no inconsistency whatsoever in their doing so.

To the best of our knowledge, each of the physical parameters (force of gravity, strong nuclear force, weak nuclear force, and so on) could have been different from what it is. So this question naturally arises: What explains the fact that these parameters have values that support life?

Now, scientists may discover that some or even all of these apparently independent parameters are linked by some underlying physical structures, as yet unknown. But due to the nature of the case, science cannot explain the ultimate (most basic) structures of the physical universe. *Once we get to the most basic structures, science can describe them, but there is nothing more basic for science to revert to.* With this in mind, the phenomenon the design argument attempts to explain may be summarized as follows:

> *Phenomenon:* The most basic structures of the physical universe support life—intelligent, conscious life; and given that slight changes in the most basic structures would alter the facts about fine-tuning, slight changes in these structures would destroy their capacity to support life.

The current scientific descriptions of fine-tuning may not be descriptions of the most basic structures of the universe. Physicists haven't finished their work, and perhaps they never will. But whatever the most basic structures of our universe are, they plainly support intelligent life. And due to the nature of the case, science cannot explain these most basic structures; it can only describe them. *So explanations at this level (if there are any) must be philosophical in nature.*

In outline form, the design argument looks like this:

1.   The physical universe is fine-tuned for life (i.e., the most basic structures of the physical universe support life, and slight changes in these structures would destroy their capacity to support life).
2.   Theism explains the presence of a fine-tuned universe better than naturalism does.
3.   In general, if hypothesis H1 explains the presence of some phenomenon better than a rival hypothesis H2 does, we have a reason to accept H1 over H2.
4.   So, the presence of a fine-tuned universe gives us a reason to accept theism over naturalism.

Notice that the conclusion is not "God exists." Rather, the point of the argument is that our fine-tuned universe gives us some reason to believe that God exists. So this argument is meant to be combined with others to form a cumulative case for theism. There is little debate about premises 1 and 3, but much discussion about premise 2. To evaluate premise 2, we must compare the naturalistic and theistic explanations of fine-tuning.

Naturalists offer a variety of explanations of fine-tuning. Here we will examine four of them. First, naturalists point out that even though our fine-tuned universe is improbable, improbable things do happen sometimes. Now "improbable things happen" is an adequate explanation in many cases, for example, when a person rolls "snake eyes" five times in a row in a game of dice. But this explanation is hardly satisfying in the case of fine-tuning, for at least two reasons: (a) Consider an analogy—call it "the electrocution scenario." In wartime, suppose that Amy is captured by the enemy and led into a very large room containing one million electrical outlets. She is forced (on pain of death) to insert a copper device into one of the outlets—but she is free to choose which one. She is informed that if she inserts the device into any of the outlets except one, she will be instantly electrocuted. With trepidation, Amy selects an outlet and inserts the device. To her amazement, she is not electrocuted. Her captors remove her from the room and place her in a prison cell, where she reflects on what just happened. Did she simply get lucky—incredibly lucky? (Improbable things do happen.) But then it occurs to her that her captors may have played a cruel trick on her. Maybe none of the outlets in the room (or only a few of them) were actually linked to an electrical source. Isn't that a more plausible explanation of what just happened? It would seem so.[9] (b) As the analogy suggests, when one can think of a plausible explanation of an event, the appeal to "improbable things happen" hardly seems adequate.[10] And given our discussion of religious experience and the cosmological argument, theism surely merits consideration as a possible explanation. Indeed, many people would judge that it has a quite significant degree of plausibility.

Second, some naturalists appeal to the so-called anthropic principle. It comes in various formulations, but the basic idea is that fine-tuning should not surprise us because a fine-tuned universe is the only kind of universe compatible with our existence. If the universe were not fine-tuned, we could not observe it. As William Craig observes, however, "This reasoning . . . is invalid. Certainly we should not be surprised that we do not observe features of the universe which are incompatible with our own existence. But it does not follow that we should not be surprised that we *do* observe features of the universe which *are* compatible with our existence, in view of the enormous improbability that the universe should possess such features."[11] Go back to the electrocution scenario. Should Amy not be surprised that she survived plugging the copper device into one of the outlets, because if she hadn't survived, she wouldn't be reflecting on the incident? Obviously not. The appeal to the anthropic principle misses the point entirely.

Third, some naturalists offer metaphysical explanations along the following lines:

The Single-Universe Hypothesis: Physical reality can take only one form, precisely the form we find our universe to have.

This hypothesis is, however, flawed for multiple reasons. First, what is "the form we find our universe to have"? That form is summed up in the terms "fine-tuned" and "life-supporting." But there simply is no logical connection between "Physical reality can have only one form" and "Physical reality is life-supporting." Thus the single-universe hypothesis does not explain fine-tuning; it simply presupposes fine-tuning. Accordingly, the single-universe hypothesis is an explanatory failure. Second, most physicists assume that the universe could be structured in various ways. So the assumption that physical reality can have just one form is very much open to doubt. Third, the claim that physical reality *can* have only one form is a large-scale *metaphysical* claim, not an empirical or scientific claim subject to observational tests. Thus, if we add the single-universe hypothesis to naturalism, we significantly complicate naturalism, which sharply qualifies the naturalist's claim to have a simpler view than theism.

The current, front-running naturalistic proposal is the *multiverse hypothesis*. The basic idea of this hypothesis is that our universe is merely one among many actual universes. There are lots of *actual* universes, with their basic physical structures varying at random. They are regarded as distinct universes because they are distinct space-times, with different initial conditions (e.g., the total amount of energy), different laws of nature (e.g., differing laws of gravity), and/or different constants (e.g., differing speeds of light). *The central idea of the multiverse hypothesis is this: Given that there are many actual universes differing randomly in regard to their basic physical structures, it is not surprising that at least one universe is life-supporting.*

To understand the multiverse hypothesis, think about playing poker. One cannot reasonably expect to be dealt a royal flush very often, but if one spends lots of time playing poker, one will probably eventually be dealt a royal flush. (A royal flush is a hand consisting of an ace, king, queen, jack, and ten, all of the same suit.) Similarly, if there are lots of actual universes whose basic physical features (e.g., laws, constants, and initial conditions) differ randomly, it is not surprising that at least one universe is fine-tuned.

Of course, no one has observed other universes. But naturalists are free to speculate. And many physicists take the idea of a multiverse quite seriously, though, as physicist-turned-theologian John Polkinghorne observes, "The many-universes account is sometimes presented as if it were purely scientific, but in fact a sufficient portfolio of different universes could only be generated by speculative processes that go well beyond what sober science can honestly endorse. An example of such a metascientific idea would be the hypothesis that the universe eternally oscillates, the big bang subsequent on each big crunch producing a world with totally different physical laws."[12] Simply put, the multiverse hypothesis, as employed by philosophical naturalists, is metaphysics, not physics.

Does naturalism together with the multiverse hypothesis — "multiverse naturalism" — offer a better explanation of fine-tuning than theism does? There are several problems to consider. (1) Obviously, multiverse naturalism complicates the naturalistic hypothesis by adding on striking new claims — not just the claim that there are many universes, but also claims about how these universes are generated. And we need mechanisms that guarantee *enough* universes whose basic structures differ in random ways. Furthermore, *if the hypothesized mechanisms are themselves fine-tuned, the multiverse hypothesis leaves a deep layer of fine-tuning entirely unexplained.*

(2) Postulating many universes does not alter the probability that our universe, the only one we've observed, is fine-tuned for life. The basic structures — laws, constants, and initial conditions — of the universes of the multiverse are supposed to vary *at random*. So any given universe is like the roll of a die. With each roll of a (fair) die, there is one chance in six that the die will turn up, say, four. It doesn't matter how many times the die has been (or will be) rolled. The outcome of each roll of the die is independent of other rolls of the die; similarly, the probability that any given universe is fine-tuned is independent of the probability that other universes are fine-tuned. Let us grant, for the sake of the argument, that if there is a vast number of universes, it is likely that *some* (at least one) universe is fine-tuned; this doesn't make it likely that *our* universe is fine-tuned. Compare: Even if it is highly likely that *someone* will win the lottery, this gives me little or no reason to suppose that I will probably win (assuming I bought one ticket). Therefore, the fine-tuning of our universe remains very improbable even if we postulate a multiverse.[13]

(3) Does postulating universes other than the one (and only) universe we've actually observed really explain the fine-tuning of our

universe? Whenever something surprising happens, can we explain it by postulating similar events with somewhat different outcomes? Suppose that Ben is the first person known to have a certain disease. The doctors are unable to help Ben. His health deteriorates rapidly, and he is in a coma for several weeks. The doctors predict that Ben will soon die. But suddenly Ben regains consciousness and returns to full health. Can the doctors explain Ben's remarkable recovery by postulating numerous *unknown* or *unobserved* cases of the disease—cases having varying outcomes? (The doctors *suspect* that there have been other cases of the disease even though they know of no one who has observed other cases.) Such an attempted explanation does not, it seems to me, make Ben's recovery less surprising. Similarly, postulating universes other than the one and only universe we've actually observed does not make the fine-tuning of *our* universe less surprising.

(4) It seems that there could be infinitely many universes, yet none that support life. Suppose that we name all the possible universes using the natural numbers: U1, U2, U3, and so on. If there are infinitely many universes, clearly there are infinitely many odd-numbered universes, but what if none of them support life? Perhaps only a few of the *even*-numbered universes support life. So it seems possible that there could be infinitely many universes (namely, the odd-numbered ones), yet none that support life. The question, then, is this: Even if we allow that there are infinitely many universes, does this (by itself) guarantee that at least one will *probably* support life? Not clearly. More importantly, if multiverse naturalists insist that they've postulated enough universes to make fine-tuning unsurprising, a second problem emerges: Multiverse naturalism explains too much, too easily; for by appeal to the multiverse we can explain any physical phenomenon P just by pointing out that, given that there are so many universes differing in random ways, it's not surprising that one of them contains P. Any arrangement of physical particles or structures is apt to be realized if we postulate enough universes. So the multiverse hypothesis can apparently explain *any* physical phenomenon. But can it really be that easy to explain each and every physical phenomenon? Surely not. It seems, then, that the multiverse approach offers a very dubious type of explanation—one that has all the advantages of theft over honest toil.

Naturalists might reply that "God did it" can explain "anything and everything," too. But this reply misses the mark for at least two reasons. First, theistic explanations must include more than merely an appeal to divine power or divine volition. They must provide plausible reasons for divine action based on divine attributes, such as love and justice. And for most physical phenomena, no such plausible reasons are available. But theistic explanations may have plausibility in at least two types of cases: (a) cases that concern very general features of the world (e.g., that contingent beings exist or that our universe supports life) and (b) cases of apparent miracles — roughly, events that apparently have a redemptive purpose and are inexplicable via laws of nature, such as a person's coming back to life after being dead for several days. Second, we already have *some* reason to suppose that God exists, namely, that supplied by religious experience and by the cosmological argument. And we have seen that a good—hence, loving and generous—God would have strong reasons to create intelligent, embodied, conscious beings in order to share good things with them — things such as beauty, physical pleasure, the delight in acquiring knowledge, the joy of personal relationships, and the satisfactions of creative activity. *Such beings would be the crowning feature of a physical world.* And a fine-tuned universe would make it possible for such beings to live.

At this juncture, naturalists may point out that an Intelligent Designer might not be morally good. And given all the evil and suffering in the world, why should we suppose that a *morally good* Intelligence lies behind our universe? Even if there is an Intelligent Designer, it might have created the world simply for its own amusement. Perhaps it even has a cruel streak. The point here could be put this way: On the assumption that theism is true, it may be likely that a fine-tuned universe exists, but it is not likely that a fine-tuned universe like ours, which contains vast amounts of evil and suffering, exists.

The problem of evil does indeed present the theist with a serious challenge. And a thorough discussion of this issue must await the next two chapters ("Why Does God Permit Evil?" and "Why Think God is Good?"). The final assessment of the design argument will depend on whether theists can provide plausible arguments to the effect that either (a) God would likely permit evil and suffering or (b) we humans are in no position to judge whether God would be likely to permit evil and suffering.

Theists generally assume that there are important connections between God and morality, but different theologians and philosophers have different views of what those connections might be. In this section and the next we'll explore two possible connections between God and morality. In both cases, however, we must work through some significant philosophical preliminaries before we can state an argument for God's existence.

Whenever we deliberate, we apparently assume that we have free will. Take a mundane case. You go to an Italian restaurant, look at the menu, and consider what to order: Will it be spaghetti or pizza? Let's say you opt for the spaghetti. Nevertheless, the fact that you deliberated indicates that you assumed you could have ordered the pizza instead. Your decision to order spaghetti marks a small "fork in the road" in your life; things might have gone otherwise, and the issue (however minor) was up to you, within your control.

Now it is widely agreed that there is a connection between free will and moral responsibility. Suppose that we hold someone morally responsible for robbing a bank or committing an act of arson. Aren't we assuming that the agent could have done otherwise? At minimum, he or she could have refrained from robbing the bank or starting the fire. Does it make sense to blame a person for performing some wrong act if he or she had no other options? Probably, for most of us, the answer is, "No, it doesn't."

This answer is currently challenged by many philosophers. They offer one or more so-called Frankfurt cases—a special kind of thought experiment—in support of their view.[14] Here is a typical Frankfurt case. Suppose a mad scientist, Dr. X, has invented a "neuro-computer" that can monitor and control the brains of other people. Dr. X wants one of his assistants, Boris, to murder someone he (Dr. X) dislikes, namely, Zoe. As it happens, Boris also dislikes Zoe and has been think-ing about killing her. (Dr. X and Boris aren't exactly the nicest people!) By using the neuro-computer, Dr. X finds out what's on Boris's mind. Dr. X could take control of Boris's brain and force him to kill Zoe, and Dr. X will do so if the neuro-computer predicts that Boris will decide not to kill her. But the neuro-computer predicts that Boris will kill Zoe, so Dr. X does not activate the control mechanism. And, indeed, Boris kills Zoe. In this scenario, it seems that Boris would be morally responsible for killing Zoe, but Boris had no alternative to killing her, because if the neuro-computer had predicted that Boris would not kill Zoe *on his own*, Dr. X would have activated the control mechanism and Boris would have killed her anyway.

Does the Frankfurt case really show that we can be morally re-sponsible for doing something when we have no other option? That seems very doubtful. First, Boris does have an alternative to *freely* kill-ing Zoe; for if Boris does not choose *on his own* to kill Zoe, Dr. X will activate the control mechanism, in which case Boris will not kill Zoe *freely*. If Dr. X activates the control mechanism, it is agreed that Boris will become merely a tool in Dr. X's hands and Dr. X will be respon-sible for the act. Second, in the absence of the neuro-computer (oper-ated by Dr. X), it is assumed that Boris *would* have options, for example, he could refrain from killing Zoe. The neuro-computer is what is supposed to remove alternative courses of action for Boris. But on reflection, this cannot be so. Here's why: If Dr. X wants Boris to act on his own, Dr. X must make his decision *not* to activate the con-trol mechanism *before* Boris makes his decision. But how could the neuro-computer infallibly predict what Boris *will* decide to do? That could happen only in a deterministic universe in which Boris's decision and action were already guaranteed by the past and the laws of nature. In that case, the neuro-computer would presuppose a deterministic universe and the Frankfurt case should be rejected by anyone who thinks determinism rules out free will. On the other hand, if Boris's actions are not determined and the neuro-computer is making merely fallible predictions, Boris might change his mind (and decide not to kill Zoe) *moments after Dr. X has decided not to activate the control mechanism*, in which case Boris has an alternative after all.[15] To sum up, the Frankfurt cases have some initial plausibility, but on reflection the principle that one is morally responsible for doing X only if one has an alternative (e.g., one can refrain from X) seems to hold up well.

But many philosophers think that free will *is* compatible with determinism. Are they right? Determinism is the idea that, given the past, only one future is possible. When you deliberate, you assume that multiple possible futures are open to you. You might phone your friend at time T, or you might read a book instead. You might turn right at the next intersection, but then again you might turn left. And so on. But if determinism is true, the appearance of multiple options is an illusion. In each case, only one of the *apparent* possibilities can be actualized.

Compatibilism is the view that our actions can be both free and determined. From this perspective, a free act is one an agent performs because he or she wants to, all things considered. For example, at the Italian restaurant, you might have had some desire for both spaghetti and pizza, but you couldn't eat both, and (on this occasion) your desire for spaghetti was stronger than your desire for pizza. So spaghetti was what you wanted, all things considered. No one coerced you— you did what you wanted to do, so your act was free. If we ask why your desire for spaghetti was stronger than your desire for pizza, the answer is that the strength of these desires was determined (necessitated) by the past and the laws of nature.

Of course, many philosophers think that free will is incompatible with determinism—this is the *incompatibilist* view of freedom. These philosophers reject the compatibilist view of a free action. In the incompatibilist view, a free action is undetermined, but it is not a mere random occurrence; it is up to the agent. More precisely, one performs an act A freely at a time T only if one performs the act at T, but *at T one has the power to refrain from doing A*. Thus, if someone robs a bank freely at time T, then at time T he (or she) has the power to refrain from robbing the bank. In short, "in order to be free, one must have the power to do something other than what one in fact does."[16] Let's refer to this briefly as "the power to do otherwise."

The most important argument against the compatibilist view is the *consequence argument*. Here is a short, intuitive version of that argument: "If determinism is true, then our acts are the consequences of the laws of nature and events in the remote past. But it is not up to us what went on before we were born, and neither is it up to us what the laws of nature are. Therefore, the consequences of these things (including our present acts) are not up to us."[17] We have no choice about the laws of nature, for example, we don't get to vote on the law of gravity. Nor do we have any choice about the state of the world, say, a billion years ago. But if determinism is true, *all* events result from the operation of the laws of nature on past conditions (including conditions present even before we were born). *All events* include those events we call our actions. And if we have no choice about the laws of nature and the remote past, we surely have no choice about what results from these factors—including our own actions. In short, we have no choice, no free will. Therefore, the compatibilist view of free will seems inadequate. If determinism is true, we do not have free will.

Compatibilists might reply that it remains true that we perform some actions because we want to. But this reply is not relevant. Compatibilists agree that we have no choice about the remote past and the laws of nature. And the consequence argument tells us, in effect, that our lack of choice about the past and the laws of nature transfers to our thoughts, intentions, preferences, desires, and actions if determinism is true.

We normally assume that having a choice involves having genuine options. At the next intersection, I might turn right, or I might turn left. And if I turn right, at that very moment I have the power to turn left. (Of course I cannot do both at the same moment, but I have the power to do either one.) If I tell a lie at time T, at T I have the power to refrain from lying. At the time I make the choice, it could go either way; it is up to me. But if determinism is true, there is really only one possible pathway into the future. The appearance of having options as I make decisions is an illusion.[18] So the idea of compatibilism (that we can be both free and determined) seems strongly contrary to our ordinary way of thinking about free choices.

What does all this have to do with theism and naturalism? Let us suppose that humans have the kind of free will needed for moral responsibility, which, as we have just seen, is apparently incompatibilist free will. Regarding this picture of free will, Paul Draper observes, "On theism, which entails that God is morally perfect, one has reason to believe that our actions are not the inevitable consequence of natural laws and antecedent conditions chosen by God. For that would mean that God is the ultimate sufficient cause of every morally wrong action we perform. More importantly, it would mean that any relationship we might have with God, indeed any response at all that we make to God, would be the result of divine manipulation."[19] In short, if a God of love exists, it seems likely that humans would have free will in the incompatibilist sense (the "power to do otherwise").

But is it likely that we have free will in the incompatibilist sense given naturalism? Arguably not. This is obviously true for any version of naturalism that involves determinism, and some naturalists are determinists.[20] But nowadays most naturalists are not determinists because, according to contemporary physics, some laws of nature are not deterministic but probabilistic. To see the difference between deterministic and probabilistic laws, compare the following:

> *Deterministic law*: Given initial conditions A, B, and C, D always occurs.
> *Probabilistic law*: Given initial conditions A, B, and C, D will probably occur, but E may occur instead.

In the case of a deterministic law, given the antecedent conditions (A, B, and C), the same result always occurs, namely, D. For example, if you heat water to 212 degrees Fahrenheit (at sea level), it always boils. In the case of a probabilistic law, more than one outcome is possible. For example, one of the laws of radioactivity is that half of the atoms in a unit of radium 226 will decay over a period of 1,602 years, but the law does not specify *which* of the atoms will decay during that period or the *precise moment* when any one of them will decay. Another example: The clicking sounds of a Geiger counter indicate the activity of electrons that are governed by probabilistic laws of nature.

While most naturalists do not endorse determinism, they do regard all of physical reality as governed by laws of nature. And the mere fact that some laws of nature are probabilistic does not bring free will into the picture. Obviously, no one would suggest that a Geiger counter has free will. Of course, the human brain is vastly more complicated than a Geiger counter, but it is still a physical system that operates entirely in accord with the laws of nature, according to naturalism. And mere complexity does not equal free will. If we had a very complex computer operating (partly) in terms of probabilistic laws, would it have free will? I see no reason to think so. Some of the outcomes would occur at random, but that wouldn't mean that the computer made free choices. Furthermore, it is implausible to suggest that a system governed by laws of nature would somehow generate a power, namely, "the power to do otherwise," which to some degree operates independently of those laws.

Now, only physical things exist, according to naturalists. So, naturalists take a *physicalist* view of the human person, that is, they deny that humans have non-physical souls. Human beings are one small part of a vast physical system. And in an entirely physical system, outcomes are a function of two factors: the initial conditions and the laws of nature. The human brain is analogous to a very complex computer. And so there seems to be no place for free will in this picture.

But don't theists agree that the human brain is a physical entity? Yes, of course. But they think that God could endow human beings with the power to make free choices. (This might involve endowing humans with a non-physical soul—that is at least one possibility.[21]) And in that case our choices wouldn't be entirely outcomes of the operation of laws of nature. Our power of free choice would be a causal factor in addition to the operation of the laws of nature.

Let's pause now to summarize the argument from free will and moral responsibility:

1. Humans are sometimes morally responsible, and they have the sort of free will that is needed for moral responsibility, namely, free will in the incompatibilist sense.
2. Free will and moral responsibility are apparently unlikely given naturalism, while they are likely given theism.
3. So the presence of free will and moral responsibility gives us a reason to accept theism over naturalism.

Most naturalists are not moved by this argument because most naturalists are compatibilists about free will. But for reasons we've just considered, the compatibilist view seems problematic. Accordingly, the argument from free will and moral responsibility seems to have some merit.

Before leaving the argument from free will and moral responsibility, let us note that, if premise 2 is true, naturalism faces a kind of problem of evil of its own; for in order to explain the presence of genuine moral evil in the world (i.e., wrong acts for which humans are morally responsible), one must have a worldview that allows for free will and moral responsibility. But, as we've just seen, naturalism seems to make no place for the type of freedom necessary for moral responsibility. So, although many suppose that the problem of evil is a problem specific to theism, naturalism also may falter in explaining the full range of evils in the world.

GOD AND MORALITY

Religious believers generally assume that there is some deep and important connection between God and morality. They also typically assume that there is an objective truth about which acts are right and which acts are wrong. An objective truth is one that holds whether or not we humans believe it, for example, the moon orbits the earth. (Note: An objective truth, as here defined, is not necessarily one that all humans believe. Not everyone believes that Mount Rainier is 14,411 feet high—after all, many people simply aren't informed of its height—but nevertheless, this is an objective truth.) Plausible examples of objective truths about moral issues include: "It is wrong to torture people just for fun (and without their consent)," "It is wrong to inflict harm on a person without a good reason for doing so," and "A person ought to keep his or her promises unless there is a very good reason not to."

Some religious believers claim that there could be no objective truth about morality if there were no God—morality would just be a matter of individual feeling or of societal norms. This suggests the following argument:

1. If there is no God, there are no objective truths about right and wrong.

2. There are some objective truths about right and wrong.
3. Therefore, God exists.

Now, most people accept premise 2 of this argument. For example, most people believe strongly that genocide is wrong and that slavery is wrong—and that the truth of these statements does not depend on whether we humans believe them.

But many philosophers would deny premise 1 of this argument. For example, many philosophers have suggested that moral truths—at least some of them—may be similar to mathematical truths, such as $1 + 1 = 2$ or No circles are squares. That is, some moral truths are *necessary truths*—they simply cannot be false under any circumstances. What makes necessary truths true? No one knows, but it is hard to deny that there are such truths. Examples include these: All husbands are married, Every even number is divisible by two, No person is a number, and Nothing is red all over and green all over at the same time. For an example of a necessary truth about morality, consider: If there are human beings, then it is wrong to torture them just for fun and without their consent.[22]

Some religious believers have suggested a different sort of connection between God and morality. This line of thinking begins with the observation that people who take morality seriously typically believe that if an act is one's moral duty, one has an overriding reason to perform the act, and if an act is morally wrong, one has an overriding reason not to perform it. (Call this the "overriding reasons thesis.") Of course, we often have reasons not to do our duty. Doing one's duty may be inconvenient or unpleasant, and it may involve making a sacrifice of some sort. For example, suppose I'm late for work. I know my boss will be upset, and reasonably so since I've been late several times recently. So I consider telling my boss a plausible lie: "There was an accident on the Ballard Bridge, and traffic was all backed up." Lying would placate my boss and get me off the hook, which would be nice. But lying would be wrong in such a situation. And because it's wrong, I have an overriding reason not to lie: My reasons to lie are outweighed, trumped, or overridden by the simple fact that lying is wrong. In general, "X is morally wrong" gives me a powerful, overriding reason not to do X, and "X is my moral duty" gives me a powerful, overriding reason to do X.

Now, if God exists, it is always in one's best interest to do one's moral duty. After all, to fail to do one's moral duty is to sin. And sin alienates a person from God. Moreover, it is never in a person's best interest to be alienated from God, for, as creatures, we have a deep need to be on good terms with God, our Creator and Judge. But if there is no God and no life after death, there do seem to be cases in which it is in one's best interest not to do one's duty. Consider the case of Ms. Poore:

> Ms. Poore has lived many years in grinding poverty. She is not starving but has only the bare necessities. She has tried very hard to get ahead by hard work, but nothing has come of her efforts. An opportunity to steal a large sum of money arises. If Ms. Poore steals the money and invests it wisely, she can obtain many desirable things her poverty has denied her: a well-balanced diet, decent housing, adequate heat in the winter, health insurance, new career opportunities through education, and so on. Moreover, if she steals the money, her chances of being caught are very low and she knows this. She is also aware that the person who owns the money is well off and will not be greatly harmed by the theft. Let us add that Ms. Poore rationally believes that if she fails to steal the money, she will likely live in poverty for the remainder of her life. In short, Ms. Poore faces the choice of stealing the money or living in grinding poverty the rest of her life.[23]

If there is no God and no life after death, it seems to be in Ms. Poore's best interest to steal the money. Moreover, if there is no God and no life after death, it seems that Ms. Poore has a stronger reason to steal the money than not to steal it. The very quality of her life is at stake. And whatever fulfillment she can achieve must be achieved in this earthly life: "You only go around once!" So if naturalism is true, it seems that "X is morally wrong" does not always provide an overriding reason not to do X.

Naturalists respond to the Ms. Poore case in various ways. (A) Some say that stealing isn't wrong in this type of case. Note, however, that this response is a departure from what most people believe about right and wrong, that is, simply being poor doesn't justify stealing. If

Ms. Poore were literally starving to death or if her children's lives were at stake, we might agree that stealing is permissible, but that's not Ms. Poore's situation.

(B) Some say that, despite appearances, it is really in Ms. Poore's best interest not to steal. She will be plagued with guilt if she takes the money. At least three points need to be considered here: (1) Some people would be plagued by guilt if they stole the money, but others wouldn't. (2) Most of us know we have done some wrong things, but as time passes, we cease to berate ourselves for these actions. Guilt feelings don't necessarily last forever. And even if they last, their strength usually fades. (3) From Ms. Poore's perspective, what she stands to gain may be worth *some* guilt feelings. After all, she does have a lot to gain. So, the point about guilt feelings doesn't really seem to defuse the Ms. Poore case.

(C) Some say that Ms. Poore should avoid stealing assuming that she doesn't want others to steal from her. Here again, we need to consider several points: (1) Stealing goes on constantly in the world. Just think of all the thefts that occur in a modern city on a daily basis! What Ms. Poore does in this one rare, special case will make her no more vulnerable to theft than she already is. Indeed, if she steals the money, she'll likely be able to live in a part of town where there is less crime and fewer thefts, in which case she'll be less vulnerable to theft than she is now. (2) Keep in mind that, by hypothesis, it's virtually certain that no one will find out that Ms. Poore took the money. So no one will have good reason to blame her or to steal from her in revenge. (3) Once again, the main question is "Is stealing worth the risk?" And Ms. Poore has a lot to lose by remaining in her impoverished condition and much to gain by stealing the money.

(D) Some say that if Ms. Poore steals the money, she will give up the virtue of honesty. And human beings are always better off if they are virtuous. Now, being virtuous is generally in a person's best interest. For example, character traits such as courage, wisdom, and moderation are generally beneficial to the person who has them — and beneficial to others too, of course. But is being *perfectly* virtuous always in a person's best interest if naturalism is true? That's the question. The cost of maintaining perfect virtue is very high for Ms. Poore — a life of poverty. One dishonest act can provide her with an entirely different and higher standard of living. If there is no God and no life after death, is perfect honesty worth a life of grinding poverty? That seems very doubtful.

(E) Still others shrug their shoulders and say, "Maybe 'X (e.g., stealing or lying) is wrong' is occasionally overridden by 'X is in my best interest.' So what if there are exceptions to the overriding reasons thesis? Furthermore, if people do their duty because it's in their best interest to do so, they aren't really being moral. Being moral involves doing the right thing because it's right—not to get a reward." There are two important points here, and both need to be considered carefully. First, is it a small matter to grant that one's best interest sometimes overrides duty? This would imply that it is sometimes irrational to do one's duty, because *doing one's duty involves acting on the weaker reason.* And if naturalism leads us to conclude that *it is sometimes irrational to be moral,* naturalism does not fully uphold the rational authority of morality. Second, theists agree that people should do what's right because it's right. The problem, however, is that, given naturalism, doing what's right is sometimes contrary to one's long-term best interest, while, given theism, one is never *ultimately* penalized for doing what's right—a God of love is able and willing to set things right in the life after death. Thus theism, unlike naturalism, fully upholds the rational authority of morality.

The moral argument under consideration has the following structure:

1. The overriding reasons thesis (ORT) is true: If an act is one's moral duty, one has an overriding reason to perform the act, and if an act is morally wrong, one has an overriding reason not to perform it.
2. If naturalism is true, the ORT is false and the rational authority of morality is not fully upheld, but if theism is true, the ORT is true and the rational authority of morality is fully upheld.
3. So the ORT gives us a reason to accept theism over naturalism.

Premise 1 seems to be true, and indeed, most ethical theorists, whether theists or not, assume that the ORT is true. Our discussion has centered mostly on premise 2. In light of the Ms. Poore case, that premise is plausible, and to the extent that it is plausible, the moral argument has merit.

Before leaving the moral argument, let's note a way in which the ORT may help us to understand God's goodness. We have previously seen that if God is almighty, he is all-knowing. And if God is all-knowing, he knows what is right and wrong, good and evil, in every circumstance. Furthermore, God knows that the ORT is true, so he knows that if an act is a moral duty (e.g., keeping a promise), he has an overriding reason to perform it. And God knows that if an act is morally wrong (e.g., breaking a promise), he has an overriding reason not to perform it. As an almighty being, God can perform acts simply by willing to do so. God does not get tired. God is not overcome by desires. So unless we suppose that God is irrational (and so acts on weaker reasons when he knows stronger reasons apply), it seems clear that God will always do what is morally required and never do what is morally wrong. And since it is not difficult for an almighty being to act on stronger reasons, it is hard to see why God would ever act on weaker reasons when stronger ones apply.[24]

At this point the reader is left with the admittedly complex task of making an overall assessment of the cumulative case for theism. There is no formula for making such a judgment. But often, for a given individual, certain points will leap out as pivotal and persuasive. Of course, the cumulative case for theism doesn't respond to the problem of evil and the problem of divine hiddenness—at least it does not do so directly. So we need to consider a more direct theistic response to those problems. The next four chapters will enable us to do that.

THREE

Why Does God Permit Evil?

The world contains *much* moral wrongdoing and *much* suffering. Is this what one would expect if a perfectly good God is in control of the world? Many people think not. This is the problem of evil, in a nutshell.

The problem of evil is generally considered the most important objection to traditional theism, the belief that there is exactly one God who is almighty, all-knowing, and perfectly good. "Evil" here refers to badness, as in "Bad things happen to good people." And we can distinguish two general types of evil (in the sense of badness). First, moral evil, that is, the wrongdoing for which humans are responsible (e.g., murder, theft, assault) and the harm or suffering that results from it. Note that both the wrong action and the resulting harm or suffering count as evils by this definition. Second, so-called natural evil, that is, the harm or suffering that results from non-human factors, such as earthquakes, tornadoes, mudslides, extreme temperatures, diseases, animal attacks, and so on. Note that the harm or suffering is what counts as bad here, not the cause thereof. Thus, if a hurricane occurs in the middle of the ocean and no one is harmed, the event does not count as a natural evil.

ROWE'S FORMULATION

A well-known critic of theism, William Rowe, has offered the following succinct formulation of the problem of evil, one that focuses on suffering in particular:

1. There exist instances of intense suffering which an omnipotent, omniscient being could have prevented without thereby losing some greater good or permitting some evil equally bad or worse.
2. An omniscient, wholly good being would prevent the occurrence of any intense suffering it could unless it could not do so without thereby losing some greater good or permitting some evil equally bad or worse.
3. [So] there does not exist an omnipotent, omniscient, wholly good being .[1]

Why accept premise 2? Consider an example. Suppose you have been seriously injured and a physician knows she could heal you in either of two ways: (A) simply by having you take one pill that has no harmful side effects or (B) by performing invasive surgery that would involve much post-operative pain over several months. A physician who opted for B in these circumstances would rightly be regarded as morally flawed — definitely not "wholly good." In the light of examples such as this, 2 seems quite plausible.

Rowe's defense of premise 1 has become a focal point in philosophical discussions of the problem of evil: "Suppose in some distant forest lightning strikes a dead tree, resulting in a forest fire. In the fire a fawn is trapped, horribly burned, and lies in terrible agony for several days before death relieves its suffering."[2] Clearly, an almighty God could prevent the fawn's suffering, for example, by painlessly euthanizing the fawn. What greater good would be lost if God did that? Theists have struggled to locate plausible answers to such questions. Of course, premise 1 can be defended by many examples involving human suffering, too. To put it mildly, it is hard to believe that every case of child abuse is necessary for some greater good. And the same can be said about instances of serious injury and cases of dread disease.

Types of Theistic Responses

Theists may respond to the problem of evil in at least four basic ways. First, they can offer a theodicy, that is, they can suggest reasons God has, or might have, for allowing evil and suffering. We'll consider some theodicies momentarily.

Second, theists may offer the "overrider" response, that is, they might simply admit that the suffering and evil in the world count as evidence against theism but insist that this evidence against theism is overridden by other evidence that favors theism. Of course, this response is only as good as the evidence for theism. And, as we saw in chapters 1 and 2, a difficulty for this response is precisely that the problem of evil can be used to cast doubt on the premises or inferences of arguments for God's existence.

Third, theists can offer the comparative response, that is, they can argue that although theism does not explain every case or type of evil, the main alternatives to theism also falter in explaining evil in terms consistent with their philosophical underpinnings; hence the problem of evil is not a good reason to reject theism in favor of the main alternative views. The comparative response is illustrated below in the case of philosophical naturalism.

Fourth, many theists are so-called skeptical theists, that is, they call into question the assumption that we humans would be likely to know God's reasons for allowing suffering, assuming God has such reasons. We humans are perhaps a bit like novice chess players who cannot fathom why a chess master has made a certain move. The novices would be foolish to reason thus: "We see no good reason for the chess master to move his rook *there*; hence, the chess master has no good reason to move his rook *there*." Similarly, because God is omniscient and the world is very complex, we would be foolish to infer that God has no good reasons for allowing suffering, since we are unable to conceive of any such reasons.

Skeptical theism is not without plausibility, but it does face difficulties. Here are four objections to it.

1. Theism is a worldview, and a worldview is supposed to help us make sense of our lives and of our place in the world. And while no worldview can explain everything, failing to explain a major feature of our experience, such as suffering, is a serious deficit, especially if there are other worldviews that can explain such phenomena well.

2.   Skeptical theism is arguably unduly skeptical. From a theistic point of view, the list of beings who might conceivably benefit from the suffering of Rowe's fawn is in fact rather short: (a) God, (b) human beings, (c) non-human animals, and (d) non-human created intelligences (either angelic or extraterrestrial).[3] And it is extremely difficult to see how any of these entities could possibly benefit from the suffering of Rowe's fawn. The suggestion that God may see such a benefit seems implausible. And, in general, implausible claims cannot be defended simply by appealing to God's omniscience. Imagine someone saying, "Torturing the innocent seems wrong to most people, but it may well be right for reasons known to God." Such an appeal to omniscience is plainly misguided. So, while it seems reasonable to be skeptical about our ability, as finite creatures, to fully understand why God permits the totality of evil and suffering, the appeal to divine omniscience and human epistemic limitation, all by itself, hardly seems an adequate response to the problem of evil.

3.   Some claim that the skepticism of the skeptical theist is arbitrary. After all, believers often seem to think they can know possible reasons why God would do certain things, such as create intelligent life forms, give humans free will, or send prophets into the world. If theists become skeptical only when they are at a loss to suggest possible reasons for divine action (or inaction), their skepticism seems arbitrary or intellectually dishonest.[4]

4.   It seems that skeptical theism can be used to defend too much. Suppose that we imagine a world far worse than the actual world, a world containing many more extreme evils than the actual world. We can still ask whether God might have reasons *beyond our ken* for allowing such evils. But surely at some point, as we imagine worlds containing more and more evil (and suffering), this way of defending theism would seem dubious. And on what principled basis could we say that skeptical theism can reasonably be applied in the case of the actual world but could not reasonably be applied in the case of "much worse" worlds?[5]

In reply to objections such as these, the skeptical theist is apt to point out that an almighty, perfectly loving God would certainly have good reasons to allow any evil or suffering he actually does allow. That's a fair point but it is relevant only on the assumption that the belief that an almighty, perfectly loving God exists is justified or warranted. And critics of theism generally think that the problem of evil calls this assumption into question.[6]

POPULAR THEODICIES

Let us now turn to some theodicies that have seemed plausible to many. I will argue that these theodicies are deficient, but they merit careful scrutiny.

The Afterlife Theodicy. The joys of heaven will outweigh or compensate for the sufferings of this earthly life. The main problem with this theodicy is that it does not tell us *why* God allows us to suffer in this earthly life. And this is what a theodicy must do. To see the problem here, imagine a husband who neglects his wife for many years and then suddenly begins to treat her nicely. While the change in his behavior is good, it obviously doesn't excuse the years of neglect. A further problem with the afterlife theodicy is that it seems to assume universalism, the idea that everyone will go to heaven eventually. If some people who suffer will not go to heaven, obviously their suffering will not be compensated by the joys of heaven.

The Counterpart Theodicy. If good exists, evil must also exist. Good and evil are logical opposites; the one cannot exist without the other. As a rough analogy, suppose construction workers build a skyscraper. The skyscraper is unavoidably big relative to, say, its first floor. A big building unavoidably has small areas within it. So the idea here is that if God creates something good, he also unavoidably creates something evil.

There are at least three problems with the counterpart theodicy (CT). First, it is inconsistent with theism. Theists hold that God created the world *freely*. And God was good prior to creating anything. (If God is outside of time, we can rephrase this point as follows: God is good independent of creation.) So, according to theism, God's goodness does not necessitate any evil at all. Good and evil are not logical opposites. The point here is that theists cannot reasonably employ the CT since it is logically inconsistent with their theology.

Second, the CT does not seem to explain the *amount* of evil and suffering in the world. Go back to the skyscraper example. Relative to one big skyscraper, there are a vast number of small areas within it. Similarly, even if good and evil are logical opposites, it might be the case that just one evil thing is sufficient to guarantee the existence of all the good in the world. But in fact the world is full of wrongdoing and suffering.

Third, the CT seems to rest on the principle that if something has a property P, then something must have the opposite of that property, non-P. For example, if something is red, something must be non-red. There are a couple of problems here. (a) Even if we accept the principle, it doesn't really support CT. If something is morally good, its non-morally-good counterpart might be, say, a rock or an electron. Rocks and electrons are not morally good things, but they aren't morally evil things, either. Non-good things are not necessarily evil things; they may be morally neutral. (b) The principle seems to be false. For example, absolutely everything has the property of being self-identical, that is, of being identical with itself. Nothing lacks the property; nothing can lack it. Furthermore, it seems that we can conceive of a world containing only non-physical entities, such as God, angels, and numbers. The presence of such non-physical entities does not necessitate the presence of any physical entities.[7]

The Knowledge Theodicy. We humans cannot recognize goodness unless there is evil to contrast it with, and recognizing goodness is itself a very great good, worth the evil necessary for it. It's important not to confuse the knowledge theodicy (KT) with the CT. The CT says nothing about our knowledge of good and evil; rather, CT posits a metaphysical or logical linkage between good and evil. On the other hand, KT posits no such metaphysical linkage; instead it makes a claim about how humans know about good and evil. Namely, we know about goodness by contrasting it with evil.

Even if there is some truth in the KT, it is open to serious objections. First, it is not plausible to claim that we could not understand goodness unless we could contrast it with genocide, child abuse, and torture. There would still be plenty of evil in the world without these extreme *kinds* of evil; they are not needed for moral knowledge.

Second, even if some evils are needed for knowledge of goodness, a great *amount* of evil is not needed. Just consider how many thefts occur in a modern city on a given day. It is not plausible to suppose that every theft is needed in order that we humans might understand the difference between good and evil.

Third, God surely understood the nature of evil prior to (or independent of) creating anything. Being omniscient, God knew that love is good, so he surely knew that very unloving attitudes and actions are evil ones. Evil is simply a departure from the standard of goodness. But if God can know the nature of good and evil apart from the existence of actual instances of evil, why can't God give humans that same ability? To say this is impossible is apparently to deny that God is omnipotent.

The Punishment Theodicy. Every instance of suffering is divine punishment for sin(s) committed by the person who is suffering; since the punishment is deserved, it is justified. This theodicy runs into immediate problems. First, it certainly appears that suffering sometimes befalls innocents, such as, infants, the mentally impaired, and non-human animals. So, the punishment theodicy (PT) is not plausible as an explanation of suffering in general.

Second, the PT seems to place too much emphasis on divine retribution. Theism, as formulated in chapter 1, says that God is perfectly loving, as well as just and wise. From this perspective, God's wrath would be like the anger of a loving parent whose patience has been severely tried by disobedient children. The parent would confront the disobedient children and perhaps punish them, but the goal would not be simply to "make them pay" or give them their "just deserts" (retribution); it would be to instruct them and to help them make better choices.[8]

The Demon Theodicy. Evil and suffering are caused by the activity of fallen angels (Satan and his cohorts). This theodicy raises many questions. First, the demon theodicy (DT), as stated, does not explain why God permits evil. DT merely posits the cause (or a cause) of evil. But why would God allow demons to wreak havoc in the world?

Second, theists generally emphasize that humans are responsible for their sins.[9] So, even if we allow that demons play a role in tempting people to sin, humans remain responsible for their own wrongdoing. And again, the DT provides no explanation of why God permits humans to do wicked things.

Third, while the DT may seem promising as an explanation of natural evil (that is, the suffering and harm that result from non-human factors such as hurricanes, tsunamis, earthquakes, and disease), there are two immediate problems with this suggestion. (a) Through advances in science, we know that natural evils are caused by the operation of laws of nature. For example, much is known about the conditions under which hurricanes form, and much is known about how bacteria and viruses cause disease. Given that natural evils are caused by the operation of laws of nature, is it plausible to suppose that demons are also the cause of natural evils? Why would demons operate in the patterned and predictable ways we call laws of nature? In describing laws of nature, such as the law of gravity or the law that gases expand when heated, are scientists in fact describing the work of demons? In short, given that natural evil is caused by the operation of laws of nature, it is not very plausible to suppose that natural evil is also caused by demons. (b) According to theism, God is the Creator of the universe. From this perspective, God not only created matter ex nihilo (out of nothing), he also sustains it in existence and causes it to behave as it does. Simply put, what we call the laws of nature are part of God's creative activity. To ascribe these laws to the work of demons is to deny that God is the one who determines the way the physical world operates.

The Consequences-of-the-Fall Theodicy. There was no evil and suffering whatsoever until humans sinned ("fell morally") and, as a consequence of their sin, the world is replete with suffering. The main problem with the consequences-of-the-fall theodicy (CFT) is that it does not explain why the sins of humans had just these consequences. And these consequences could occur only if God causes them or at least permits them. Why would God cause or permit such consequences? If the consequences are regarded as punishment, then we are back to the PT.

Some have suggested that the consequences of the fall are meant to have an educational function. They are meant to teach us how much we need God and how desperate our situation is without God's help. This seems more promising than the PT, but still raises several questions. First, throughout the world, a great many people do not believe that a God of love exists. What lesson can they draw when a tsunami strikes or a loved one dies of some dread disease? Aren't they likely to see such events as evidence against the idea that a loving Being is in control of the universe? That seems to be the lesson that is often drawn. So, taken as a form of education, evil seems apt to backfire, leading people to the wrong conclusions.

Second, in the course of history, a vast number of little children (including babies) have died long before they were capable of drawing any theological conclusions about the suffering and evil in the world. So what is the point of their lives and of any suffering they experienced? Did they live, suffer, and die just so others could learn to draw the right conclusions about the human predicament? If so, it seems the little children were used *merely* as a means to an end. And that would call God's perfect goodness into question.

Third, as noted previously, natural evil is caused by the operation of laws of nature. And the laws of nature are part of God's work as Creator. Are we supposed to believe that God changed the laws of nature when humans sinned? There is reason to doubt this. Scientists now know that our universe is "fine-tuned" for life.[10] This means that a world containing slightly different laws of nature probably would not support life at all. From this perspective, it seems likely that natural evils, or at least their causes (lightning, volcanic eruptions, temperature extremes, etc.), have been present as long as there have been forms of life capable of suffering.

Fourth, the CFT does not explain the suffering of animals. Unless we deny what science claims based on the fossil record and the techniques of radiometric dating, animals existed millions of years before humans came on the scene. There were predators killing other animals, and there were disease and death. It can hardly be doubted that predation and disease sometimes caused suffering in the animal world long before there were any humans in existence.

THE SOUL-MAKING THEODICY

John Hick's "soul-making" theodicy is perhaps the most promising one on offer. According to Hick, "God's purpose was not to construct a paradise whose inhabitants would experience a maximum of pleasure and a minimum of pain. [Instead] the world is . . . a place of 'soul making' or person making in which free beings, grappling with the tasks and challenges of their existence in a common environment, may become 'children of God' and 'heirs of eternal life.'"[11] From this perspective, God has given us the power of making significant free choices. We can choose to help or harm one another. God could have made robots, without free will. But God wants us to freely choose the way of love— love of God and love of neighbor. Our freedom makes human life profoundly meaningful and provides the opportunity to develop virtues such as love, compassion, generosity, patience, courage, prudence, hope, mercy, and moderation. God might have made a world from which suffering was excluded, but in such a world, humans would arguably have lived lives of much less moral and spiritual significance than in the actual world. While we may at times envy those who have relatively easy lives, we tend to admire those who have faced serious hardship and suffering with courage, patience, compassion, and hope. Similarly, we admire and honor those who have sacrificed to help others who are suffering and in need. In short, a world with the many challenges and evils our world contains is one in which human beings can develop their best traits and capabilities.[12]

But theists claim that there won't be any suffering in heaven. So why didn't God put us in heaven to begin with and skip this vale of suffering? From a theistic point of view, this question overlooks the great value of becoming a certain kind of person, namely, a virtuous person. As Hasker notes, "A courageous woman is different from a coward, even when no danger is present; the love of a person who has learned compassion and self-sacrifice has a distinctive quality even when no one is presently suffering. . . . Heroes in many walks of life are often . . . honored long after age and/or changed circumstances have made a repetition of their heroic achievements impossible. . . . Such persons are valued for what they *are* and for what they *have done* rather than for what they may yet do."[13] Beyond this, theists typically believe that a virtuous character is necessary for the sort of close relationship with God that heaven involves. And many theists believe that the moral rigors of this earthly life prepare us for important spiritual tasks we'll be called on to perform in the life after death.

If God wants us to be virtuous, why didn't he create us as virtuous in the first place? By giving us free will, God "gives us a say" in the kind of persons we will be. Our character is not imposed on us by another.

The soul-making theodicy, however, does seem to come up short in some cases. For example, it is apparently inapplicable in the case of Rowe's fawn. And the deaths of small children, who have had little or no chance to develop the virtues, do not seem to be explained by the soul-making theodicy.

But the soul-making theodicy can and should include the idea that natural evil is caused by the operation of laws of nature. After all, an environment governed by laws of nature seems to be needed for soul-making because free action requires an environment that is predictable to a significant degree. Just consider a simple act such as walking across a street. Such an act is taken on the assumption that the street won't suddenly evaporate, that gravity won't fail, and that one's legs won't turn to jelly. Furthermore, the challenges and dangers of the natural world provide much of the stimulus for soul-making.

But couldn't almighty God create an environment governed by natural laws that do not produce devastating hurricanes, debilitating diseases, and so on? With this suggestion, however, the critic of theism wanders into highly speculative territory, for contemporary science tells us that our universe is "fine-tuned" for life. Extremely minor changes in the fundamental laws of nature would very likely produce a universe that would not support life at all. So no one can say with confidence that God could create a physical universe that both supports life and is governed by laws of nature that do not produce natural evils.

But almighty God can do miracles, so God can always intervene to prevent suffering (e.g., God could relocate Rowe's fawn so that it doesn't get burned). Yes, but as Hasker points out, God's "constant interference . . . would negate the uniformity of natural order," which seems necessary for free action and soul-making.[14] Of course, the critic of theism may claim that a wholly good God would be obligated to intervene in order to prevent the most intense instances of suffering. As Hasker points out, however, this claim needs to be backed up by some plausible moral principle that distinguishes the natural evils God is obligated to prevent from those God is not obligated to prevent. And drawing up a plausible principle of this type is no easy philosophical task.[15]

The soul-making theodicy seems inapplicable to the suffering of non-human animals. And many have felt that "nature red in tooth and claw" fits poorly with the idea that the almighty Creator is also a God of love. But in regard to the suffering of animals, I think the following points merit consideration. First, would the world be a better place without the animals, including the predators? Many of us see the "animal kingdom" as wonderful in spite of the facts concerning predation. Second, we need to be wary of making dubious value judgments. As Hasker observes: "One may be led to hold that it would be better that there be neither hawks nor hares, than that hawks should live by preying on hares; and the destruction of the rain forests may come to seem, on the whole, a beneficent act, in that it greatly reduces the number of creatures that will suffer, die, and be preyed upon."[16]

Third, we should be cautious in making assumptions about the extent of animal suffering. For example, it may be that in a great many cases the victim of predation goes into severe shock and feels little pain. The famous ethologist Jane Goodall, who can hardly be accused of a lack of sympathy for animals, remarks: "Cape hunting dogs, commonly known as wild dogs, and jackals also kill by the method of rapid disembowelment. We . . . hate to watch it and yet, though it seems longer at the time, the victim is usually dead within a couple minutes and *undoubtedly in such a severe state of shock that it cannot feel much pain.*"[17] Furthermore, as we move down the evolutionary scale, to animals with nervous systems and brains very different from our own, such as insects, worms, and jellyfish, we have at best only very weak reasons to suppose that they can feel pain. Reacting to potentially damaging stimuli does not necessarily signal the sensation of pain. (Even in humans, an automatic nervous response can occur in the absence of pain.) Moreover, feeling pain is one thing; suffering is another. Suffering involves (at least) the memory of past pain and the anticipation of future pain. And while I am confident that animals with more highly complex brains (e.g., dolphins, chimps, wolves, cougars, deer, elk, etc.) can suffer, I doubt that animals with much less complex brains (e.g., insects, most mollusks, and fish) can suffer. So, in my opinion, the serious problem of animal suffering arises in connection with animals' having relatively complex brains.

Fourth, consider these questions about the suffering of animals. (1) If there is a Creator-God, is it plausible to suppose that he has a great interest in the animals, given that he has created so many different kinds of them?[18] (2) Among the animals with more highly complex brains, do the hardships and dangers of life in the wild seem to call for the development of rudimentary virtues, that is, tendencies to act that are beneficial for the agent and often for conspecifics too—for example, courage, prudence, patience, perseverance, and a willingness to co-operate? And if so, might there be a kind of rudimentary soul-making going on among animals with relatively complex brains? (3) Further-more, if a loving Creator-God exists, would it be unsurprising if he has some further plans, beyond this earthly life, for those animals ca-pable of developing rudimentary virtues—some way of honoring them and rewarding them for the virtues they have manifested, perhaps granting them a more exalted mode of existence?[19] (4) Finally, while such rudimentary soul-making would by no means explain all animal suffering (think of Rowe's fawn), might it account for much animal suffering? I am inclined to answer all of these questions cautiously but affirmatively.

ROWE'S SECOND PREMISE RECONSIDERED

At this point it is also worth noting that reflections on the moral life may lead theists to deny Rowe's second premise, which I will here sim-plify slightly: An omniscient, wholly good being would prevent the occurrence of any intense suffering it could, unless it could not do so without thereby losing some greater good.[20] Suppose a theist—let's call him Theo—who accepts Rowe's second premise is considering whether to inflict suffering on someone. Theo reasons as follows: "If the suf-fering is not necessary for a greater good, God will prevent me from inflicting it. But if I am successful in inflicting the suffering, it is nec-essary for some greater good—a greater good that will be lost if the suffering does not occur." Or again, suppose Theo tries to prevent some suffering but fails; he then reflects, "Oh well, the suffering will result in a greater good. It's all for the best." Hasker points out that these ways of thinking about suffering undermine morality. Given Rowe's second premise, to attempt a virtuous act would often be to attempt an act contrary to the greater good. And when we think about people inflicting suffering (or harm) on others, we do not generally suppose that if the suffering (or harm) is inflicted, it was necessary for some greater good. So, from this perspective, if God allows us to choose between good and evil, we ought to think that the evils are often gratuitous, that is, not necessary for any greater good.[21]

But if the evils are necessary for the moral life, they are not gratuitous after all, right? Here we must make an important distinction. Taken collectively, as a group, evils are necessary, but taken individually they are not. That is, no specific instance of suffering, harm, or evil is necessary for the moral life. In that sense, evils are gratuitous. Furthermore, it is not plausible to suppose that there is some optimal amount of harm or suffering that God must allow so that if God allowed even one fewer case of harm or suffering, the moral life would not be possible. Thus, reflection on the moral life provides reasons to doubt Rowe's second premise.[22]

GOD'S REASON FOR ALLOWING SUFFERING BEYOND SOUL-MAKING

In addition to the purpose of soul-making, God may have a reason to allow suffering and evil that concerns God's own goodness. In the absence of evil and suffering, God's goodness would be to a large degree *merely dispositional*, that is, it would to a large degree consist in an *unrealized tendency* to act or to have certain attitudes. God would be disposed to empathize with those who suffer, but he would never in fact empathize if no one suffered. God would be disposed to be patient with those who sincerely but imperfectly struggle with temptation, but he would never actually forgive anyone if no one ever sins. God would be disposed to work against evil if the situation called for it, but the situation would not call for it. And if the most profound sort of love requires that the lover be vulnerable to rejection by the beloved and also vulnerable to the suffering of the beloved, then in a world without suffering and evil God's vulnerability would be merely dispositional; it would never be realized in practice.

Merely dispositional virtues, never expressed or realized in practice, are arguably not as praiseworthy or valuable as virtues that have actually borne fruit. For example, suppose that God were to place humans in a perfect paradise with no evil or suffering. In such an environment, some humans might still have the *disposition* to act with courage or compassion, but there would be no opportunity for such action. And it seems to me that such merely dispositional character traits would not be as praiseworthy and valuable as character traits that have been put into action.

Thus, it seems to me that God would have reason to permit the existence of evil and suffering so that his goodness would not remain to a large extent merely dispositional. God would have reason to permit evil, to confront it, and eventually to defeat it. I am not suggesting that God would permit evil without regard for the well-being of his creatures, but I am suggesting that God would have a reason beyond soul-making to permit evil and suffering, namely, so that his goodness might be far less merely dispositional than it would be otherwise. Simply put, the praiseworthiness and value of God's goodness depends partly on what God does.

If God decided to "take on" evil, it seems to me that God would probably not just allow a few minor evils but rather would allow serious evils and many of them.[23] Furthermore, I suggest that a God of love would defeat evil not simply by force—by a "snap of the divine fingers"—but primarily through "soft power"—the appeal to conscience, teaching, preaching, special messengers, and so on. Again, I am not suggesting that a loving God would allow evil simply to render his own goodness less dispositional and without regard for his creatures' well-being. But I am suggesting that a good God would have reason to allow evil and suffering beyond the purpose of soul-making. God's glory (or splendor) is an important value from the standpoint of theism even if that value is not countenanced by non-theists.

Am I suggesting that God improves over time if he creates a world and confronts evil and hence, that prior to creation God is not the greatest possible being? No, I am suggesting that the greatest possible being is one whose goodness becomes much less merely dispositional given the circumstance of creation and the presence of evil. In that sense, I am suggesting that there is a kind of development in the goodness of the greatest possible being. To assess whether a being is the greatest possible being we must consider its entire "life history," so to speak. To put the point negatively, the being who is God might have decided not to create and not to confront evil, but in that case he would not have been the greatest possible being; God's greatness depends partly on what God does.

The above discussion, though brief, illustrates several important things, it seems to me. First, it shows that the problem of evil raises very challenging questions for theism. Second, many popular theodicies are deeply flawed; they explain little or no suffering and evil. Third, the soul-making theodicy explains quite a bit of evil, both moral and natural. But fourth, theists have difficulty in producing a theodicy that explains all instances of harm and suffering in a satisfying way. For example, it seems to me that the question "Why doesn't God intervene more often to prevent suffering?" is not given a fully satisfying answer.

The Comparative Response

At this point theists might have recourse to a moderate version of skeptical theism. Should we really expect to be able to discern God's reason for permitting *every* instance of evil? No worldview can explain everything. And many theists think that by combining the soul-making theodicy with a moderate form of skeptical theism they have an adequate response to the problem of evil.

But there is also another possibility. Theists might offer a version of the comparative response. This response could be combined with a theodicy, such as the soul-making theodicy, and it could also be combined with a version of skeptical theism. (In fact, one can combine all three responses.) According to the comparative response, the main alternatives to theism also falter in explaining evil in terms consistent with their philosophical underpinnings; hence, the problem of evil is not a good reason to reject theism in favor of the main alternative views. I will now briefly illustrate the comparative response in the case of philosophical naturalism, which I take to be the chief contemporary rival of theism. (A developed version of the comparative response must await the discussion of theories of the mind in chapters 10 and 11.) Recall that naturalism is the view that there is no God or anything like God (e.g., no angels or non-physical souls) and that everything is physical.

Let me begin by calling attention to a point that emerged in the discussion of free will in chapter 2. To explain the presence of genuine moral evil in the world, one must have a worldview that allows for free will and moral responsibility. But if the arguments of chapter 2 hold up, this requires free will in the incompatibilist sense (the "power to do otherwise"). In this view, free will is logically incompatible with determinism. If one performs an act A freely at time T, one must be able to refrain from performing A at T; that is, one must have the *power* at time T to act otherwise than one in fact does. And to be morally responsible in acting at a given time T, one must have genuine options at T. But given determinism, there is only one possible pathway into the future; the appearance of options is illusory. And a person can't rightly be blamed (or praised) for doing something if he or she is unable to refrain from doing it due to the causal laws governing physical reality.

Now, in chapter 2 we saw that while some naturalists are determinists, most contemporary naturalists are not because, according to physicists, some laws of nature are probabilistic rather than deterministic. To see the difference, consider the following:

> *Deterministic law:* Given initial conditions A, B, and C, D always occurs.
> *Probabilistic law:* Given initial conditions A, B, and C, D will probably occur, but E might occur.

In the case of a deterministic law, given the initial conditions (A, B, and C), the same result always occurs. For example, if the temperature lowers to 32 degrees Fahrenheit, the water always freezes. In the case of a probabilistic law, more than one result is possible given the initial conditions. For example, the law may tell us that some percentage of atoms of an element (such as radium) will decay over a certain period of time while leaving it open *which* atoms will decay and precisely *when*. Geiger counters illustrate the operation of probabilistic laws because the clicking sounds of a Geiger counter indicate the activity of electrons governed by probabilistic laws.

According to naturalism, only physical things exist. So naturalists take a *physicalist* view of the human person, that is, they deny that humans have non-physical souls. Human beings are one small part of a vast physical system. And in an entirely physical system, all outcomes are a function of two factors: the initial conditions and the laws of nature. Thus, given naturalism, it seems that our thoughts, feelings, desires, intentions, acts, and so on result from past states of the physical world and the operation of the laws of nature. But no human has any choice about the past and the laws of nature. Is there any room for free will in this picture?

Naturalists may respond that people obviously often do what they want to do, without being coerced, and in that sense people often act freely. But if we ask why a person, say Jill, wanted to perform act A (say, shoot Jack), the answer will be along these lines: Jill's desire to shoot Jack was the outcome of the operation of the laws of nature (including the laws governing human brain activity) on past states of the physical world. Is this a situation in which Jill has genuine free will? It seems not. No one would suggest that a Geiger counter acts freely simply because it operates in accord with probabilistic laws of nature. And while of course a human brain is vastly more complex than a Geiger counter, mere complexity is not a guarantee of free will. Would a very complex computer that operates partly in accordance with probabilistic laws have free will—"the power to do otherwise"? I see no reason to think so. Thus, it just doesn't seem plausible to suppose that humans would have (incompatibilist) free will on the assumption that naturalism is true. And if the arguments of chapter 2 hold up, this means naturalism falters in accounting for moral responsibility. But moral evil is the wrongdoing for which humans are morally responsible. So naturalism arguably falters in explaining moral evil. And this is not a small matter.

What about natural evil? And what about suffering in general? Can naturalism explain the presence of suffering? To explore this question, it will be helpful to elaborate a bit on the phenomena of pain and suffering. It is widely agreed that the phenonema of suffering include at least the following:

A. Certain subjective conscious experiences, for example, the hurtfulness of physical pain; the feeling of being miserable; the agony of anxiety; the dreadful feeling of depression; and the raw fear of more suffering to come.

B. Cases in which pain and suffering enter into causal relations. For example: (1) A person experiencing severe chronic pain may opt for suicide as a means of avoiding any further feelings of an extremely un-welcome sort. Here pain and suffering seem to be among the causes of behavior. (2) The belief that others have been harmed or killed can cause suffering in the form of deep sadness, anxiety, or despair. Here a mental state (a belief) is apparently the cause of (or among the causes of) mental pain and suffering. (3) After an earthquake, a family may sleep outside and suffer in the bitter cold because they fear that after-shocks will cause their house to collapse. Here physical pain and suf-fering apparently result (in part) from the mental state of fear.

Just as theists struggle to explain why God would permit certain types of suffering, naturalists may struggle in providing an adequate explanation of A and/or B. But for naturalists the problems arise be-cause of questions about their theories of the mind. Because naturalists offer many different theories of the mind, a full development of the comparative view involves an examination of the various naturalistic theories of the mind. There is no way to conduct such an examination briefly, and a more extensive look at naturalistic theories must await the discussion in chapters 10 and 11. Here I can only illustrate the basic approach by considering two kinds of naturalistic theories of the mind.

Epiphenomenalism. Epiphenomenalists hold that mental states (e.g., thoughts, desires, feelings, intentions, and choices) are caused by physical states (e.g., brain states), but mental states themselves cause nothing. From this perspective, mental states are analogous to the shadows cast by a car as it moves down a road; the shadows are caused by the car's blocking the sun's rays, but the shadows do not, in turn, have any causal effect on the car's motion. (Mental states do not cause physical states, such as brain states.) Nor is the shadow at a given mo-ment caused by the shadow from the preceding moment; the shadows are caused by the car. (Mental states do not cause other mental states.)[24] Epiphenomenalists admit the reality of mental states, including sub-jective conscious experiences of pain. But by denying mental states any causal powers, epiphenomenalists must deny all of the phenomena included in B above. Relatively few naturalists explicitly endorse epiphenomenalism; the clash with common sense is simply too great.[25] It is hard to believe, for example, that the feeling of pain does not cause victims of torture to scream or to feel fear. Nevertheless, our discussion in chapters 10 and 11 will consider arguments to the effect that some commonly held naturalistic theories of the mind lead to epiphenomenalism *by implication*.

Reductive Physicalism. Reductive physicalists claim that mental states are wholly *reducible* to physical states, that is, mental states are nothing over and above physical states. An example of reductive physicalism is the mind-brain identity theory, the view that mental states are identical to brain states. (Just as water is H_2O, mental states are simply brain states.) A standard objection to this theory is that it fails to account for subjective conscious experiences. No amount of information about the brain, neurons, dendrites, axons, and so on tells us *what it is like* to feel a sharp pain or to smell ammonia. We might put the point this way: Suppose we could provide an extraterrestrial visitor with a complete set of biological facts about the human body, including all the neurobiological details about the workings of the human brain. If we confine ourselves to these physical facts, we will leave out something important, namely, such subjective conscious experiences as the feeling of pain or the experience of smelling ammonia.

A common reply is that the complete physical description does not leave out these subjective conscious experiences; it merely refers to them using a different (i.e., neurobiological) description. But here many philosophers agree with John Searle: A description of the world in third-person physical terms such as scientists provide is not a complete description of the world. What is left out is precisely the subjective, first-person, conscious phenomena, for example, *what it is like* for a person to experience pain or the smell of ammonia.[26] And Thomas Nagel makes the same point with his famous question "What is it like to be a bat?" Imagine a researcher who can fully describe, in neurobiological terms, the workings of a bat's brain. Her account leaves out what it is like to experience the world in the way a bat does. And thus an interesting and important feature of reality has been omitted.[27] Facts about first-person, conscious experiences are not metaphysically reducible to facts about neurobiology.

Furthermore, the identity theory explains mental causation by reducing it to physical causation. But does this provide us with a satisfying explanation of mental causation? Consider that one mental state can apparently be causally linked to another mental state partly by virtue of their informational contents. For example, think of undergoing a sequence of thought such as the following:

Some pasta would taste good tonight → I think I'll go to an Italian restaurant

In such cases, one thought plausibly gives rise to (i.e., causes) the next. But the causal links surely somehow involve the *informational content* of the mental states. For example, no one with a minimal knowledge of ethnic cuisines is apt to move from "Some pasta would taste good tonight" to "I think I'll go to a Japanese restaurant." Brain states, however, are linked by neurobiological factors; the account is given in terms of axons, dendrites, chemical synapses, electrical synapses, neurotransmitters, ion channels, and so on. So, we *seem* to have two very different causal chains here: one that involves the informational content of the mental states and one that involves the purely neurobiological factors.

An analogy may be helpful at this point. Suppose you plug a thumb drive into your computer so you can remind yourself of the lyrics of a song. The lyrics are classic: "My baby left me. I'm so sad. And life is bad." Now, there are two sequences here. First, the lyrics of the song form a sequence of thoughts involving informational content, one thought leading to the next. Second, there is a complex series of electronic events in the thumb drive involving silicon chips, capacitors (which store a charge), and transistors (each of which can be switched on or off, controlling the movement of electrons). The two different kinds of sequences coincide perfectly because the thumb drive is designed so that the processes within it can reproduce the words of the song. But plainly there are two *distinct* kinds of sequences here, and it seems to me that the thumb drive analogy strongly suggests that a thought sequence is a very different thing than any sort of causal sequence that can be spelled out in terms of electrical events—including the electrochemical events in the brain.

Moreover, since the identity theorist insists that there are not two distinct causal chains, but just one, it seems to me that instead of providing a satisfying explanation of mental causation, the identity theory in fact changes the subject. The causal story becomes an entirely physical, neurobiological story. But in my estimation, this leaves us with a very unsatisfying account of mental causation—at least in cases in which mental states are apparently causally linked (in part) by way of their informational content. It is a bit like trying to explain the lyrical sequence "My baby left me → I'm so sad" by producing a detailed description of the complex sequence of electronic events within the thumb drive. The informational aspect of the causal linkage is not illuminated.

Here ends the illustration of the comparative response to the problem of evil. But as we shall see in chapters 10 and 11, objections similar to those I've summarized for epiphenomenalism and the mind-brain identity theory have been raised against all the main naturalistic theories. Of course, many naturalists think that there are ways of getting around these problems. So they think they face no serious problem of evil. But it's not as if there is a consensus among philosophers as to how physicalists can refute the well-known objections to their views. Note also that many theists think that *they* have ways of getting around the problem of evil; for instance, many theists *think* they have an adequate theodicy. Many other theists believe that a combination of theodicies (which explain much but not all evil) together with a moderate version of skeptical theism gives them an adequate response to the problem of evil. So do neither naturalists nor theists face a serious problem of evil? Or would it be more correct to say that both face difficulties in explaining the phenomena of suffering and evil? Proponents of the comparative approach claim that both do.

To sum up, the problem of evil is a very important objection to traditional theism. Theists try to respond in various ways. Though many theodicies fail badly, the soul-making theodicy explains quite a bit of evil. The overrider response is only as good as the positive evidence for the existence of a perfectly good God. Skeptical theism seems weak unless it can be successfully combined with a plausible theodicy that explains much of the evil in the world. Finally, via the comparative response, theists seek to put the problem of evil into perspective by arguing that rival metaphysical positions face quite significant problems of evil of their own.[28]

FOUR

Why Think God Is Good?

Stephen Law challenges theists to explain why the hypothesis of an almighty, omniscient, perfectly good God (the "good-God" hypothesis) is more reasonable than the hypothesis of an almighty, omniscient, supremely evil God (the "evil-God" hypothesis).[1] Law claims that arguments offered for the good-God hypothesis often fail to provide much (if any) evidence for God's goodness. For example, even if the fine-tuning of the universe provides grounds for believing that a powerful intelligence created the universe, the motives of the Creator might well have been evil, for example, an evil God might create a universe involving conscious beings in order to enjoy their suffering, their wickedness, and the harm they do one another.[2]

Law is not arguing for the existence of an evil God. In fact, he thinks the hypothesis of an evil God is unreasonable.[3] Thus he thinks that if the good-God hypothesis is not significantly more reasonable than the evil-God hypothesis, both are unreasonable. The challenge for theists, then, is to show that the good-God hypothesis is significantly more reasonable than the evil-God hypothesis.

Law emphasizes parallels between the good-God and the evil-God hypotheses. As is well known, the presence of evil poses a difficulty for the good-God hypothesis. Similarly, the presence of good (e.g., beauty, pleasure, moral virtue) poses a difficulty for the evil-God hypothesis. But just as the good-God hypothesis can be defended via theodicies, such as the soul-making theodicy, the evil-God hypothesis can be defended via "reverse theodicies."[4] For example, evil God gives humans free will so that they can be genuinely responsible for wicked actions, but of course free will carries with it the risk that humans will sometimes choose to perform virtuous or right actions. If evil God did not give us free will, we would be puppet-like beings. And "the behavior of such puppet beings lacks the dimension of moral responsibility that transforms such acts into actions of the most depraved and despicable kind."[5]

But why would evil God create natural beauty? "To provide contrast. To make what is ugly seem even more so."[6] And the "need for contrast also explains why evil god bestows lavish lifestyles and success upon a few. Their happiness is designed to make the suffering of the rest of us even more acute."[7]

Law argues that there is a symmetry between the good-God hypothesis and the evil-God hypothesis. In general, moves used to defend the good-God hypothesis can be mirrored by equally plausible (or equally implausible) moves in defense of the evil-God hypothesis. Law's "reverse theodicies" and his explanation of the presence of beauty (on the assumption that an evil God exists) illustrate this point. But what about miracles and religious experience? Don't they support the good-God hypothesis (and not the evil-God hypothesis)? Not so, according to Law:

> Suppose the evil-god hypothesis is true. This malignant being may not want us to know of his existence. In fact, it may help him maximize evil if he deceives us about his true character. An evil and omnipotent being will have no difficulty duping human beings into believing he is good. Taking on a "good" guise, he might appear to one corner of the world, revealing himself in religious experiences and performing miracles in response to prayers, and perhaps also giving instructions regarding what his followers should believe. He might then do the same in another part of the globe, with the exception that the instructions he leaves regarding what should be believed contradict what he has said elsewhere. Our evil being could then stand back and watch the inevitable conflict develop between communities to whom he has now misleadingly revealed himself, each utterly convinced by their own stock of miracles and religious experiences that the one true all-good god is on their side. Here we have a recipe for ceaseless conflict, violence and suffering.[8]

But surely an evil God would place us in a far worse situation than we find ourselves in. Wouldn't an evil God "just send us straight to hell"? Here Law responds that "a mirror puzzle faces those who believe in a good god. Given that a heavenly environment would be profoundly more joyful than this earthly environment, why doesn't a good god send us straight to heaven?"[9]

What about our grasp of the moral law, of right and wrong? Surely an evil God would have no interest in providing us with the knowledge of good and evil. Not so, according to Law, for "by providing us with both free will and knowledge of good and evil, an evil god can allow for the very great evil of our freely performing evil actions in the full knowledge that they are, indeed, evil."[10]

Some theists will insist that there are no objective moral values apart from the commands of a good God. But this claim faces Plato's Euthyphro dilemma:

> Suppose we say that God, as divine law-maker, decrees that certain things, such as stealing and murder, are wrong. Does God decree this because He recognizes that stealing and murder are, independently, wrong, or are they wrong only because He decrees them to be so? The first answer makes God redundant so far as setting up a standard of right and wrong is concerned—murder would have been wrong anyway, whether or not God exists, or, indeed, whether or not God Himself happens to be good or evil. But then the objective . . . wrongness of murder would obtain anyway, even if there were an evil God.[11]

The second answer—that acts such as stealing and murder are wrong only because God decrees them to be so—"appears to make the moral wrongness of murder arbitrary and relative. Notice that this is a problem whichever of our two god hypotheses we favour."[12] Thus, the Euthyphro dilemma blocks any attempt to support the good-God hypothesis over the evil-God hypothesis by means of a moral argument.

Although Law does not mention this, we might also note that the problem of divine hiddenness would seem to favor the evil-God hypothesis. If a perfectly loving God exists, he wants all created persons to have a personal relationship (analogous to friendship) with him. But

such a relationship is impossible for created persons if they do not believe that God exists. And many people do not believe that God exists
through no fault of their own. For example, they may have been
brought up in a religion that does not involve the belief that God exists,
such as Theravada Buddhism. Or they may simply find the standard
arguments for God's existence unconvincing. An almighty, loving God
could certainly make his existence known to all created persons and
would surely do so (except perhaps in the case of persons, if any, who
do not want to have a relationship with God). So, if a good God exists,
why are there so many people who, *through no fault of their own*, do
not believe that God exists? Theists have struggled to provide a satisfying answer to this question. But the presence of *inculpable* non-theism
is easily explained by the evil-God hypothesis. (By "non-theism" here
I mean "not believing that good God exists." Thus, non-theism includes
atheism, agnosticism, polytheism, the belief in a morally indifferent
God, ignorance of the very concept of a perfectly good God, and so
on.) For example, while an evil God might dupe some groups into
thinking that he is good, he might dupe others into thinking that there
are no supernatural beings at all, or into thinking that Deism or polytheism is true. And an evil God might simply bewilder others, making
them suspend judgment with regard to the existence of any sort of God
or gods.

Law admits that there may be *some* asymmetries between the good-
God and evil-God hypotheses: "For example, if we suppose free will is
itself an intrinsic good, then the reverse free-will theodicy involves an
evil god imbuing us with the good of free will. While an evil god may
still be able to maximize evil by giving us free will, he will nevertheless
have to pay a price (introducing that intrinsic good)—a price for which
there is no parallel in the standard free-will theodicy."[13] According to
Law, however, the effect of such "asymmetries appears to be compara-
tively minor, having little effect on the overall balance of reasonableness."[14] After all, if we are "to have a full range of choices between good
and evil, God, whether good or evil, must introduce pain, suffering,
and death not just as possibilities but as realities."[15] And "if it is prima
facie plausible that free will is an intrinsic good, it is no less plausible
that pain, suffering, and death are intrinsic evils."[16] In short, while it is
true that an evil God would have to use some intrinsic goods to achieve

his purposes, it is equally true that a good God would have to use some intrinsic evils to achieve his ends.

To sum up, if we take into account all the phenomena typically used to build a case for the good-God hypothesis, we see that the evil-God hypothesis explains these phenomena about as well as the good-God hypothesis does. So, the good-God hypothesis is apparently not significantly more reasonable than the evil-God hypothesis. But most would agree that the evil-God hypothesis is unreasonable. This being so, the good-God hypothesis is also unreasonable.

Naturally, we need to consider some possible replies to Law's evil-God challenge. But before taking up possible replies, I think three preliminary comments will be helpful.

PRELIMINARIES

First, in assessing hypotheses, we must take into account two main factors: (1) their explanatory power and (2) their prior probability. We assess the explanatory power of a hypothesis by asking, "If the hypothesis were true, to what extent would it make the phenomenon in question probable or unsurprising?" But in deciding which hypothesis among rivals is best, we also need to consider the *prior probability* of the hypotheses, roughly, how plausible they are independent of ("prior to considering") the phenomenon we are trying to explain. To illustrate the difference between explanatory power and prior probability, consider the following example. Suppose the door to Smythe's apartment has been forced open; her computer and some expensive jewelry are missing. (This is the phenomenon we are trying to explain.) Now consider two hypotheses:

H1: Someone stole Smythe's computer and jewelry.
H2: Someone, under the guidance of—and with the assistance of—a good God, stole Smythe's computer and jewelry.

These hypotheses are equal in explanatory power—if we assume that they are true, they render the phenomenon completely unsurprising, and they do so to the same degree. But the two hypotheses differ in prior probability. Burglary is not uncommon, so H1 is a plausible hypothesis. H2 is much less plausible for at least two reasons. First, for any given instance of a morally wrong act (such as an instance of burglary), a *good* God probably would not guide and assist anyone in performing it.[17] Second, H2 is intuitively more complicated than H1, and a complication is *unnecessary* if it is not needed to explain the phenomenon in question. Thus H2 contains unnecessary complications. And most would agree that a hypothesis that contains *unnecessary* complications is less plausible than a rival hypothesis that contains no such complications—philosophers call this *the principle of simplicity*.[18] For these two reasons, H1 has a much higher *prior* probability than H2.

Second, Law's arguments focus on showing that the good-God and evil-God hypotheses are similar in explanatory power. He has done nothing to show that the two hypotheses are similar in prior probability. Hence, we need to consider the possibility that the two hypotheses differ in prior probability.

Third, I would like to note that I do not share the opinion that the evil-God hypothesis is *obviously* unreasonable. No doubt it seems laughable to many or even most philosophical naturalists, who deny that God (or anything supernatural) exists. And even to those who are quite open to theological hypotheses, the evil-God hypothesis may seem "too bad to be true"—a worst-case scenario that tops them all, a metaphysical "conspiracy theory" than which none greater can be conceived! Furthermore, if one hasn't thought much about the evil-God hypothesis, one might easily assume that it has little by way of explanatory power. But Law has argued with great plausibility that the evil-God hypothesis has considerable explanatory power. And for this reason, I think it deserves to be taken seriously.

Now let's consider some possible replies to Law's evil-God challenge.

THEOLOGICAL VOLUNTARISM

Theological voluntarism (TV) is the view that an act (motive, character trait, etc.) is right or good if, *and simply because*, the almighty Creator approves of it, and an act (motive, character trait, etc.) is wrong or evil if, *and simply because*, the almighty Creator disapproves of it. From the perspective of TV, the evil-God hypothesis seems to be metaphysically impossible, for presumably, if evil God exists, he approves of his own actions, in which case, according to TV, his actions are right; they are not evil.

Could we imagine that evil God always disapproves of his own actions, thus making them wrong or evil? If evil God disapproves of his own actions for adequate reasons, surely the reasons are what make evil God's actions wrong, and not merely the fact that he disapproves of them—contrary to TV. On the other hand, if evil God disapproves of all of his own actions for no reason, his disapprovals are quite mystifying, in which case the evil-God hypothesis is very implausible. In fact, a being who disapproves of all of his own actions for *no reason whatsoever* strikes me as deeply irrational. Moreover, if evil God disapproves of all of his own actions for weak (inadequate) reasons, then, once again, his disapprovals are mystifying; for a being who consistently disapproves of his own actions for inadequate reasons is surely irrational.

But why not assume that evil God is irrational? Because doing so would make Law's entire argument collapse. Notice that Law's evil God is a being who consistently acts for reasons that make perfectly good sense *given his evil purposes*. If we suppose that evil God is irrational, we can make no predictions about what he might do or bring about. All bets are off. An irrational evil God might well act contrary to his own purposes, and he might do so consistently. Or inconsistently. In short, the hypothesis of an irrational God has very little explanatory power. There's no way to know (or even to make reasonable guesses about) what such a being might do.

To sum up, if the almighty Creator always approves of his own acts, then, according to TV, his acts are right or good, not wrong or evil, in which case the Creator is good and certainly not supremely evil. And if the almighty Creator sometimes approves of his own acts and sometimes disapproves, then, given TV, he is morally imperfect but not *supremely* (maximally) evil. Furthermore, if the almighty Creator always disapproves of his own acts for adequate reasons, those reasons surely contribute to the wrongness of the acts and the acts are not wrong *simply because* the Creator disapproves of them—contrary to

TV. But if the almighty Creator disapproves of all of his own acts for no reason or for inadequate reasons, he is irrational—in which case there is no telling what he might do, and the evil-God hypothesis is low in explanatory power (contrary to what Law claims). Therefore, from the standpoint of TV, a *supremely* evil God is either impossible or irrational, and hence the evil-God hypothesis is either very low in prior probability or very low in explanatory power.

Does this give us a strong argument against the evil-God hypothesis? Unfortunately, it does not. Instead, we have a reductio ad absurdum of TV.[19] No matter what the God of TV does, as long as he approves of his own actions, they are good or right. The God of TV could create millions of persons and immediately place them in the torment of hell forever—for no just cause and with no chance of escape—and still be doing the right thing! In short, the God of TV can do *anything* we might expect a supremely evil God to do and yet still count as good. But this only means that TV gives us an utterly inadequate account of divine goodness.

THE COHERENCE OF THE EVIL-GOD HYPOTHESIS

Keith Ward has argued that the concept of a wholly evil God is incoherent, for a wholly evil God "would have to realize all disvalues. So it would have to be maximally weak, maximally ignorant, in maximal pain and misery, and maximally depressed."[20] Furthermore, "It would know that it would be better if it did not exist. . . . [So] if it was omnipotent, it would commit suicide. But it is too weak to do so. A very miserable, and weak, and ignorant God would not be maximally evil anyway, since it would be unable to cause maximal evil successfully, so the idea of a supremely worthless being is incoherent."[21] Obviously, a being could not be omnipotent, as evil God is supposed to be, and also maximally weak. Nor could a being be omniscient, as evil God is supposed to be, and also maximally ignorant. But before we accept Ward's reasoning, we should note that a similar type of argument can be applied to the concept of a greatest possible being. And of course, most theists regard God as the greatest possible being.

If the greatest possible being must *realize all positive values*, he would have to be physically beautiful and a superb athlete. In that case, however, the greatest possible being would have to be a physical entity. But physical entities are governed by laws of nature, and so they are not omnipotent. Also, physical entities are typically regarded as *contingent* in nature, that is, they do exist but could fail to exist under certain circumstances. By contrast, the greatest possible being is typically regarded as a *necessary* being—one that cannot fail to exist under any possible circumstances.[22] Thus, in elaborating the concept of the greatest possible being, we encounter trade-offs. Since a being apparently cannot be both physical and omnipotent, we must ask whether physical beauty or omnipotence is of greater value. Traditional theists clearly regard omnipotence as of greater value than physical beauty, and from this perspective the greatest possible being is omnipotent but not physically beautiful. Similarly, since a being apparently cannot be both physical and necessarily existent, traditional theists claim that the greatest possible being is not physical but exists of necessity. No being can realize *all* of the positive values.

We face similar trade-offs in developing the concept of an evil God. We must ask, "What attributes would make a being as evil (bad) as possible?" And Law's nightmarish concept of a being who is omnipotent, omniscient, and thoroughly malicious (i.e., thoroughly bent on causing undeserved harm and suffering) seems a plausible candidate for the post "as bad as possible." What could be worse? I confess that Law's evil God seems to me as bad as bad can be, even if he does have some admirable attributes, such as omniscience and omnipotence. After all, these attributes make him extremely dangerous—far more dangerous than he would be if he were abysmally ignorant and a total wimp. Thus, as far as I can see, Ward's attempt to show that *the concept of an evil God is incoherent* fails.

OMNISCIENCE AND THE EVIL-GOD HYPOTHESIS

Ward also argues that an omniscient God will not cause suffering, for if he is omniscient, "God will know what it is like for another being to feel suffering."[23] So if "God has feelings, then God knows what suffering is like, and knows, whenever others suffer, exactly what their suffering feels like. This entails that God will feel that suffering with perfect empathy. That is what total omniscience involves."[24] Therefore, an "omniscient God will . . . not cause pain to others, since that entails some corresponding lessening of pleasure in God."[25] On the other hand, if God has no feelings, he could take no pleasure in causing harm and suffering and so presumably has no reason to inflict harm and suffering on others.

But if X knows what Y's suffering feels like, does it necessarily follow that X's pleasure is lessened? I think not. A torturer may know what his victim's suffering feels like. The torturer may have been tortured in the same way himself, or he may have experimented on himself so that he knows what the pain is like. And yet he may enjoy torturing his victim. Or he may be indifferent to the victim's suffering — he just doesn't care. And it seems to me that it is part of the nature of an evil person that he takes pleasure in the suffering of others or is indifferent to it. Moreover, a person's pleasure in the suffering of another may be greater than it would otherwise be precisely because he does know what the experience is like.

Perhaps Ward would reply that human torturers, unlike omniscient beings, are not perfect in empathy. But why suppose that an omniscient being must be empathetic? An omniscient being may well understand the suffering of others without vicariously experiencing their feelings or feeling sorry for the sufferers. Consider an example. Suppose Jane has just stubbed her toe. I know what stubbing one's toe feels like. I know it hurts a lot. But do I thereby necessarily empathize with Jane? No. Maybe I dislike Jane and secretly enjoy the fact that she's in pain. Even if, in order to understand Jane's pain, I must at some previous time have experienced the pain of stubbing my toe, understanding her pain does not require that I experience it vicariously or feel sorry for her.

There are deep questions here about what omniscience involves and about a non-physical being's knowledge of physical pain and suffering: (A) Does omniscience consist simply in knowing every true proposition (and believing no false ones)? Or does it also involve knowledge by acquaintance, that is, personal experience? (One might know a lot of true propositions about Paris without having experienced the city firsthand.) (B) And *how* could a non-physical being know what it is like to experience physical pain, for example, a sharp pain in the knee or a migraine headache? More generally, how would a God have knowledge of the mental states of his conscious creatures? (If mental telepathy is at least logically possible, then presumably an omnipotent God can communicate directly with created minds, and if thoughts can be communicated in this way, perhaps feelings and emotions can be, too?) These are good questions, but they arise for the good-God hypothesis as well as for the evil-God hypothesis. Accordingly, I see no special problem for the evil-God hypothesis in this vicinity.

To sum up, as far as I can see, an evil, omniscient God might know that his creatures are suffering, and know what their suffering is like, and yet take pleasure in their suffering or be indifferent to it. Thus, a God's omniscience is not by itself a guarantee that he will not cause suffering.

THE OVERRIDING REASONS THESIS

Moral theorists generally agree that if an act is morally required, one has overriding reason to perform it, and if an act is morally wrong, one has overriding reason not to perform it. Let's call this the "overriding reasons thesis" (ORT, for short). To clarify the meaning of the ORT, let me offer an example. Suppose I am late to work and I have no good excuse for being late, but a plausible lie occurs to me: "There was a bad accident on the way to work and traffic was tied up." Now, I may well have a reason to lie—perhaps lying will keep me out of trouble with my boss. But of course I have a moral reason not to lie, namely, that lying is wrong—at least in this type of case. And if lying is wrong in this case, then, given ORT, I have a stronger reason not to lie than to lie—however tempting it might be to tell a lie.

Morally serious people in general assume or presuppose that the ORT is true. If an act is morally required (all things considered), one must perform it and, *simply because the act is morally required*, one has a stronger reason to perform it than any reason one might have not to

perform it. Furthermore, if an act is morally wrong, one must not perform it and, *simply because the act is morally wrong*, one has a stronger
reason not to perform it than any reason one might have to perform it.

Does ORT hold *on the assumption that evil God exists*? Whether
it does or does not, there is a serious problem for the evil-God hypothesis. Let me explain.

First, let's assume that the ORT holds given that evil God exists.
Evil God is omniscient, so evil God has an exhaustive knowledge of
morality; he knows (in complete detail) what is morally required, what
is morally permissible, and what is morally wrong. Furthermore, if the
ORT is true, evil God knows that it is true. So evil God knows that he
has an overriding reason to do those things that are morally required
and an overriding reason not to do those things that are morally wrong.
*Moreover, evil God is all-powerful; so it is not hard for him to do what
is morally right.* Why, then, doesn't evil God behave morally? Why
does evil God characteristically do evil (morally wrong) things?

We humans often fail morally because we get tired, scared, or confused, or we may be caught off guard or overcome by desire. But an
omniscient and omnipotent being does not suffer from such weaknesses. As an omniscient being, evil God always knows what is morally
required of him—he is never confused or caught off guard. And as an
omnipotent being, he is always able to do what is morally required
simply by willing to do so—an omnipotent being doesn't get tired or
scared or overcome by desire. Notice, too, that, given ORT, in order
to commit morally wrong or evil acts, evil God would have to act on
weaker reasons when he is perfectly aware that stronger (moral) reasons apply. Therefore, the suggestion that an omnipotent and omniscient being *who knows the ORT is true* would characteristically act in
evil ways is deeply puzzling. The motivational structure of such a
being seems strange and implausible; for this reason we must assign
Law's evil-God hypothesis a relatively low *prior* probability, that is, a
lower prior probability than the good-God hypothesis, since good
God always acts on the strongest reasons that apply (including when
moral reasons are the strongest ones that apply).[26] (Recall that the prior
probability of a hypothesis is, roughly speaking, the plausibility it has
independent of—"prior to considering"—the phenomenon one is trying to explain.)

A further problem arises here. As we've just noted, given the ORT, in order to commit morally wrong or evil actions, evil God would have to act on *weaker* reasons when he is perfectly aware that stronger, overriding, moral reasons apply. So there is an obvious sense in which a supremely evil God would be irrational. But if evil God is irrational, Law's argument seems to break down, for there is no predicting what an irrational god might do. Law's argument proceeds by providing reasons why evil God would create conscious beings, provide them with free will, give them knowledge of good and evil, create beauty, and so on. But a god who often acts on weaker or inferior reasons, *when he could just as easily act on stronger or superior reasons*, is not a god whose acts can be explained by identifying apparently strong reasons why he would do thus and so. From this perspective, the evil-God hypothesis seems to be *low in explanatory power* (in addition to being low in prior probability).

Could Law respond as follows? "Evil God acts on the strongest reasons except when they are moral reasons; so, evil God may be irrational in one sense, but his motivations are not really very puzzling. Moreover, we can offer reasonable hypotheses about what evil God would do—as reasonable as the hypotheses we can offer regarding what good God would do. So, the evil-God hypothesis has as much explanatory power as the good-God hypothesis." There are at least two problems with this response. First, it complicates the evil-God hypothesis. We are now supposing that evil God acts on the strongest non-moral reasons but not on the strongest reasons in general. Clearly, that's a more complicated motivational structure than the motivational structure of a being who always acts on the strongest reasons. This complication makes the evil-God hypothesis less simple in one important respect than the hypothesis of an omnipotent being who always acts on the strongest reasons. So, by the principle of simplicity, this version of the evil-God hypothesis has an important demerit. Second, the postulated selective irrationality is mystifying. Why does evil God act on inferior or weaker reasons when overriding moral reasons apply? Note: "Because he is evil" is not an explanation. As an omnipotent being, evil God can do what is morally required simply by willing to do so; it's not as if he is overcome by wicked desires, too weak to break a bad habit, or anything of that sort. So the suggestion that evil God acts on the strongest reasons unless they are moral reasons is mystifying and hence implausible. For these reasons, the hypothesis of an evil God *who acts on the strongest applicable reasons except when they are moral reasons* has a relatively low prior probability.

By comparison, the idea that an omniscient, omnipotent being would always act on the strongest reasons is both simpler and non-mysterious. In every situation such a being knows what the strongest relevant reasons are and can act on them simply by willing to do so; therefore, that's what he does. And, given ORT, this means we should expect an omniscient, omnipotent being to always act in morally right or virtuous ways. Accordingly, we ought to assign the good-God hypothesis a significantly higher prior probability than the evil-God hypothesis.[27]

Now, if the good-God and evil-God hypotheses are about equal in explanatory power, as Law argues, then if the good-God hypothesis has a significantly higher prior probability than the evil-God hypothesis, the good-God hypothesis is more reasonable than the evil-God hypothesis. I conclude that, assuming ORT holds, the good-God hypothesis is indeed more reasonable than the evil-God hypothesis.

Let me briefly comment on two matters that may cause some to question my reasoning to this point:

1. My argument assumes that there are objective truths about what is morally required and what is morally wrong. (Here an *objective truth* is roughly one that holds whether or not anyone believes it.) But as our discussion of theological voluntarism indicates, we must make this assumption even to make sense of the evil-God hypothesis: A God must violate an objective standard of moral goodness or rightness in order to count as evil in any relevant sense. So the assumption that there are objective moral truths is entirely legitimate in context. It is also independently plausible, though this is not the place to defend that claim.

2. It is sometimes suggested that moral standards do not apply to an omnipotent and omniscient being—that such a being is "beyond good and evil." But first, if moral standards don't apply, the evil-God hypothesis is a non-starter. We cannot speak sensibly of an omnipotent, omniscient being *who is also evil* if moral standards do not

apply to beings who are omnipotent and omniscient. Second, the suggestion is implausible. Moral standards apply to persons who are exceptionally strong physically or extremely powerful politically. So, being very powerful seems not to place one outside the moral realm. Similarly, moral standards apply to geniuses just as they apply to persons of average intelligence. And moral standards apply to extremely knowledgeable persons just as they apply to persons who have a relatively limited knowledge base. So having greater intelligence or knowledge than others in no way places one outside the sphere of right and wrong. Third, theologians and philosophers often claim—with great plausibility—that a God (omnipotent and omniscient) who would act in certain ways would be *unjust* or *unloving*, for example, a God who consigns those who die as infants to eternal hell or a God who breaks his promises. Accordingly, the claim that an omnipotent and omniscient being is "beyond good and evil" seems both ungrounded and implausible.

So far, then, my argument apparently holds up: If the ORT is true, the evil-God hypothesis has a significantly lower prior probability than the good-God hypothesis. And so the good-God hypothesis is more reasonable than the evil-God hypothesis.

But what if the ORT is not true *on the assumption that evil God exists*? And indeed, it may well be that if evil God were to exist, the ORT would be false; for evil God might severely penalize morally virtuous persons while he rewards the wicked (or at least gives them lesser penalties). And in such a scenario, it might be true that people often or typically have overriding reason *not* to do their moral duty. If, however, the ORT is false given that evil God exists, then the evil-God hypothesis is, in one very important respect, lacking in explanatory power; for, as previously noted, moral theorists and morally serious people in general claim (or presuppose) that the ORT does hold. And I take this to be strong evidence that the ORT is true. So any view that leads us to deny the ORT (or even to have serious doubts about it) is problematic. By contrast, given the good-God hypothesis, the ORT is to be expected. Doing what is morally required often involves sacrifices on the part of the agent, but a good God can and will ensure that ultimately—in the long run (which includes the life after death)—no one ever really "gets ahead" by performing wrong acts, and no one ever loses true blessedness by performing right acts.

Two clarifications may be needed here: (a) I am not suggesting that one can earn heaven by being morally virtuous. According to many theists, no one is that good; salvation is by divine grace—*unmerited* favor. Nevertheless, despite appearances, it is never to one's advantage to do wrong; doing wrong is sinning, and sinning separates one from God, which is never to a creature's advantage. (b) I am not suggesting that we should perform right acts in order to get a reward; we should do the right thing simply because it's right. But I am claiming that a good God would ensure that doing one's duty never *ultimately* penalizes the agent.

To sum up, I've argued that the ORT spells trouble for the evil-God hypothesis. (A) Assuming that the ORT is true and that evil God knows that the ORT is true, it is deeply puzzling why evil God does evil (wrong) things. After all, as an omnipotent being, evil God could act on the stronger (moral) reasons just by willing to do so. But if evil God's motivations are deeply puzzling, we must assign the evil-God hypothesis a relatively low prior probability—lower than that of the good-God hypothesis. (B) Furthermore, if the ORT is true, evil God is irrational since he frequently acts on weaker reasons when he knows that stronger (moral) ones apply. But Law's evil God is clearly meant to be rational and to consistently act in accord with his own purposes. (C) If Law were to claim that evil God is selectively irrational, acting contrary to the strongest reasons only when (overriding) moral reasons apply, the prior probability of the evil-God hypothesis is still relatively low for two reasons: (i) the postulated motivational structure of evil God is more complex than that of good God and (ii) it remains mystifying to suggest that an omnipotent being acts on weaker reasons when he can act on stronger reasons simply by willing to do so. (D) Finally, on the assumption that an evil God exists, the ORT is arguably false or at least very questionable. But according to moral theorists and morally serious people in general, the ORT does hold. This means that the evil-God hypothesis—unlike the good-God hypothesis—suffers from an important explanatory failure in regard to the ORT.

In conclusion, given the ORT, the good-God hypothesis has a higher prior probability than the evil-God hypothesis. Furthermore, the evil-God hypothesis calls the ORT into question, while the good-God hypothesis upholds it; this signals an important explanatory failure on the part of the evil-God hypothesis. For these reasons, it seems to me that the good-God hypothesis is much more reasonable than the evil-God hypothesis.

An Epistemological Problem?

Suppose that Eva is in a locked room by herself. Statements written on note cards are slipped into the room every few minutes. The statements are about matters concerning that Eva has no prior information; moreover, Eva has no independent way to check or corroborate the statements. Furthermore, suppose that Eva believes (never mind why) that the source of the written statements is a thoroughly wicked, evil person. If Eva really believes that the source is a thoroughly wicked, evil person, should she judge that the information she is receiving is *reliable* — that it is true for the most part? Surely not. On the assumption that the source is thoroughly evil, she would be very foolish to conclude that the information was reliable. Instead, she would rightly judge that, given the source, the information is not to be trusted.

Now let's suppose that you believe the evil-God hypothesis. Given that hypothesis, your cognitive faculties are created by a supremely evil person. They might be created directly, or they might be created indirectly via processes evil God controls. But given the evil-God hypothesis, your situation is similar to Eva's: The ultimate source of all your information is a supremely evil person. And on the assumption that a maximally evil God created your cognitive faculties (either directly or indirectly), the reliability of those faculties is questionable. They might yield more falsehood than truth, possibly a lot more falsehood than truth. And they might be designed to keep you confused or in error about the things that matter most to you. Thus, given the evil-God hypothesis, it seems that you are led into a state of radical doubt. Any of your beliefs might well be mistaken. But notice that this applies to your belief in the evil-God hypothesis itself. You believe it and it seems true to you, but it might very well be among the mistaken beliefs you hold. In this way, the evil-God hypothesis is self-defeating — it calls itself into doubt.

Obviously, a self-defeating hypothesis must be assigned a very low prior probability relative to a rival hypothesis that is not self-defeating (but otherwise comparable). And the hypothesis of a good God is not self-defeating (but is otherwise comparable to the evil-God hypothesis). A good God would have good reason to give us cognitive faculties that are generally reliable, that is, that yield truth for the most part (if employed as God intended in the circumstances they were designed for). After all, the purposes of a good God would surely be advanced by our having knowledge of the existence of other human persons, of what helps and harms them, of right and wrong, of how to navigate our environment, of how to find food and water, and so on.

Law claims that evil God would want us to have a lot of knowledge, for example, knowledge of right and wrong, knowledge of how to harm and help others, and so on. But in making such claims Law is assuming that his cognitive faculties provide reliable information about what evil God would want. And Law is assuming that his capacities for logical inference are generally reliable. But of course, given the evil-God hypothesis, Law is putting his trust in cognitive faculties created by a supremely evil person. So, from the standpoint of the evil-God hypothesis, Law's trust in his cognitive faculties is not justified.

Probably no one reading this chapter regards his or her own cognitive faculties as generally unreliable. But this trust in one's own cognitive faculties would be misplaced if they were created by a supremely evil God. Thus all or most of us tacitly assume that we are not created by an evil God. The evil-God hypothesis would lead us into a radical form of skepticism, and for this reason it should be regarded as far less reasonable than the good-God hypothesis.

Could Law lodge a protest along these lines? "We have no choice but to trust our cognitive faculties—even if there is an evil God. What else can we do? For example, when you are crossing a street and you see a truck coming, you would do well to wait till the truck passes by! Moreover, the experiences of others generally confirm what our own cognitive faculties tell us. So, even if there is an evil God, we can trust our cognitive faculties." Now, I agree that we have little choice but to trust our cognitive faculties. But it doesn't follow that our cognitive faculties are reliable. Nor does it follow that the evil-God hypothesis, if we accept it, does not cast doubt on the reliability of our cognitive faculties. The question still stands, "If all my beliefs come to me directly or indirectly from a supremely evil person, are my beliefs for the most part true?" And it seems to me that a "yes" answer is poorly grounded. Any thoughts I have in regard to what an evil God would want or do are thoughts produced by cognitive faculties that, by hypothesis, are given me by an evil God—which casts doubt on all such thoughts. And if I turn to other humans for cognitive assistance, I am relying on *evil-God-given* cognitive faculties when they indicate (i) that other humans exist, (ii) what other humans say, (iii) whether other humans are lying or sincere, and so on. A checking procedure that is entirely dependent on faculties given me by an evil God is surely a checking procedure of quite dubious merit. The lesson, it seems to me, is this: While, from a pragmatic point of view, we have little choice but to rely on our cognitive faculties, it is possible to adopt a metaphysical hypothesis that calls the reliability of our cognitive faculties into question, and any such hypothesis should be assigned a very low prior probability.

To sum up, in this chapter I have argued that the good-God hypothesis is much more reasonable than the evil-God hypothesis for three main reasons. First, ORT is presumably true. But the evil-God hypothesis apparently calls ORT into question since an evil God might well severely punish the morally virtuous and reward the morally vicious (or at least give them lesser punishments). In such a scenario, it is far from clear that moral reasons would override prudential (self-interested) reasons. Thus, the evil-God hypothesis—unlike the good-God hypothesis—seems to be an explanatory failure as regards ORT. Second, if ORT is true and evil God knows it's true, evil God's motivations are mystifying, for he often acts on weaker reasons when he knows that stronger (moral) reasons apply, and he can act on the stronger reasons just by willing to do so. From this perspective, the evil-God hypothesis is puzzling and implausible; hence, it must be assigned a relatively low prior probability (lower, that is, than the good-God hypothesis). Third, I have argued that the evil-God hypothesis is self-defeating. Can we trust our cognitive faculties if they are designed and created by evil God? I don't think so. If we accept the evil-God hypothesis, we accept a hypothesis that calls all of our beliefs into question, and that includes the evil-God hypothesis itself if we believe it. Such a self-defeating hypothesis must be assigned a much lower prior probability than the good-God hypothesis. For these three reasons, it seems to me that the good-God hypothesis is clearly more reasonable than the evil-God hypothesis. And if so, Law's "evil-God challenge" has been fully met.

FIVE

Why Is God Hidden?

Part I

John Schellenberg's well-known hiddenness argument can be outlined as follows:

1. If a God of love exists, reasonable non-belief (that is, not believing that God exists) does not occur.
2. But reasonable non-belief does occur.
3. So a God of love does not exist.[1]

Here God is understood to be the God of traditional theism—perfectly loving, almighty, and all-knowing. Assuming that there is at most one God, the hiddenness argument, if sound, supports atheism. But "non-belief" here includes atheism, agnosticism, never having conceived of God, polytheism, and so on.

What is "reasonable" non-belief? "Non-belief is reasonable," according to Schellenberg, "if and only if it is not the result of culpable actions or omissions on the part of the subject."[2] So a reasonable belief is (roughly) one held *responsibly*, that is, with due diligence in regard to seeking and assessing the relevant evidence.[3]

Schellenberg offers examples of people who do not believe that God exists *through no fault of their own*. (1) There are "individuals—primarily from non-Western cultures—who have never so much as entertained the proposition 'God exists' . . . , let alone considered the question of its truth or falsity."[4] And in many cases this failure to entertain the proposition is evidently not the fault of the individuals in question; they may never have heard of the concept of a perfectly loving, all-powerful, all-knowing God. (2) There are people who have thoughtfully engaged in reflection on God's existence but who find the evidence for it unconvincing. Perhaps they have read books about God's existence and discussed the issue with a priest, pastor, rabbi, or imam, but the arguments for it strike them as weak or inconclusive. And perhaps they even want to believe that God exists (or formerly did believe), but their honest assessment is that the evidence simply does not favor "God exists."[5] They may judge that the evidence supports atheism, or they may find the evidential situation unclear—that is, the evidence does not definitely favor either "God exists" or its negation. And these individuals are apt to find themselves unable to believe. Is this their fault? Surely not in every case. One examines a range of evidence and comes to believe—or not. One cannot simply choose to believe something if one judges that the evidence does not support it.[6] (3) There are converts to non-theistic religions, such as Theravada Buddhism. Upon making a study of a non-theistic religion, some people find the teachings compelling. And once again, it seems implausible to claim that such people are always at fault in some way for believing as they do.[7] Thus, premise 2 is quite plausible.

Why does Schellenberg think premise 1 is true? In a nutshell, he thinks that a God of love would want to have a personal relationship with all created persons. And one cannot have a personal relationship with God unless one believes that God exists. What does a "personal relationship" involve in this context? Schellenberg claims that "God, if loving, seeks *explicit, reciprocal* relationship with us, involving not only such things as Divine guidance, support, and forgiveness, but also human trust, obedience, and worship."[8] Why, according to Schellenberg, would God seek such a relationship with human persons? Partly because it would be a great blessing to us. A personal relationship with God would provide a "sense of security" and "the joy that may come from the conviction that one is rightly related to what is ultimately real."[9] Beyond this, if God is indeed loving, he would seek a personal relationship (analogous to friendship) with each created person for *its own sake* since such a relationship is intrinsically good.[10]

Schellenberg claims that a God of love would provide enough evidence to make "God exists" probable, but not necessarily enough evidence to make it highly probable or certain.[11] Thus, Schellenberg is not claiming that if God exists, he will overwhelm us with spectacular miracles or provide us with "knockdown" philosophical proofs of his existence. But God will provide enough evidence to make his existence probable. Schellenberg thinks that religious experience would likely be a loving God's means of revealing himself to everyone. In order for religious experience to serve this purpose, however, it would have to have two main features: (a) Virtually all persons would have to have it, and (b) there would be uniformity in its description, specifically, all (or virtually all) subjects would describe their experiences as involving or including the presence of God—an almighty, all-knowing, perfectly loving being.[12]

What would the world be like if God exists, on Schellenberg's view? Roughly, there would be evidence (or experiential grounds) readily available to everyone that clearly and decisively rendered "God exists" more probable than not. (I say *roughly*, because we must make exceptions to "everyone"—for babies, very young children, the mentally impaired, and perhaps for anyone who has through past sinful choices blinded himself or herself to God's presence.) In short, in Schellenberg's view, "God exists" would be a generally accepted truth if God exists; it would be denied (or not believed) only by unreasonable people.

Given that *reasonable* atheism and agnosticism are ruled out if God exists, then, in Schellenberg's view, "God exists" must be uncontroversial if God exists. For we cannot speak of controversy about a proposition P when all who deny P, or withhold judgment regarding P, are unreasonable in doing so. There is a Flat Earth Society, but there is no genuine controversy about whether the earth is flat.

Objections to Premise 2

Is There Enough Evidence? Some may claim that there is enough evidence to establish the belief that God exists; so, if a person does not believe, it is through some fault in his or her cognizing—a fault for which he or she is responsible, such as a failure to examine the available evidence or a failure to reason carefully.

Here we must remember that in order to have enough evidence for God's existence, one must have enough evidence for the existence of a being who is perfectly loving, all-knowing, and almighty. So, for example, even if an argument from design provides good evidence for an intelligent Creator, why think the Creator is all-knowing? Presumably a Creator of the universe must be very knowledgeable, but why think it must know *every* truth? And obviously a Creator must be powerful enough to create the universe, but what evidence shows that the Creator has maximal power—that there is no state of affairs that God is unable to bring about due to a lack of power?[13] In short, the claim that an almighty, omniscient, perfectly loving God exists is a very strong claim.[14]

And while some non-theists may culpably fail to consider the evidence or to reason about it carefully, this charge hardly applies in every case. Some non-theists have considered the evidence for God's existence with much greater diligence and care than many theists. These non-theists simply judge the evidence to be insufficient.

Moreover, the fact that God's existence is controversial strongly suggests that the evidential situation is ambiguous. If the evidence *clearly* favors God's existence, why do so many who have examined the evidence find it unconvincing? Is it plausible to suppose that *every* non-theist is so biased as to be unable to see that the evidence clearly favors theism *if indeed it does clearly favor theism*?

In addition, it seems to me that, given the problem of evil, a person can reasonably doubt that there is a perfectly loving God. The basic question here is "If God is perfectly loving and almighty, why does he not intervene more often to prevent horrendous evil and suffering?" Theists generally admit that they have at best only partial answers to this question. And atheists and agnostics generally regard the problem of evil as a major reason for their lack of belief. If *very powerful* arguments for the existence of a perfectly loving, all-knowing, almighty God are not available, then, given the problem of evil, it seems to me that atheism and agnosticism can be reasonably held positions.[15]

Even if we grant that there is not enough evidence to make non-theism unreasonable, however, these reflections on the evidence for theism point to a problem for Schellenberg. He claims that a God of love would provide humans with enough evidence to make "God exists" probable, though not necessarily with enough evidence to make it highly probable. But given the problem of evil, what sort of evidence (or experiential grounding) would be needed to *make it clear to everyone* that God probably exists? As noted above, Schellenberg thinks that religious experience (suitably qualified), would do the trick. That seems very doubtful to me. Given the actual use atheists and agnostics make of the problem of evil in dialogue, I think many of them would regard the problem of evil as a strong reason to doubt the veridicality of religious experiences of God, even if everyone had such religious experiences (and described them in similar terms). Would these atheists and agnostics be unreasonable in so responding? Not necessarily, it seems to me. The problem of evil does provide *some* reason to doubt the veridicality of alleged experiences of God (almighty and wholly good); the question is how strong a reason to doubt? And reasonable people might disagree on the answer. Similarly, I think many atheists and agnostics would judge that the problem of evil raises serious doubts about God's existence even if there are cogent *probabilistic* arguments for God's existence. For even if God's existence is probable given some premises, it may reasonably be argued that it is improbable given the phenomena of evil and suffering. In what sorts of worlds, then, would God's existence be regarded as probable *by everyone* (i.e., every inhabitant)? Consider the following possibilities:

A. Worlds in which there is no problem of evil but in which *everyone* is provided with arguments (and/or experiential grounds) that make God's existence probable, all things considered.
B. Worlds in which everyone is provided with a proof that God exists — where a proof is an argument that (i) uses only premises all (or nearly all) rational people accept and (ii) proceeds by making only valid (i.e., logically necessary) inferences that all (or nearly all) rational people endorse.
C. Worlds in which frequently occurring, dramatic, beneficial miracles are witnessed by everyone.

It seems to me that B and C are not actually worlds in which the hiddenness problem would be absent. Regarding B, I believe that some atheists and agnostics would argue that the problem of evil should cause us to doubt that the premises of the alleged proof are all true and/or that the inferences of the alleged proof are all valid. Would these non-theists be unreasonable in taking this line? They would be giving a lot of weight to evil and suffering as evidence, but is that *unreasonable*? Not obviously, it seems to me. They might be making a mistake, of course, but the mistake might well be a reasonable one; many mistakes are reasonably made. Regarding C, some non-theists would likely argue that, given the problem of evil, there are reasons to doubt that God is either omnipotent or perfectly loving. For example, perhaps God is doing his best but is unable to overcome evil. Would that be an unreasonable position to take? Again, not necessarily, as far as I can see. Thus, it seems to me that worlds in which the problem of divine hiddenness is absent are worlds in which the evidential situation is very different from the evidential situation Schellenberg has suggested. And I think it is plausible to suppose that worlds containing evil and suffering (in the amounts and kinds we find in the actual world) are almost bound to be worlds in which reasonable non-theism is possible.[16]

Is Unbelief Due to Sin? Some have suggested that unbelief is always due to sin. This suggestion could be taken in at least two ways. First, it might be suggested that for every case of non-belief, the individual in question fails to believe because of his or her own sinful acts and attitudes; hence, non-belief is always the fault of the non-believer. But even if there are cases in which the individual's sin blinds him or her to God's existence, it is not plausible to claim that this is so in every case of non-belief. One thing to keep in mind here is that many non-theists seem to be as morally virtuous as many theists. This being so, individual sinfulness hardly provides a convincing explanation of non-belief. Furthermore, as Schellenberg notes, "There are doubters who have agonized long years over matters of faith, hoping that belief may come to them. Why . . . should this be the case if all doubt is due to a sinful rejection of belief?"[17] Simply put, given that some non-believers are positively biased *in favor* of belief, it isn't very plausible to regard every case of non-belief as a result of the sin of the non-believer.

Second, it might be suggested that sin creates a cultural climate that lays down obstacles to believing that God exists. Undoubtedly, there are cultural influences that run contrary to the belief that God exists. There are polytheistic cultures. There are forms of religion (e.g., some types of Hinduism) that teach that ultimate reality cannot be categorized in terms of human concepts. (Note that God's existence is formulated using such human concepts as power, knowledge, and love.) There are religions, for instance, Theravada Buddhism, that are, as a matter of principle, either agnostic or atheistic.[18] And, of course, nowadays philosophical naturalism is a powerful cultural force that runs counter to the belief that God exists.[19] A person who is brought up under the influence of such cultural forces may well find God's existence highly implausible. After all, we humans are greatly affected by what we are taught when young and by what the surrounding culture reinforces through art, music, literature, film, religious instruction, philosophy, and so on. But on what grounds could a theist claim that a person is at fault for being strongly influenced by such cultural factors? None of us escapes the power of culture. (If you are a theist, just stop and consider whether your religious beliefs would *likely* be different than they are had you been brought up in a cultural setting dominated by a non-theistic religion or philosophy.) In short, even if we assume, for the sake of the argument, that all anti-theistic cultural influences result from sin or sinful attitudes, it does not follow that people are at fault for being susceptible to these influences. Furthermore, the claim that all non-theistic cultural influences result from sin is by no means obviously true. What good reason is there to claim that every non-theistic cultural influence stems from sin? When people try to understand ultimate metaphysical issues, they tend to come up with widely varying answers. And even if one assumes that all non-theistic cultural influences are mistaken, is there no room here for honest mistakes? Given the complexity of ultimate metaphysical issues, surely humility demands that we all make allowances for the possibility of well-intentioned errors.

OBJECTIONS TO PREMISE 1

Is Belief Really Necessary? Some have questioned Schellenberg's assumption that one must believe that God exists in order to have a personal relationship with him. But is it possible to have a personal relationship with someone if one does not believe that he or she exists? Andrew Cullison offers the following scenario:

> Suppose Bob recently discovers that he has been (for several years) hallucinating people and from his perspective developing very sophisticated, complex relationships. After several months in the hospital the doctors have determined that Bob has been cured. They are confident that he will no longer hallucinate. Julie is one of the doctors. Bob is skeptical that Julie is real. He even says on several occasions, I really don't believe you exist. However, Bob thinks to himself, Julie (if real) would be the most amazing person I have ever met, and I am confident that we could have a long lasting relationship. I could never forgive myself if I didn't give her exactly the kindness she deserves (if I discovered she were real), so I'll continue this relationship.[20]

This scenario seems at least logically possible. And perhaps it suggests that one can have a personal relationship with another if one *merely hopes* she exists. (If one believes that P, one is confident that P is true, while if one *merely* hopes that P, one is not confident that P is true — one might even think P is unlikely given the evidence.[21])

But even if it is possible to have a personal relationship with X when one *merely hopes* that X exists (and so does not believe that X exists), at least two questions arise here. First, isn't rationally believing that God exists better than merely hoping that God exists? After all, if one merely hopes that God exists, one can only hope one has a personal relationship with God. So if God exists, why would God leave us merely hoping for his existence when he could presumably provide us with solid grounds for believing that he exists? That question needs to be answered, and the answer is far from obvious.

Second, many things might be hoped for. Some might hope that the universe is governed by the law of karma (without God), that ultimate reality is undifferentiated being, that the finite God of process theology exists, or even that the physical universe is the ultimate reality. Why is the theist's hope more reasonable than these hopes? And if the theist's hope is not more reasonable, why would a loving God leave us in such a situation? The answers to these questions are, once again, far from obvious.

Does Hiddenness Make Room for Faith? When confronted with the problem of divine hiddenness, many believers respond along these lines: "Of course God is hidden. There would be no room for faith if God's existence were a matter of common knowledge." This response is a popular version of a solution offered by the Danish philosopher Søren Kierkegaard.[22] For Kierkegaard, genuine faith must involve risk. Believers take a big risk in believing that God exists because the existence of a perfectly loving, almighty God is improbable: "Without risk there is no faith. Faith is precisely the contradiction between the infinite passion of the individual's inwardness and the objective uncertainty. If I am capable of grasping God objectively, I do not believe, but precisely because I cannot do this I must believe."[23] Kierkegaard's solution immediately raises this question: What is so great about faith if it is understood to involve believing improbable or weakly grounded propositions? Outside of religious contexts, such believing is called *wishful thinking*. And wishful thinking is commonly regarded as faulty and foolish thinking. Kierkegaard would answer as follows:

> If strong objective evidence of God's existence were made generally available, we would be *deceived* in two related ways. First, we would be deceived into thinking that we had a proper understanding of religious truth—that the answers were clear and striving unnecessary. Second, we would be deceived into thinking that God could be fully understood in terms of objective categories. . . . The results of such deception would be disastrous for beings disposed (as we are) to avoid the strenuosity of subjectivity. For we would become *complacent*, thinking that we had arrived when really there was still a lot to be done. . . . Our knowledge of God would be *superficial* since the most that can be known of God objectively is still radically incomplete: God is Spirit and can only be known through the activation of our own spirit of inwardness. Our relationship with God would be *shallow*, not deep, personal and strenuous as befits a relationship with the infinite Subject.[24]

But Kierkegaard's proposed solution is open to a number of objections. First, if the evidence does not favor theism, does it favor some other view, such as philosophical naturalism? If so, why not believe the view that is best supported by the evidence? Kierkegaard seems to assume that we should believe that God exists even if the evidence does not favor this proposition. Note, however, that a similar assumption could be made by those who accept some non-theistic view of the world, for example, the view that the world is governed by an impersonal law of karma (and not by a personal God). Should we accept such a view *even if* we judge that the evidence does not favor it? It seems to me that the answer is clearly "No, we should not."

Second, Kierkegaard seems to assume that we have direct voluntary control over our beliefs; hence, we can believe that God exists even if we think this proposition is improbable given the evidence. But most philosophers think we do not have this sort of direct control over what we believe. One cannot simply "will to believe" that which one judges to be improbable (all things considered). For example, if you think that polytheism is poorly supported by the evidence, can you, just by an act of will, get yourself to believe that there are many gods? And if you think that reincarnation is poorly supported by the evidence, can you, just by an act of will, get yourself to believe that reincarnation occurs? On reflection, I think most people will agree that they do not have this kind of control over their beliefs.

Third, Kierkegaard's understanding of faith overlooks an important distinction. We have to distinguish between (a) believing that God exists and (b) believing in God—that is, trusting God. A person who is confident of God's existence may still take great risks in trusting God and devoting himself or herself to doing God's will. For example, it is plausible to suppose that famous religious figures such as Abraham, Muhammad, and the apostle Peter were confident of God's existence; they did not regard God's existence as unlikely or improbable. Yet they reportedly took great risks in serving God and in trying to do God's will, in some cases risking their very lives. The point here is that Kierkegaard is mistaken in supposing that God must be hidden if faith is to involve risks. Faith involves believing *in* God, not just believing *that* God exists. And even if God weren't hidden, doing God's will could still involve great risks.

Fourth, reflection on famous religious figures such as Abraham, Muhammad, and the apostle Peter also calls into question other claims

Kierkegaard makes. Again, I think it plausible to suppose that these famous figures were confident of God's existence; they did not regard his existence as unlikely or improbable. Should we then conclude that they were complacent, that they had a shallow relationship with God and a superficial understanding of him? The suggestion that these paradigms of faith were deficient in these ways is implausible, to put it mildly.

Does Hiddenness Make Room for Free Will? According to Richard Swinburne, there is a very strong connection between knowing that God exists and obeying God (hence, acting morally). Suppose that the existence of God was common knowledge:

> Knowing that there was a God, men would know that their most secret thoughts and actions were known to God; and knowing that he was just, they would expect for their bad actions and thoughts whatever punishment was just. . . . Further, in seeing God, as it were, face to face, men would see him to be good and worshipful, and hence would have every reason for conforming to his will. In such a world men would have little temptation to do wrong—it would be the mark of both prudence and reason to do what was virtuous. Yet a man only has a genuine choice of destiny if he has reasons for pursuing either good or evil courses of action, for . . . a man can only perform an action which he has some reason to do.[25]

According to Swinburne, then, if God's existence were an item of common knowledge, our free will would be radically infringed. We would lack any reason, or at least any weighty reason, to reject God's love or to turn from doing God's will. There would be no real choice between good and evil or between devotion to God and devotion to something else (e.g., to oneself or to worldly pleasure). Thus, divine hiddenness is a necessary condition for the presence of significant creaturely freedom.

But an immediate problem arises for Swinburne's solution. It seems that people can in fact firmly believe that God exists and yet not trust and obey him. As an illustration, consider the story of the Exodus in the Bible.[26] In that story, the Israelites were delivered from slavery in Egypt by numerous miracles, such as the ten plagues and the parting of the Red Sea. Within the framework of the narrative, the children of Israel believed that God exists and had good reason to do so (namely, the miracles). But this belief did not result in trusting and obeying God; they immediately turned from God to worship a golden calf.

Of course, it would seem to be irrational to believe that a *perfectly good* being exists and yet not trust such a being. (If you can't trust a perfectly good being, whom can you trust?) But humans are apparently capable of irrational behavior. For example, a person may know that smoking is not in her long-term best interests. She may know that continued smoking is apt to lead to serious health problems. And yet she may continue to smoke. We humans are only too able to act against our own best interests. We may value the pleasure of the moment (lighting up a cigarette) over our long-term health and happiness, and that seems irrational. Similarly, even a person who believes that God exists may (at least temporarily) value the pleasures of sin or the delight in doing his or her own will over the value of a good personal relationship with God. In general, from a theistic point of view, the psychology of temptation involves the all-too-human ability to act for an inferior or weaker reason when a better or stronger one is available. Thus, it seems that divine hiddenness is not a necessary condition for creaturely freedom.

But would we be free *in a significant sense* to disobey God if doing so were irrational? Well, again, consider the case of those who firmly believe that God exists. To take another biblical example, consider King David.[27] The biblical narrative certainly presents David as one who believed that God exists and, indeed, as one who trusted deeply in God—or at least as one who *typically* trusted deeply in God. And yet David committed adultery with Bathsheba and ensured the death of her husband, Uriah, by having him abandoned in the forefront of a battle. Now, was David's choice to commit these acts not significant if he was aware that God disapproved of them? But David certainly believed that adultery and murder were contrary to God's will. (If having Uriah abandoned in the forefront of a battle wasn't *strictly speaking* murder, it was morally equivalent to murder.) If David engaged in self-deception, convincing himself that he hadn't sinned, he was being irrational.[28] In that case, were his acts not *significantly* free? That seems like the wrong conclusion to me. On the other hand, if David committed these actions while consciously believing that God disapproved of them, was he acting irrationally? Yes, I think so; for in David's worldview, violating God's law is foolish. So, if David performed the acts while consciously believing they were contrary to God's will, were his acts not significantly free? Again, that seems to me the wrong conclusion to draw.

Swinburne claims that if we *knew* that God exists, we would have "little temptation to do wrong." But I suspect that many people of faith down through the ages *thought* they knew that God exists. (They may have been mistaken, but they thought they knew.) And a great many people of faith have certainly *believed very firmly* that God exists. And yet people of faith have often faced great temptations and have often sinned. This being so, I very much doubt that if we knew that God exists, we would have "little temptation to do wrong."

Perhaps Swinburne would emphasize the manner of knowing—he speaks of "seeing God, as it were, face to face." In that case disobeying God might be compared to stealing a car while a police officer is watching—a behavior even most habitual criminals would avoid. Schellenberg would reply that God could make his existence known without providing us with an overwhelming "face to face" encounter. But even if very vivid experiences of God's presence are necessary for knowledge of his existence, such experiences would not need to be constant or even frequent in order to justify or warrant the belief in God. So the "police officer" analogy is not apt. And even if a person is convinced of God's existence through vivid religious experiences, it seems to me that given human nature, there can still be significant temptation.[29] Famous religious figures, such as Abraham, Muhammad, and the apostle Peter, had vivid religious experiences, but these individuals are not usually regarded as morally perfect or sinless.

Can Humans Know God's Reasons? If an all-knowing God exists, we humans stand to God rather as a small child stands to his or her parents; the child may often not understand why the parents do what they do, for example, why they say "No" when the child wants more candy or wants to play on the stairs. So-called skeptical theism is the view that we humans should not assume that we would be likely to know God's reasons for permitting evil, suffering, and reasonable non-theism— assuming God has such reasons. As applied to the issue of divine hiddenness, skeptical theism calls into question the following inference:

> *No-see-um Inference:* We see (know of) no good reasons why God
> would permit reasonable non-theism. So there are no good reasons
> why God would permit reasonable non-theism.

No-see-ums (or biting midges) are a type of insect that cannot be seen
with the naked eye, but are notorious for the itchy bites they can deliver.
"I see no no-see-ums in my tent, so there are none" is a fallacy that
campers would do well to avoid. But it should be noted that not all inferences of this general type are logically flawed, such as "I see no milk
in the fridge, so there is none." The difference is that in the case of a carton or bottle of milk—unlike the case of no-see-ums—a person with
normal vision can see the entity in question (namely, the carton or bottle
of milk) if it's there. The question, then, is whether, given our cognitive
capacities, we humans are in a position to know what an omniscient
God's reasons for allowing reasonable non-theism would (or might) be.

Is the skeptical theist assuming that God exists? *If* we can assume
that an almighty, omniscient, *perfectly loving* God exists, we can safely
assume that he has good reason (or reasons) for permitting every actual
case of reasonable non-theism—even if we are unable to state his rea-
son(s). A loving God would not be hidden from us unless there were
a good reason (or good reasons) for him to be hidden. But we must
keep in mind that we are discussing the hiddenness argument—an
argument in support of atheism. So we cannot simply assume that God
exists; that would be begging the question. Instead we must think of
skeptical theism, in this context, as a conditional claim, namely, *if God
exists, his reasons for acting would be to a large extent (or perhaps entirely) beyond our ken.*

Does skeptical theism provide an adequate reason to doubt the first
premise of the hiddenness argument: "If a God of love exists, reasonable
non-belief does not occur"? First, it seems that skeptical theism can be
used to defend too much. To see this point, let's think about the skeptical theist's strategy as it applies to the problem of evil: God may have
reasons *beyond our ken* for allowing evil and suffering. Now, suppose
we imagine a world far worse than the actual world, a world containing
many more horrendous evils than the actual world. We can still ask
whether God might have reasons *beyond our ken* for allowing such
evils. But surely at some point, as we imagine worlds containing more

and more evil (and suffering), this way of defending theism would seem highly suspect. *And on what principled basis could we say that skeptical theism can reasonably be applied in the case of the actual world but could not reasonably be applied in the case of "much worse" worlds?*[30] It's hard to think of a good answer to that question.

Second, skeptical theism seems at odds with the way theists themselves often think about God. Theists usually think they can see reasons why God would do certain things, such as create a world that contains life, create agents with free will, or send prophets into the world. But as Schellenberg observes: "Isn't the Skeptical Theist required to say that there might be great goods we cannot understand on account of which God does none of these things? If he does not wish to say this, isn't he required to admit that sometimes there can be clear reasons for supposing that some claim about what a God would do is correct, which renders pointless investigation into reasons God might have to do some contrary action?"[31] The point, of course, is that skeptical theism seems to be an arbitrary application of doubt. If the general approach were applied consistently, theists would be unable to make many claims they want to make about God.

Third, as Schellenberg notes, if we just can't know what reasons God would have for allowing reasonable non-theism, perhaps God would have overriding reasons *not* to allow reasonable non-theism.[32] It may be tempting to argue that since reasonable non-theism occurs, God must have a good reason to allow it. But this argument presupposes that a God of love exists, which begs the question against Schellenberg. His point is that if we humans are largely (or entirely) ignorant of God's reasons for acting, then for all we know a loving God would have good reason not to allow reasonable non-theism.

Fourth, it is well to keep in mind that theism is an important worldview or worldview component. A worldview is a comprehensive philosophical position, one that provides a fundamental outlook on the world and on human existence. And a worldview is supposed to help us make sense of human life and of our place in the world. So to the extent that theists cannot explain important phenomena such as reasonable non-theism, suffering, and evil, theism exhibits weakness as a worldview. (By way of contrast, philosophical naturalists have no difficulty in explaining the phenomenon of divine hiddenness: "Since there is no God, it is hardly surprising that there is no compelling evidence for God's existence and that non-theism is entirely reasonable.") So a heavy reliance on skeptical theism weakens theism's merits as a worldview.

Given the above reasons, it seems to me that skeptical theism *by itself* does not provide a strong objection to the hiddenness argument. But so far I've been considering skeptical theism as a "stand-alone" response to the problem of divine hiddenness. What if it were combined with arguments for theism (and/or experiential grounds for theism) that made the belief that God exists *reasonable*? Would that make a difference? Yes, I believe it would, but I also believe it would force us to modify skeptical theism quite significantly. Let me explain.

I'll start by noting that philosophers often hold positions on controversial issues, such as whether humans have free will, whether humans have souls as well as bodies, or whether euthanasia is ever permissible. Philosophers defend their views with arguments, but they do so knowing that many other philosophers will find their arguments unconvincing. In this situation, can philosophers, in holding their views, be reasonable? It seems to me that they can, provided that they handle the available evidence *responsibly*—taking all the available evidence into account, reasoning the issues through carefully, avoiding inconsistencies, and avoiding personal biases as far as possible, for instance, by doing their best to consider the issues from opposing points of view.

Now, even if God is hidden—that is, even if it is reasonable for some (or many) people not to believe that God exists—it may also be reasonable for others to believe that God does exist, provided that they hold the belief that God exists in a responsible manner. The belief that God exists might be based on arguments, on religious experience, and/or on an appeal to authority (such as the authority of a religious tradition). But the appeal to authority, if reasonable, would presuppose that the authority bases its claims on evidence (that is, arguments and/or religious experience); therefore, arguments and/or religious experience would seem to be the *ultimate* basis for a reasonable belief that God exists, assuming such is possible.

In chapters 1 and 2 we examined a cumulative case argument for the existence of God, an argument that included an appeal to religious experience along with a cosmological argument, a design argument, an argument from free will, and a moral argument. I think the discussion in chapter 1 strongly suggests that religious experience, all by itself, is not a sufficient ground for the belief that God exists. One reason for this is that people in different religious traditions have different experiences, and some of those experiences seem to be at odds with the experience of a personal God. For example, the mystical experiences of some Buddhists and Hindus seem to them to indicate that ultimate reality is not personal in nature, contrary to the experience of theistic mystics. In my view, it doesn't follow that theistic mystical experience should be tossed aside as worthless, but it does mean that we need some reason to think that theistic mystics are on the right track. And I think "some reason" here will need to include some arguments for God's existence.[33] Thus, in my opinion, theism needs some argumentative support if it is to be held reasonably. (I do not mean to imply that every believer, in order to be reasonable, has to examine theistic arguments and base his or her belief on them directly. Many believers lack the time, inclination, or even the ability to engage in a critical examination of the theistic arguments. In my view, these believers can reasonably rely on the authority of a religious tradition *if that tradition contains within it sufficient evidence to render the belief that God exists reasonable*.)

As far as I can tell, however, the most important, plausible versions of the theistic arguments depend on claims about what God would have reason to do.[34] For example, the design argument depends on the claim that a loving (hence generous) God would have reason to create intelligent conscious life, for a generous God would want to share blessings such as beauty, creative activity, and loving personal relationships; therefore, God would have reason to create a fine-tuned universe that supports life. And the argument from free will depends on the claim that a God of love would have reason to give intelligent creatures the power to make significant choices, such as the choice to do good or evil and the choice to devote oneself to God. Since these arguments involve claims about what an almighty, wholly loving God would have reason to do, they presuppose that humans can have reasonable beliefs about what a loving God's reasons for doing certain things would be. (Note: This is not the claim that humans can somehow magically "peer into" the divine mind; rather, it involves the claim to understand, to some significant degree, the nature of love.) But skeptical theism, as formulated above, calls into question our ability to know or to have reasonable beliefs about what God would have reason to do—God's reasons are to a very large extent (or perhaps entirely) beyond our ken.

Perhaps, however, a more moderate form of skeptical theism can be proposed. Let us call it simply moderately skeptical theism: *We should not expect to know God's reasons (actual or even possible reasons) for allowing every case of reasonable non-theism and every case of evil (including suffering).* Moderately Skeptical Theism would call into question no-see-um inferences such as the following:

a.   We see (know of) no good reasons why God would permit *all* of the cases of reasonable non-theism the world contains. So, there are no good reasons why God would permit all of the cases of reasonable non-theism the world contains.

b.   We see (know of) no good reasons why God would permit the *totality* of evil and suffering in the world. So, there are no good reasons why God would permit the totality of evil and suffering in the world.

Given that God is omniscient and hence that we stand to God rather as small children stand to their parents, moderately skeptical theism seems sensible. And it allows that theists might make reasonable claims about God's reasons for taking certain actions, claims such as those made in advancing the cosmological and design arguments.

If we allow that the belief that God exists can be reasonably held, theists can make use of moderately skeptical theism. They can argue that a loving God would remain hidden only if he had good reason to do so. And they could employ moderately skeptical theism to explain why they should not be expected to know God's reasons—actual or even possible reasons—for allowing *every* case of reasonable non-theism.

But this application of moderately skeptical theism is not by itself an adequate response to the problem of divine hiddenness. The critic of theism might allow that theists should not be expected to know God's reasons (actual or possible) for allowing *every* case of reasonable non-theism. And yet the critic might go on to claim that if theists cannot provide plausible reasons why God would allow *much* of the reasonable non-theism the world contains, then theism is deficient, perhaps seriously deficient, as a worldview (or worldview component). Even if we assume, then, that moderately skeptical theism can be part of the solution to the problem of divine hiddenness, it apparently needs to be supplemented with a plausible account of why God allows much of the reasonable non-theism the world contains. The next chapter is an attempt to provide such an account.

SIX

Why Is God Hidden?

Part II

If a God of love exists, wouldn't he make himself known to everyone? This important question lies behind John Schellenberg's hiddenness argument:

1. If a God of love exists, reasonable non-belief (that is, not believing that God exists) does not occur.
2. But reasonable non-belief does occur.
3. So a God of love does not exist.[1]

In the previous chapter I asked a series of questions about Schellenberg's argument: Is there enough evidence for God's existence so that God is in fact not hidden? Is non-theism in general caused by sin (and hence the responsibility of those who don't believe)? Must one believe that God exists in order to have a personal relationship with him? Must God remain hidden in order to make room for faith or for free will? Can finite creatures such as humans reasonably expect to know God's reasons for remaining hidden? These are all good questions, but I've suggested that the answers do not clearly yield a refutation of the hiddenness argument. So in this chapter we will consider an additional response to the hiddenness argument.

Before plunging into yet another response to the hiddenness argument, however, it is good to remember something discussed in chapter 1, namely, that the hiddenness argument can be used to defend naturalism.

For naturalism has no difficulty in explaining the fact that many people do not believe that God exists *through no fault of their own*. Since, according to naturalists, there is no God, it is hardly surprising that many people do not believe that God exists. And of course it's not their fault, no more than they are at fault for not believing in Santa Claus, unicorns, or "engine-angels." Non-theism is entirely reasonable. And to the extent that theists have difficulty in explaining the presence of reasonable non-theism, naturalists can claim that the so-called hiddenness of God (a.k.a. reasonable non-theism) provides a reason to accept naturalism over theism.

The General Problem of Ignorance

Perhaps we can achieve a helpful perspective by considering a more general problem related to the problem of divine hiddenness, which we might call the general problem of ignorance:

A. If a loving God exists, he would want us to have justified beliefs on any subject in which such beliefs would be beneficial. (For the purposes of this argument, a belief counts as justified only if it is *clearly favored* by the available evidence.)
B. So if a loving God exists, he would place us in a situation in which justified, beneficial beliefs were readily available.
C. There are many subjects on which having justified beliefs would be beneficial but on which such beliefs are not readily available (because we lack sufficient evidence).
D. So a loving God does not exist.

Premise C is obviously crucial here. Consider some examples:

1. It would be beneficial to have justified beliefs regarding the cure for dread diseases such as cancer, smallpox, or Alzheimer's. But we lack such beliefs. And as regards many other diseases, there were no known cures for most of the history of the world.
2. It would be beneficial to have a justified belief regarding which religion (if any) is the true religion and an understanding of which

religions (if any) advocate importantly false beliefs. The diversity of religions causes much confusion and has been at least partly the cause of animosity—and in some cases wars—between cultures.

3.   Many of the issues we care deeply about are philosophical in nature and very controversial. It would be beneficial to be able to identify the justified and unjustified beliefs of this type. Then we would have fully justified answers to questions such as: What happens when we die? Is morality relative to cultures? Is euthanasia ever permissible? Is the death penalty sometimes justified? When is war justified (if ever)? What sorts of political structures best promote human flourishing?

4.   On a more personal level, wouldn't it be beneficial to have a justified belief about whether to marry or whom to marry and which career(s) to pursue? Much human misery has resulted from wrong answers and uncertainty about these matters.

These reflections on premise C underscore the following point: If God exists, he is not in general much concerned with providing humans with an environment free of uncertainty and controversy. But is the general problem of ignorance a powerful objection to theism? If it is, theism is apparently quite easy to refute.

One thing we need to be careful about here, I think, is relying too heavily on "heavenly parent" analogies. Any good human parent who knew how to cure his or her dying child of some dread disease would certainly act on that knowledge and save the child if at all possible. And an almighty, omniscient God can cure any disease instantly; nevertheless, many children die of diseases every day. So, although many theists speak of God as their "Heavenly Father," the term "father" must be regarded as highly metaphorical in this context. Otherwise, theism is manifestly false and hardly worth discussing. One crucial difference between God and a human parent is that God, as Creator, is responsible for selecting the main structural features of the environment creatures will inhabit. Will there be a physical reality, and if so, what laws of nature will it operate by? What sorts of creatures will there be? Will there be a limit on the length of a creature's life? What sorts of challenges and dangers, if any, will the environment contain for creatures? What sorts of choices, if any, will creatures be allowed to make? What sorts of cognitive powers will creatures have? In answering such questions, a Creator makes decisions no earthly parent makes, decisions that determine the sorts of challenges all creatures must face; and to that extent, the parent analogy is out of place. To cite one simple example: If God allows burglary, he allows something any human would be duty bound to prevent if he or she could do so at little or no personal cost.

Is there a reason why God might place us in an environment in which many beneficial beliefs are unavailable to us (due to the lack of evidence)? Is there a good reason why God might want rational creatures to live under conditions of significant uncertainty? Let's consider some answers to these questions.

Ignorance and Evil. Fairly obviously, the general problem of ignorance is an aspect of the problem of evil. Or at least it is closely related to the problem of evil because much suffering and loss result from (or occur because of) human ignorance. So it may be helpful to view the problem of ignorance in a wider context.

Suppose that God does not allow evil. What would be lost? From the standpoint of the soul-making theodicy, the presence of evil and suffering makes our environment very challenging, and to meet those challenges well, we must develop virtues such as patience, hope, courage, humility, moderation, wisdom, generosity, fairness, and sacrificial, forgiving love. Thus, a world without evil and suffering would be one from which the best and most admirable character traits of human beings would be absent.

Objection: "If God wants virtuous persons, why doesn't he just create virtuous persons?" Answer: Our characters are formed as we make choices over time; thus God offers us the opportunity to "have a say" in the kinds of persons we become. Instead of having our characters imposed on us, we are given a significant choice in the matter.

Objection: "But if it weren't for evil and suffering, we wouldn't need the virtues, right? Alternatively, we would need different virtues, at least for the most part. And a world without evil would be a better world than the one we've got, right?" Answer: Granted, to develop virtues such as courage, compassion, generosity, patience, moderation, hope, and sacrificial, forgiving love, we must live in a very challenging environment. But these virtues in particular are of extraordinary value, apparently the finest and most admirable qualities humans can attain. Moreover, a person without these virtues may well lack the spiritual depth or maturity necessary for the fullest sort of intimacy possible with a perfectly good God. So would a world without these virtues be a better world? That's far from clear.

Will there need to be evil and suffering in heaven, then? No, for at least two reasons: (1) Virtues such as compassion, generosity, and courage are of value even when there is not presently a reason to exercise them. We admire and honor people who have performed great acts of courage or love even if present circumstances do not call for similar acts.[2] (2) Also, while it may be good, all things considered, for humans to live in very difficult circumstances during one phase of their existence, it is plausible to suppose that it would not be good for humans to live in such circumstances forever.

The soul-making theodicy arguably accounts for quite a bit of evil. Unfortunately, it comes up short in some cases, e.g., what about children who die very young, before they have a chance to develop the virtues? And is really horrendous evil, such as genocide, necessary for the development of the virtues? Fair enough. But for present purposes there is no need to claim that the soul-making theodicy accounts for all evil and suffering, only that it accounts for quite a bit of evil and suffering.

Divine Goodness and Evil. Perhaps we can go a step further if we think about God's own goodness. In the absence of evil, God's goodness as a response to evil would be merely *dispositional* (i.e., merely a *tendency* to act in certain ways or to have certain attitudes). For example, God would be disposed (or have the tendency) to empathize with those who suffer if the situation called for it. But if there is no suffering, such empathy is out of place. And God would be disposed to oppose or to work against evil if the situation called for it. But opposing evil makes no sense if there is no evil. And God would be patient with and forgiving of those who sincerely (but imperfectly) struggle with temptation *if* there are agents struggling with temptation. But such patience and mercy are out of place if no one ever faces temptation. Furthermore, if the most profound sort of love requires that the lover be vulnerable to rejection by the beloved and vulnerable to the suffering of the beloved, then in a world without evil and suffering

God's vulnerability would be merely dispositional; it would never become manifest or be realized in practice.

It is plausible to suppose that merely dispositional virtues, never expressed or realized in practice, are simply not as praiseworthy and valuable as virtues that have actually borne fruit. For example, suppose that God were to place humans in a paradisal environment with no evil or suffering. In such an environment, some humans might still have the disposition to act with courage or compassion, but they would never in fact act courageously or compassionately because there would be no opportunity to do so. It seems to me that such merely dispositional character traits would not be as praiseworthy and valuable as character traits that have been expressed in action and have actually been a force for good in the world. This claim about merely dispositional character traits also has an application in regard to divine goodness. Compare the following hypothetical deities:

1. Deity A would act in a loving way if the circumstances called for it, but through all eternity, the circumstances never call for it because Deity A creates nothing. (To make this hypothetical clear, "loving acts" are here understood to be acts intended to benefit *others*; self-love doesn't count.)
2. Deity B would act in a loving way if the circumstances called for it, and in fact Deity B has been in many such circumstances and has always acted in a loving way.

Deity B, is, I suggest, more praiseworthy than Deity A; Deity B has a more valuable form of goodness. A deity's goodness depends partly on what the deity does.[3]

With the above thought experiment in mind, it seems to me that a perfectly good God's life will have a certain narrative structure. Prior to (or independent of) creation, God's goodness will be in many (most?) respects merely dispositional.[4] Prior to (or independent of) creation, God may realize an appropriate self-love.[5] But prior to (or independent of) creation, God's goodness *as a response to creatures and to evil* must be merely dispositional. Now, an almighty God could decide not to permit any evil. In that case evil would never be more than an unactualized possibility. And God would be avoiding confrontation with that which is, in its essence, contrary to the divine goodness. Moreover, much (if not most) of what religious believers regard as divine goodness would remain merely dispositional—mercy, compassion, and grace; the inclination to forgive, to redeem, to sanctify, to strengthen, to comfort, to instill hope, and so on. From this perspective, God would have reason to permit evil, and to confront and defeat it, so that the divine goodness as a response to evil would not be merely dispositional, but would be expressed in action. Let us call this type of goodness "active goodness."

Thus, it seems to me that the most praiseworthy sort of deity—with the most valuable sort of goodness—would create and indeed would create agents who can do evil, and thus make evil a reality. Moreover, if God decides to confront evil, it makes sense that he would not take on just a few evils and only minor ones; rather, God would take on (and eventually defeat) very serious amounts and kinds of evil. From this perspective, we ought to expect much evil and some great evils.[6] But I must hasten to add that I am not suggesting that God would permit evil just to express his own goodness in action and without regard for the well-being of his creatures. The point is that *in addition to allowing evil and suffering for the purpose of soul-making, God has reason to allow evil and suffering so that his goodness might be active goodness (i.e., far less merely dispositional than it would otherwise be).*

Furthermore, I suggest that the most praiseworthy sort of deity would confront evil not merely through omnipotence or force (a "snap of the divine fingers"), but primarily through moral and spiritual means, such as teaching, preaching, appealing to conscience, sending special messengers, and so on. And the most praiseworthy sort of deity—with the most valuable sort of goodness—would eventually defeat evil by, for example:

a. Converting as many as possible to the way of holy love,
b. Helping as many as possible to develop the moral virtues,
c. Assisting and guiding those who seek to prevent, eliminate, or diminish suffering, and

d.   Ultimately securing the blessedness (flourishing) of all who have
     sided (consciously or unconsciously) with God's program of holy
     love.

(This list is meant to be merely illustrative, not complete.[7])

Am I suggesting that God needs evil? In one sense, clearly not. God
exists independent of evil and can decide not to permit it. But if God's
goodness as a response to evil is to be more than merely dispositional, obviously God must permit evil. And I am suggesting that God's goodness
is greater if his goodness as a response to evil is active—that God actually
confronts and eventually defeats evil. A God who allows, confronts, and
eventually defeats evil is greater than a God who avoids confronting and
defeating evil. But wouldn't it be better if God never allowed any evil at
all? No, it wouldn't. What would be lost would be (a) creatures having
spiritual depth and moral virtues (of the sorts listed above) and (b) the aspect of divine *greatness or glory* that results from God's confronting and
defeating evil.

Objection: "You are suggesting that God improves over time if he
creates a world and confronts evil. This implies that prior to creation
God is not the greatest possible being, and hence, prior to creation,
God is not God, which is absurd." Answer: I am not denying that God
is the greatest possible being. I am suggesting that the greatest possible
being is one whose goodness becomes active—much less merely dispositional given the circumstance of creation and the presence of evil.
In that sense, I am suggesting that there is a kind of development in the
goodness of the greatest possible being. To assess whether a being is
the greatest possible we must consider its entire "life history," so to
speak. Prior to creation God *is* the greatest possible being given that he
will create, permit serious evil, and confront and defeat the evil. To put
the point negatively, the being who is God could have decided not to
create and not to confront evil, but in that case he would not have been
the greatest possible being. God's greatness depends partly on what
God does.

From the standpoint of the soul-making theodicy, in a world without evil and suffering human goodness would be far more shallow and
far less admirable than it is. I am suggesting that there is a different but
analogous point with regard to divine goodness. In a world without

evil and suffering, divine goodness would be far more dispositional and hence less praiseworthy and valuable than it actually is (assuming that God exists). Why does this matter? From a theistic standpoint, God's glory is one of the most valuable features of reality. And God's glory consists at least partly in the splendor of divine attributes that have been manifest in praiseworthy action.

Objection: "By your logic, we ought to expect the world to contain much more evil than it does. We can easily imagine a world containing more instances of horrendous evil than the actual world contains. And if God exists, by your logic, God would confront and defeat this greater quantity of evil." Answer: There are at least two things wrong with this objection. First, for any amount of evil we imagine, we can always imagine more. So there is apparently no upper limit on the amount of evil, just as there is no greatest natural number. However much evil God allows, he could allow more. Thus, it seems that there is unavoidably an element of arbitrariness with regard to the quantity of evil God allows. Second, the suggestion that the challenge of evil isn't great enough strains credulity. The amounts and kinds of evil in the world are so daunting that they constantly tempt us to become bitter or cynical or to give up all hope. God will confront serious evil, but he will not create a world from which goodness is largely absent, mostly powerless, or generally overcome by evil.

Now, if God has decided to confront and defeat evil that is serious (in both amounts and kinds), it is not surprising that we live in a world in which ignorance and uncertainty are common. For as we have already noted, ignorance exposes us to many evils. And many would claim that ignorance is itself a bad thing, quite apart from any suffering or loss it occasions.[8] So if God has decided to confront and defeat evil, it is not surprising that ignorance and uncertainty are in the mix. Note, too, that conditions of uncertainty call for humility and wisdom. And where controversy is present, empathy, tolerance, and mutual respect are called for, as well as humility and wisdom. In addition, ignorance can often be overcome by intelligent people working together cooperatively; in this way, ignorance calls for trust and good will. Thus, ignorance provides an occasion for developing many important virtues.

At this point I suggest that we have before us a reasonable response to the general problem of ignorance: God permits ignorance as part of

Cary Area Public Library
1606 Three Oaks Road
Cary, IL 60013

the "package" of evils (or evil-conducive factors) he has decided to confront and ultimately defeat. As a result, divine goodness can be expressed in actions that confront and eventually defeat evil, thus making the divine goodness active (far less merely dispositional than it would otherwise be). In addition, to respond well to ignorance and uncertainty, humans must acquire many important, praiseworthy, and valuable virtues. Thus, ignorance is part of the challenge of evil that God permits for the purpose of soul-making.

BACK TO SCHELLENBERG

But does this response to the general problem of ignorance give us a response to the problem of divine hiddenness? Schellenberg would insist that it does not. If we do not believe that God exists, then, from a theistic perspective, we are cut off from the greatest good for finite persons, namely, "knowledge by acquaintance of God."[9] And if God loves every person, then "anyone who is (i) not resisting God and (ii) capable of meaningful conscious relationship with God is also (iii) in a position to participate in such relationship (able to do so just by trying)."[10] And to be in this position, one must believe that God exists.

There are at least four problems with Schellenberg's reasoning here. First, I do not think that, even from a theistic viewpoint, *knowledge by acquaintance of God* is the greatest good for finite persons. According to most theists, the greatest good is having God's blessing or approval, and having it in such a way that, should one die, one would find oneself in an eternal, harmonious relationship with God. And a person can have God's blessing or approval without believing that God exists—at least this is so if one's lack of belief is not one's fault. *Indeed, if one lacks the belief that God exists through no fault of one's own, a God of love and justice surely would not withhold his blessing and approval simply because the belief that God exists is absent.* God's blessing and approval may rather depend on one's devotion to the way of holy love, since that would presumably be a loving God's approved way of living.[11]

Second, should we accept the claim that if a loving God exists, those who are capable of a personal relationship with God (and who

are not resisting God) are able to relate to God personally "just by trying"? Schellenberg makes an extensive use of the analogy of a loving
parent to convince us of this conditional, but as we have already seen,
there are good reasons to be wary of that analogy in this context.[12] We
must go on to ask, "If A genuinely loves B, would A ever do anything
that would prevent B from being able, just by trying, to consciously
relate personally to A?" I think the answer is, "Yes." For example, as
Daniel Howard-Snyder points out, A might know that B's interest in
the relationship is calculating — B is interested only because of what he
thinks he can get out of the relationship.[13] Then A might well wish to
avoid the relationship, *at least for a time.* And fairly obviously, many
have sought God in hopes of gaining some immediate advantage for
themselves and not out of any deep regard for God's moral beauty. So
it seems to me that Schellenberg's reasoning depends ultimately on
some questionable generalizations.

Third, if God has decided to confront and defeat serious evil,
including evils that depend on (or consist in) ignorance, why is it
unthinkable that God would allow reasonable non-theism to occur? If
God exists, reasonable non-theism is lamentable — a bad thing. But does
it rank with the worst evils? That seems very doubtful. Of course, if our
epistemic situation in this earthly life were the only epistemic situation
we will ever be in, many would be cut off from a conscious relationship
with God permanently if God is hidden.[14] But according to most theists,
our present epistemic situation is not permanent. In the life after death
it will presumably become clear to everyone that God exists.

Furthermore, do we need some specific reason to account for the
presence of reasonable non-theism as opposed to other evils? I don't
think so. No more than we need some specific reason to account for
the presence of theft as opposed to lying or arson. No more than we
need some specific reason to account for the presence of the suffering
due to toothaches as opposed to suffering due to the flu.

Here I should note that some religious believers hold that a person's
salvation depends on his (or her) having certain theological beliefs *prior
to death* — among them the belief that God exists. The problem of divine
hiddenness seems to me to present a strong objection to such exclusivist
views. For unless people are always at fault if they lack theistic belief —
which, as we've seen, is implausible, the exclusivist position implies that

some people miss out on salvation *through no fault of their own*. (Surely some non-theists have been such that if God's existence had been made clear to them, they would have put their faith in God.) I see no plausible way to square such an outcome with the claim that God is perfectly loving and just.[15]

Fourth, we need to consider some ways in which theistic belief can go wrong. Some people who believe that God exists become unduly focused on God's knowledge and righteousness. They become vividly aware that God knows their every thought, word, and deed. Having a sensitive conscience, they get bogged down in feelings of guilt and shame. Some other believers tend to focus on God's power and righteousness in such a way that they tend to behave morally but are motivated primarily by fear of divine punishment. Still other believers, focused on divine justice, may become very judgmental and critical of other people. Yet other believers may make divine grace an excuse for being morally lukewarm. And some believers may imagine that their faith in God guarantees that their moral and political opinions are superior to those of non-believers. Finally, some who believe that God exists resent his demand for devotion because they want to serve themselves. In short, the belief that God exists can be beneficial, but it can also have effects that arguably cancel or at least greatly qualify its benefits. Perhaps, then, some people are better off without theistic belief, at least for a time, and possibly even for the duration of their earthly lives. From this perspective, God would have good reason to make reasonable non-belief in his existence possible. But this means that the first premise of the hiddenness argument is false or at least dubious.

Still, if salvation involves a conscious personal relationship with God, aren't many deprived of salvation if God is hidden? Here we need to consider at least two points: (1) According to most theists, our ultimate salvation will come in the life after death. And, as mentioned previously, if in this earthly life a person does not believe that God exists *through no fault of her own*, a loving God presumably would not *on this ground* deny her salvation in the afterlife. (2) A person's relationship with God should be viewed developmentally, as moving through levels or stages over time. If this is so, for many people, the first stage of the relationship may involve no belief that God exists. It may instead center on one's relationship with God's creatures—and on whether one is devoted to the way of holy love, a loving God's approved way of living. The main point here is that we should not assume that those without a *conscious personal* relationship with God are necessarily without a vital spiritual connection to God involving his blessing and approval.

But wouldn't it be better for us all to have a *conscious* personal relationship with God? After all, theists usually claim (or at least assume) that their personal relationship with God in heaven will be a *conscious* one. At least two points need to be considered here: (a) As we have already seen, theistic belief can go wrong in various ways, so it's not clear that everyone is *at all times* better off by having the belief that God exists. (b) Why must God eliminate every case of reasonable non-theism in this earthly life? The final defeat of evils will occur in the life after death.

Moreover, reasonable non-theism may have a useful place in the divine economy. It seems obvious that significant numbers of people live their lives in ways that are habitually opposed to the standard of holy love. This is why we have to lock our homes, use passwords, avoid taking walks late at night, tell our children not to talk with strangers, help those fleeing the cruelty of tyrannical rulers, fund police departments, and so on. But if non-theism were unreasonable, those who live in habitual opposition to the standard of holy love could be seen by everyone to be unreasonable and foolish—they would be on the level of people who deny that the earth is round. For if it is unreasonable to doubt or deny that a *perfectly loving and almighty* God exists, living in opposition to (or in disregard of) the standard of holy love is manifestly foolish and unreasonable. On what reasonable grounds could one fail to trust and to devote oneself to such a God? (None as far as I can see.) As things stand, however, we find ourselves in an environment in which the belief that God exists is controversial. Those who do not wish to follow the way of holy love can reasonably doubt or deny God's existence. For example, they might believe that an uncaring deity rules the cosmos, or they might simply be skeptical of theism. (Note: I am not for a moment suggesting that non-theists tend to be immoral or unloving; I'm merely pointing out that those who live in habitually unloving ways can rationally doubt or deny the existence of a perfectly loving, almighty God.) God could have set things up so that those who reject the way of holy love are manifestly foolish and unreasonable, but God has not done so. In this way God has avoided making the choice between devotion to holy love and its alternatives the choice between being reasonable and being unreasonable. God could have "stacked the cards" (epistemically) much more strongly in favor of the divine will. But I suggest that a loving God might well want created agents to follow the way of holy love simply or primarily because they see that love is good.

But wouldn't those who have lived lives in opposition to love have lived differently if they had known that God exists? In my estimation, a "Yes" answer overestimates the role of religious and philosophical beliefs in human motivation. It also overlooks the fact that some very unloving people have been theists.

Two Additional Hiddenness Problems

Some hiddenness arguments focus on specific forms of non-theism thought to be especially problematic. For example, Stephen Maitzen argues that the uneven distribution of theistic belief is particularly problematic for theism. Maitzen illustrates the problem by noting that Saudi Arabia is 95 percent Muslim; hence, nearly all of its citizens are theists, while Thailand is 95 percent Buddhist; hence; nearly all of its citizens are non-theists.[16] Moreover, the explanations for non-belief among individuals do not explain these demographic facts, for instance, resistance to God is presumably more or less equally distributed across cultures—it's not that Thais are vastly more resistant to God than Saudis. Nor are Thais vastly more likely than Saudis to respond to God in a calculating way for their personal advantage. And so on. The demographic facts regarding theistic belief are to be explained via cultural factors, not via theology or philosophy.

But if God has decided to confront evil in the form of ignorance and uncertainty, then, as regards religious issues that are un-settleable via the available evidence, it is predictable that cultural factors will powerfully influence human belief. And while this would be a problem if salvation depended on an individual's religious beliefs prior to death, many theists would deny that salvation depends on any belief one lacks *through no fault of one's own*. So, if it makes sense to suppose that God has decided to confront serious evil, including ignorance and uncertainty, it seems to me that the demographic facts regarding theistic belief do not present theism with a pressing problem.

Jason Marsh argues that "natural non-belief" is particularly problematic for theism. It seems likely that from the beginning, human groups held a diversity of religious beliefs, for example, a belief in forest spirits, multiple gods, an indifferent deity, a cruel God that demands human sacrifice, and so on. Marsh provides the following brief summary of the research of sociologist Rodney Stark: "On Stark's own estimation, which is based on ethnographic data for roughly four hundred 'pre-industrial' cultures, a huge portion of these cultures ([but] from what I can tell, less than 50 percent) have apparently affirmed a High God, *with far fewer affirming an active or moralistic High God that cares about the morality of human beings* [italics added]."[17]

Marsh argues that philosophical naturalism can explain the following apparent fact better than theism can:

> *Apparent Fact:* For a variety of biological, cognitive, and environmental reasons, early humans . . . originally lacked a concept of God and were religiously restricted to concepts of limited, and sometimes mean, supernatural agents. As a result, many early humans . . . failed to believe in God or in anything like God.[18] [And this failure was due to natural causes, not to resistance to God.]

Of course, one might well question how sure we can rightly be about the religious beliefs of early (that is, prehistoric) humans, but I grant the plausibility of the view that the religious beliefs of early humans were very diverse, with many (or most) lacking the concept of an almighty, perfectly good God.

But once again, on the—I think plausible—hypothesis that God has decided to confront serious evil, including ignorance and uncertainty, it is not clear to me that philosophical naturalism gains an easy victory over theism in explaining the "Apparent Fact." If God chooses to confront serious evil, he may well allow human existence to begin in very deep ignorance (the truly "dark" ages), including profound religious uncertainty. And God expects humans to use their God-given intellectual gifts to evaluate the diversity of religious ideas produced.

God may occasionally provide assistance through special messengers (e.g., prophets), but not in such a way as to provide decisive evidence for theism. And as regards issues in which clarity is ultimately needed, God can provide that in the life after death.

OUR EPISTEMIC SITUATION

Our epistemic situation, as humans, seems to me to be this: The evidence concerning God's existence is ambiguous in the sense that it can be given more than one reasonable interpretation. (By a "reasonable interpretation" I mean one held *responsibly*, that is, with due diligence in regard to seeking and assessing the relevant evidence.) Thus, the evidential situation regarding theism is similar to the evidential situation regarding some other well-known philosophical questions. For example, philosophers disagree about which ethical theory is best, about which theory of the mind (or soul) is best, and about what makes a person the same individual over time. In my view, on each of these issues, more than one position can be held in a reasonable way. Similarly, in my estimation, theism, atheism, and agnosticism can all be held in reasonable ways.

As regards the issue of God's existence, however, we do face a momentous choice: whether to live as if God exists or not. If we opt for a life that includes the disciplines of prayer, worship, and seeking God's will, we live as if God exists. If we opt for a life without these disciplines, we live as if God does not exist. In that sense, there is no middle ground. The person who believes that God exists can of course opt for a life devoted to God. It also seems to me, however, that the person who thinks the evidence favors neither theism nor atheism can *adopt theism as a position* and live as if it's true. Adopting theism as a position and acting as if it's true is not the same thing as believing, for the confidence that God exists is lacking. But it seems that a personal relationship with God would be possible on this basis (assuming that there is a God).

To sum up, I have tried to show that the hiddenness arguments are not conclusive. I have suggested that our epistemic situation, which includes much ignorance, uncertainty, and controversy, fits in well with the idea that God has decided to confront and defeat serious evil. And therefore, while naturalism has a plausible explanation of reasonable non-theism, it seems to me that theism has a reasonable alternative explanation. If that is right, the appeal to divine hiddenness does not provide strong support for naturalism.

SEVEN

How Is God Related to Ethics?

How is God related to ethics? This is a major question for theists, one they must answer if they are to have a comprehensive view of the world. And theists have proposed a number of answers to this question. In what follows I will discuss three main proposals: theological voluntarism, divine command theory, and natural law theory. I will argue that a version of natural law theory is more defensible than the alternatives.

The label "natural law theory" has been used to refer to various philosophical ideas, but for our present purposes it refers to theories of ethics with these four features:

1. *The moral law is grounded in human* nature.[1] Human beings cannot flourish or be genuinely fulfilled unless they heed the moral law, and no *true* system of morality undermines human nature, that is, prevents human beings from flourishing. It is a fundamental moral principle that we should promote human flourishing. Thus, the moral law is "natural" in the sense that it is grounded in human *nature*. This does not mean, however, that humans are always or even usually inclined to do what is right; natural law (NL) theorists are well aware that being or becoming a good person takes a lot of effort. Also, since any plausible system of morality requires that individuals make some sacrifices for others, NL theorists must explain how such sacrifices are compatible with human flourishing.

2. *The good is prior to the right*; that is, principles concerning right action, such as "You should not commit murder," are based on the

goods necessary for human flourishing or fulfillment.[2] NL theorists do not all agree on which goods are necessary for human flourishing, but a typical list would include life, health, friendship, creative activity, knowledge, beauty, and pleasure.[3] We should seek these goods, but we need guidance in doing so. For one thing, we need an appropriate balance of the goods, and we need some guidance in finding that balance. For another, there are often trade-offs, and how should we handle them? For example, in a given situation, seeking one good, such as pleasure, may be incompatible with seeking another good, such as knowledge, and in many situations, seeking one person's good may conflict with seeking the good of another person; for example, we may not have enough flu vaccine for everyone who needs it.

3. *The most important truths about morality are knowable by human beings.*[4] Here NL theory collides with moral skepticism. NL theorists need not claim, however, that every human being knows the most important moral truths. Humans who are severely mentally impaired may lack even the *ability* to know moral truths. And a child raised by morally corrupt adults may have deeply misguided ideas about right and wrong. But most human beings are *capable* of knowing the most important moral truths. That said, *humans need instruction to gain a good working knowledge of moral truth, just as they need instruction to have a good working knowledge of mathematics.*

4. *The moral law is universal*; it applies to all human beings.[5] Thus, NL theory conflicts with normative relativism, the idea that acts are right (or wrong) simply because they are approved of (or disapproved of) by the society in which they occur. For example, the moral codes of some societies permit acts and attitudes that are sexist in nature, but the mere fact that the members of a society generally endorse such a code is no defense of it from the standpoint of NL theory. If the code hinders the flourishing of many people, NL theory calls that code into question. Similarly, the NL theory conflicts with moral subjectivism, the idea that acts are right (or wrong) simply because they are approved of (or disapproved of) by the agent, that is, the person who performs the act. No doubt Adolf Hitler approved of the many acts he performed to exterminate Jews and other minorities. But given

that his acts were destructive of flourishing for millions of people, from the standpoint of NL theory, Hitler's self-approval provides no defense of his actions whatsoever. However, while NL theorists hold that *everyone* should promote human flourishing, NL theorists do not deny that flourishing is, to some degree, dependent on—and hence relative to—a person's social or cultural context. This is so because humans can flourish only in communities or societies and because social structures to some extent dictate the terms of fulfillment. For example, in a preliterate society, human fulfillment does not depend on being able to read, but in a society in which gainful employment typically involves reading, a person's fulfillment does usually depend on his or her being able to read—and thus, hindering a person's attempts to learn to read becomes a moral issue.

In what follows I want to expand on these basic elements of NL theory, contrast NL theory with some main alternatives, identify some of its strengths, and consider some key objections to it.

THEOLOGICAL VOLUNTARISM

Many theists have been NL theorists; noteworthy examples include Thomas Aquinas and C. S. Lewis.[6] NL theory, however, provides a view of the relationship between God and ethics that contrasts sharply with some other views theists have advocated. One such view is theological voluntarism (TV):

> TV: Something (e.g., an act, motive, or character trait) is right or good if and only if, *and simply because*, the almighty Creator approves of it, and something is wrong or bad if and only if, *and simply because*, the almighty Creator disapproves of it.[7]

Many believers are attracted to TV because it plainly makes God the moral standard-setter, the ultimate source of moral value and moral obligation. But there are many objections to TV. The most famous objection is this: Suppose the almighty Creator approves of, say, child abuse or torturing people just for the fun of it. According to TV, such acts would then be right. But it is implausible to suppose that such acts could be right. So TV is implausible or false.

Defenders of TV might reply, "But God would never approve of child abuse or of torturing people just for fun." Unfortunately, this reply misses the point. Given TV, if God did approve of such acts, they would be right. God would have done nothing wrong in approving of them. God's approvals and disapprovals are the ultimate standard in ethics. Furthermore, even if God currently disapproves of child abuse, nothing prevents him from approving of it in the future. Ethics is entirely dependent upon God's will.

A second objection runs as follows: When God approves (or disapproves) of some act, does God do so for a reason? It is natural to suppose that the answer is "Yes." But then, contrary to TV, the act is not right (or wrong) *simply because* God approves of it (or disapproves of it). It is surely the *reason* that makes the act right, good, wrong, or evil, as the case may be. On the other hand, if God's approvals and disapprovals are not backed by reasons, they are purely arbitrary; they are, in effect, divine whims. But ethical decisions are the most important, or among the most important, decisions we make. Can ethics really depend in the end on mere whims? God approves of "loving thy neighbor," but he might just as well have approved of "hating thy neighbor"—is there no *reason* why God approves of love over hate? That's hard to believe.

Here is a third objection: TV asserts or presupposes that *whatever an almighty Creator wills (or approves) is right*. But why should we accept this proposition? Is it supposed to be a necessary truth, like "No circles are squares" or "All husbands are married"? (A necessary truth is one that cannot be false under any circumstances.) Notice that the proposition ascribes just two attributes to God—being almighty and being the Creator; it does not ascribe moral goodness, justice, or love to God. And the problem is that there is no obvious logical connection between "An almighty Creator wills (approves) X" and "X is right." Might does not make right. Nor does the act of creation obviously give one total control over right and wrong; this point is underscored by possible substitutions we might make for X, such as racism, sexism, child abuse, adultery, and so on. Keep in mind that according to TV there are no limits on what an almighty Creator might will or approve, for there is no moral standard independent of God's will.

A fourth problem with TV concerns what it implies about the nature of divine goodness. Think of the worst acts an evil deity might perform, such as breaking its promises, torturing little children, rewarding the wicked while punishing the virtuous, deceiving creatures, making any form of happiness impossible for them, and so on. According to TV, if God approves of these things, they are right or good. So the God of TV could do all of these things while remaining good. But a theory that implies that God can be good even though he does all the terrible things an evil deity might do is a theory with a deeply flawed conception of divine goodness.

Finally, proponents of TV apparently presuppose that there can be no moral law without a personal lawgiver, that is, a person in authority who issues a command. They apparently regard "There is no moral law without a personal lawgiver" as a necessary truth. But critics of TV question this claim. Instead, many of them would claim that there are necessary truths about right and wrong, such as "It is wrong to intentionally inflict intense pain on a person without his or her consent and merely for sadistic pleasure." From this perspective, the moral law is somewhat similar to the laws of logic. One very basic law of logic says that if a proposition P is true, and P implies Q, then Q is also true. (Example: "Lincoln was a husband. If Lincoln was a husband, then Lincoln had a wife. So, Lincoln had wife.") This law of logic holds of necessity, and it does not need to be issued by a personal "logic lawgiver." Similarly, according to many critics of TV, an act can be morally right even if it has not been commanded by a personal lawgiver, and an act can be morally wrong even if it has not been forbidden by a personal lawgiver.

NECESSARY MORAL TRUTHS?

The claim that some truths about morality are necessary truths is controversial but very important in this context, so let us stop a moment to examine it more carefully. It is often assumed that truths about morality depend on the existence of human beings and hence are merely contingent truths (i.e., true but not necessarily true).[8] This line of reasoning might be summed up as follows: "There would be no moral truths if there were no humans. But humans do not exist of necessity. In fact, we know that there was a time when there were no humans. And it makes no sense to suggest that there were truths about right and wrong before humans came into existence." But this line of thinking overlooks the possibility that moral truths can be conditional (if-then) in nature. Think about it like this. Suppose we describe an action that we consider to be clearly wrong. We make a list of all the features that make the act wrong, for example:

A. The agent inflicts intense pain on another person.
B. The agent does so *intentionally*.
C. The agent inflicts the pain knowing full well that doing so is against the will of the victim.
D. The agent inflicts the pain *merely* because he enjoys making the victim suffer. (The pain is not deserved, nor is it an unavoidable side effect of beneficial surgery, etc.)

Now, it is very plausible to suppose that any act with all of these features is wrong. In fact, it seems clear that no act with all of these features *could* be morally permissible. But then it apparently follows that there is a necessary truth along these lines: "If human beings exist, then any action with features A, B, C, and D is wrong." (Keep in mind that a conditional is hypothetical in nature. So this conditional does not imply that humans exist, and it can be true even if there are no human beings. A conditional can be true even though its if-clause is false; for example: "If Abe Lincoln is only four feet tall, he is less than seven feet tall.")[9]

In this connection, using the phrase "other things being equal" to mean "exceptional cases aside," Judith Jarvis Thomson has argued that the following are necessary moral truths: "Other things being equal, one ought not cause others pain," "Other things being equal, one ought to do what one promised," and "Other things being equal, one ought not act rudely." If we keep the "other things being equal" qualification in mind, these examples are plausibly regarded as necessary truths.[10]

But if there are truths, don't they have to be put into human language? And if so, don't all truths depend on the development of human language(s)? Here we must distinguish between sentences and propositions. Consider the English sentence "Grass is green" and its German equivalent, "Das Gras ist grün." In their ordinary uses, these sentences express the same truth (or falsehood). Sentences belong to a human language—in this case, to English and German, respectively. But propositions do not belong to any human language; they are simply truths or falsehoods. And they may or may not be expressed in human language. The geometrical truth expressed by "No circles are squares" (using the words with their ordinary meanings) would hold even if it had not been expressed in any human language. So why couldn't there be truths about morality that have not been expressed in any human language? It seems there could be.

But aren't moral truths dependent on human nature? And isn't it at least possible that human nature will change as humans evolve? If so, aren't all moral truths contingent truths, and hence not necessary after all? Let us grant that human nature may change over time. But then, instead of talking about human nature, we can talk about creatures with the needs and capacities that are *currently* characteristic of human beings. We can then rephrase the above argument. If we do that, we will again wind up with conditionals that appear to be necessary truths about morality—that is, truths about right and wrong for creatures with the needs and capacities *currently* characteristic of human beings. From this perspective, it is plausible to suppose that at least some truths concerning what is morally right (or morally wrong) are necessary truths. And, as we will see momentarily, the apparent fact that there are necessary truths about morality makes a difference as we sort through views concerning the foundations of morality.

DIVINE COMMAND THEORY

The objections to TV have led many theologians and philosophers to reject it. Nevertheless, many also think there is something right about TV insofar as it posits a strong connection between ethics and the will of God. Accordingly, some theologians and philosophers have suggested an alternative view that makes a *loving* God's commands the source of moral obligation. This view is called divine command theory (DCT):

DCT: An act is obligatory (morally required) if and only if, *and because*, it is commanded by a loving God; and an act is morally wrong if and only if, *and because*, it is forbidden by a loving God.[11]

DCT seems clearly to avoid the first objection to TV: A *loving* God would not command cruel acts such as child abuse and torturing people just for fun. DCT also seems to get around the third objection to TV because it is plausible to suppose that *if an omnipotent, omniscient, and perfectly loving God commands X, then X is right*. Nevertheless, DCT faces significant objections.

First, in claiming that the commands of a *loving* God create moral obligations, defenders of DCT are assuming that love is good or that love is a virtue, that is, a good character trait. But what makes love good? The answer cannot be simply that God approves of love. That is the answer TV gives, but as we have seen, that answer implies that morality is arbitrary: God might have approved of hate, in which case hate would be good. So, from the standpoint of DCT, it seems that love is necessarily good—it cannot be bad or evil or morally neutral. (We are speaking here, of course, of the type of love that involves caring about what is in the best interests of others.) But then it seems that, from the perspective of DCT, "Love is good" is a necessary truth; like "1 + 1 = 2," it cannot be false under any possible circumstances. Accordingly, a critic of DCT might agree that "Love is good" is a necessary truth and suggest that fundamental moral truths in general are necessary, thus questioning the need to ground moral obligation in divine commands. (Recall the purported examples of necessary moral truths given in the previous section.)[12]

Second, suppose that God issues no commands applicable to a certain action or type of action, say, child abuse or animal abuse. In that case, DCT implies that the act (or type of act) is neither obligatory nor wrong. But wouldn't child abuse and animal abuse be wrong even if God had issued no applicable commands? Defenders of DCT might reply that God has issued certain general commands that cover all particular cases. For example, "Love thy neighbor" rules out child abuse, and God has commanded us to love our neighbors. But this reply misses the point of the objection. A theory of ethics can reasonably be criticized for what it implies about *hypothetical* situations, that is, situations that haven't occurred but conceivably could. And according to DCT, God issues commands freely—he is not forced or obligated to do so; therefore, it is *possible* that God would issue no command concerning child abuse, in which case child abuse would not be wrong, according to DCT.

Now, defenders of DCT might reply that it is inconceivable that a *loving* God would fail to issue commands about child abuse. But why is that inconceivable? Defenders of DCT do not think that God is morally obligated to issue commands; rather, they hold that divine commands are the source of all moral obligation. And remember, according to DCT, the fact that an act is unloving or even hateful does not make it wrong; an act (or type of act) is wrong *if and only if* (and because) God forbids it. And again, according to defenders of DCT, God issues commands freely; he could have refrained from issuing any commands at all.

Third, we still have to ask whether divine commands are issued for reasons—they either are or they aren't. Let's consider both possibilities. If divine commands are issued for reasons, and the reasons are good reasons, then it is plausible to suppose that the reasons make the actions obligatory (or wrong if the act is forbidden). For example, suppose that God were to forbid rape because it is very harmful and shows a total lack of respect for the victim. Then it would be plausible to suppose that rape is wrong for the stated reasons and would be wrong even if God had not forbidden it.

On the other hand, if divine commands are not issued on the basis of reasons, the commands are arbitrary. But why would a *loving* God place restrictions on our behavior for no reason at all? The suggestion seems to make no sense. Imagine a deity who says, in effect, "While there is admittedly nothing inherently problematic about killing innocent people, stealing, lying, and adultery, I forbid you to do such things!"

Might divine commands be based on reasons, but on reasons too weak (by themselves) to make the acts right (or wrong)? If, however, divine commands are based on weak reasons, we have to ask, "Why would a loving God restrict our behavior on the basis of weak reasons?" Wouldn't that amount to demanding that we "jump through hoops" unnecessarily? It would seem so, and such demands would not seem to be loving—rather they would seem to be manipulative in nature. Moreover, why would a divine command *based on weak reasons* generate a genuine moral obligation? Presumably, it wouldn't.

There is, however, an important complication we need to consider at this juncture. Suppose that a parent sets bedtime at 9:00 p.m. and tells her children to go to bed then, but the children respond, "Come on, Mom. Why 9:00? Why not 9:10?" The parent's response is likely to be some form of "Because I said so." What can we learn from this type of case? I assume that children have a moral duty to obey the reasonable commands of their parents. And "Go to bed at 9:00 p.m." might well be a reasonable command depending on various circumstances, such as the ages of the children. Yet there is an element of arbitrariness in the command, since "Go to bed at 9:10 p.m." might also be a reasonable command. On the other hand, "Go to bed at 7:00 p.m." might well be an unreasonable command, so the arbitrariness here clearly has limits. Let's assume that the parent's selection of 9:00 p.m. as bedtime is reasonable. The parent's reason for selecting this time—presumably, the health and well-being of the children—does not rule out other reasonable times, such as 9:10 p.m. In that sense, the parent's reasons don't by themselves fully determine the content of the command—which is presumably the point the children are trying to make! What is going on? One way to look at the situation is this: There is a general moral principle along the lines of "Children should obey the reasonable commands of their parents."[13] And if the parent's command is reasonable, it should be obeyed even if there is an element of *unavoidable* arbitrariness in it. With this example in mind, let's return to the DCT.

Theists assume that in many respects humans stand in relation to God in the way that young children stand in relation to their parents.[14] From this perspective, it is plausible to suppose that there is a general moral truth along these lines: "Humans should obey the commands of a loving God—even when there is an element of unavoidable arbitrariness in the command." (I am assuming that a loving God would not issue unreasonable commands.) Now, there might well be an element of unavoidable arbitrariness in some divine commands. For example, if God commands people to give 10 percent of their income to charitable causes (i.e., to tithe), presumably he might have selected a somewhat different percentage, say, 9.9 or 10.1 percent.[15] In this limited sense, God's reasons for issuing *some* commands might be insufficient to fully determine the content of the commands. And yet the divine command would create an obligation, just as the parent's command "Go to bed at 9:00 p.m." creates an obligation for her children. From this perspective, the DCT contains an important element of truth. *Some* actions may be obligatory *partly* because a loving God has commanded them.[16]

But notice two things: (1) Many moral requirements seem to be based on sufficient reasons, apart from any divine command: One ought not torture children, one ought not intentionally kill innocent humans, one ought not steal, one ought not rape, one ought to love God, one ought to love one's neighbor, and so on.[17] Thus, the claim that acts are obligatory *because* they are commanded by a loving God is at best a partial truth. Many acts would seem to be obligatory for reasons that apply whether or not God issues a relevant command. (2) What is the status of the principle that *if humans exist, they ought to obey the commands of a loving God*? Obviously, it would make no sense to suggest that we should obey God's commands *because he commands us to do so*. Is the stated principle instead a necessary truth? That seems plausible, but if so our discussion of the DCT seems to point us toward the idea that morality is *ultimately* grounded in necessity rather than in divine commands.

BACK TO NATURAL LAW THEORY

Very well, TV and DCT are apparently problematic views. But what is the relation between God and ethics according to NL theory? Fundamentally this: God chooses to bring into existence human beings, creatures who can act freely and on the basis of reasons.[18] These creatures have certain characteristic capacities (such as the power to think rationally and the power to make choices) and certain characteristic needs (for food, drink, companionship, creative activity, and so on). By bringing creatures of this type into existence, God creates beings that have moral obligations; it cannot be otherwise, for such beings can mistreat one another. Humans can deliberately deny others the good things needed in order to flourish, that is, to be what humans were meant to be. For example, humans can be denied adequate food and drink and thus be deprived of health. Or they can be severely injured and thus deprived of the ability to walk, to speak, or even to think (in the case of brain injury). They can be denied the liberty to form friendships. And of course they can be killed, and thus deprived of life itself.

According to theists who endorse NL theory, humans cannot truly flourish or be fulfilled apart from a right relationship with God, their Creator. It is bad for a human being to be alienated from his or her Creator. Thus, true human flourishing must be described, in part, in theological terms.

It must be stressed that NL theorists do not regard human flourishing or fulfillment as a matter of mere subjective opinion. To put this point negatively, it is quite possible for a person to be mistaken about what is in his own best interest or in the best interest of others. Flourishing or fulfillment essentially involves three things:

a. Having one's genuine needs met. (Here we must distinguish between genuine needs and mere wants or desires.)
b. Having well-functioning capacities of the sort characteristic of human beings. (The relevant capacities include, for example, the ability to think rationally, the power to make free choices, the ability to speak, the ability to walk, the ability to see, the ability to hear, and the ability to enter into loving relationships.)
c. Having well-developed individual talents or abilities, such as, musical or artistic talent, athletic ability, leadership ability, technical abilities, and intellectual gifts. (Note: Since talents and abilities differ from person to person, it follows that fulfillment is *to some extent* person-relative.)

According to theists who endorse NL theory, human beings cannot be completely fulfilled in this earthly life; ultimate fulfillment must await an afterlife in which redeemed human beings will exist in harmony with God and with one another. Nevertheless, there is a kind of fulfillment appropriate to this earthly life, and we should seek it.

The Good. By holding that the good is prior to the right, NL theorists reject deontological theories of ethics, in which truths concerning right action are taken to be the most basic truths about ethics. The most famous deontological theory is Immanuel Kant's, in which

the fundamental ethical principle is the so-called categorical imperative, which might be paraphrased as follows:

> *Categorical Imperative*: You may perform an act only if the prin-
> ciple upon which you are acting is one you can coherently will
> everyone to act upon in the circumstances in question.[19]

To illustrate, suppose you are considering whether to act on the following principle or maxim: "I will borrow money and promise to pay it
back while knowing that I will not be able to pay it back." Kant argued
that if everyone tried to act on this maxim, no one would loan money,
and therefore no one could act on the maxim; hence, you cannot coher-
ently will that everyone act on it.

The point here is not that NL theorists necessarily reject Kant's
categorical imperative. The point is rather that NL theorists believe that
our thinking about ethics gets off on the wrong foot if we try to identify principles of right and wrong independently of truths concerning
what is good, that is, what is worth having or seeking. NL theorists regard claims about *what is good* as the most basic truths concerning the
moral life.

Most of us can probably agree that many things are good—worth
having or seeking—for example, life, health, food, drink, pleasure, companionship, creative activity, and beauty. But of course human beings
do not agree entirely in regard to what is good for a human being to
have or to seek. For instance, theistic NL theorists insist that companionship with God, the Creator, is among the goods humans should
seek, but obviously no atheist would agree with that. Bear in mind,
however, that any theory of ethics is forced to make controversial
claims at certain points, so it is surely unreasonable to demand that an
ethical theory be acceptable to everyone.

As noted above, for NL theorists, true fulfillment consists in (a)
having one's genuine needs met, (b) having well-functioning capacities
of the sort characteristic of human beings, and (c) having well-developed
individual talents and abilities. True fulfillment or flourishing is the fundamental good to be sought. And one person's fulfillment or flourishing
is as important as another's. Thus, when acting, one must take into

account not only one's own flourishing but the flourishing of everyone affected by one's action.

The idea of fulfillment or flourishing is undoubtedly somewhat vague, and NL theorists are well aware that people often disagree about its nature. Such disagreements cannot be eliminated; they are simply part of the human condition. But most of us would probably agree that some people have come much closer to true fulfillment than others. For example, by taking addictive drugs, one may (for a time) obtain much pleasure, but in doing so one is apt to lose out on health, knowledge, creative activity, and so on. So taking addictive drugs is surely not the path to flourishing. And one reason we find biographies and autobiographies profoundly interesting is that they enable us to think in very concrete terms about human fulfillment. They help us to think more clearly and specifically about what true fulfillment consists in. So the search for a clearer and deeper understanding of flourishing is bound to be ongoing, but honest dialogue about it can be seen as itself part of the moral life. To arrive at a viable conception of true fulfillment, we must think as clearly as we can about what our genuine needs, as humans, are, and we must also think as clearly as we can about what it takes to nurture the capacities characteristic of human beings, including our capacities for knowing, for creative activity, and for loving relationships.

Philosophers distinguish between intrinsic and instrumental goods. An instrumental good is one that is good as a means to some other good. An intrinsic good is one worth seeking for its own sake, not *merely* as a means to something else. Money is an example of an instrumental good. Money isn't worth seeking for its own sake, but it is worth seeking as the means to other good things, such as food, shelter, and clothing. Philosophers in the NL tradition regard true fulfillment or flourishing as an intrinsic good.[20] It is worth having for its own sake, not merely as the means to something else. Other goods may be intrinsically good too, however; for example, many philosophers regard pleasure and companionship as intrinsic goods. These goods may be regarded as worth seeking for their own sake but also worth seeking as means to (or as aspects of) true fulfillment.

Some philosophers have argued that there is only one intrinsic good. For example, hedonists argue that pleasure is the only thing worth having for its own sake. And any genuine good is a form of pleasure—

a "mental" pleasure if not a physical pleasure. Philosophers in the NL tradition do not claim that all goods reduce to one basic type, such as pleasure. And, as we have seen, true fulfillment or flourishing plausibly consists in the possession of a variety of distinct goods in an appropriate balance.

The Right. Like NL theorists, consequentialists hold that the good is prior to the right, but they also hold that we are morally obligated to *maximize* the good. Utilitarianism is the best-known form of consequentialism.[21] Utilitarianism comes in various forms, one of which philosophers call "act-utilitarianism."

> *Act-Utilitarianism*: An act is morally required or obligatory if, and only if, no alternative act would produce more utility (roughly, happiness) than it does.

In other words, an act is morally obligatory if, and only if, it maximizes utility. But what exactly is utility? Different utilitarians characterize it in different ways, but here is one way: An action is apt to please or satisfy some people while displeasing or dissatisfying others. To determine the utility of an action, add up the satisfaction of all those who will be affected by the action and then add up all the dissatisfaction (if any) of those affected by the action. The utility of the act is the sum of satisfaction minus the sum of dissatisfaction. Consider this example: Suppose lawmakers are voting on a bill that will raise the age at which citizens can receive social security payments. If the bill passes, the retirement age will be raised, and that will help to keep the social security system financially viable; of course, many citizens would be pleased by that result. But those nearing the *currently* legal age of retirement are apt to be displeased if the age is raised, so they would be displeased if the bill passes. What is the right thing for the legislators to do? They must consider the sum of satisfaction for all affected if the bill passes (*minus* the sum of dissatisfaction) and compare that with the sum of satisfaction if the bill fails to pass (*minus* the sum of dissatisfaction). It is the moral duty of the legislators to vote for the bill if passing it would yield the most utility. On the other hand, it is their duty to vote against the bill if not passing it would yield the most utility.[22]

Unlike consequentialism, NL theory does not require that we maximize the good. Maximizing the good may be the right thing to do in some cases, but it is not in general required. As we have seen, true fulfillment consists in (a) having one's genuine needs met, (b) having well-functioning capacities of the sort characteristic of human beings, and (c) having well-developed individual talents and abilities. It does not involve *maximizing* pleasure, knowledge, companionship, and so on. Neither does it consist in obtaining *the greatest possible sum* of goods combined. This is important because one standard objection to utilitarianism is that it makes morality too burdensome. Suppose you are thinking about going to a movie. From a utilitarian perspective, you must consider other acts you might perform, other ways you could spend your money, such as, sending a check to a charitable organization. If sending the check would produce more utility than attending the movie, you are morally obligated to send the check—unless there is some other act that would produce even more utility. In thinking about such cases, many conclude that utilitarianism makes morality too demanding, placing a burden on agents that goes beyond what true morality requires.

We should promote true fulfillment, but whose? Not just the agent's, of course. The flourishing of everyone affected by the action must be taken into account. And no one's flourishing or fulfillment is more important than anyone else's. So how do we *know* which acts are right and which are wrong? NL theorists can approach this issue in several ways. First, many theists employ "You should love your neighbor as yourself" as a master rule.[23] From the perspective of NL, this rule makes sense because, if we love someone, we care about his or her best interests (i.e., flourishing) and we are willing to act in such a way as to promote his or her best interests. A proper self-love ensures that one will seek fulfillment for oneself. But the type of care or concern one has for one's own fulfillment should be extended to others. One person's flourishing is just as important as another's.

One might reply that "Love your neighbor as yourself" is a rather vague principle that leaves many ethical questions unanswered. NL theorists acknowledge that the principle does not provide clear answers in every case. But they would make two further observations: (A) Our usual problem, as human beings, is not that we do not know what is right. In the course of our daily lives, more often than not, we do know the right thing to do. We may often not *want* to do the right thing, because doing so takes effort and sacrifice, but that's a different matter altogether. (B) It is most unlikely that any ethical theory can provide us with a set of formulas that will give us the correct answer to all questions about right and wrong. It is simply unrealistic to expect any ethical theory to meet this demand.

NL theorists, however, have more to say about our knowledge of right and wrong. They also stress that human beings cannot achieve true fulfillment unless they cultivate certain moral virtues.[24] The virtues are character traits, habits of thinking and/or acting. Examples include wisdom, moderation, courage, justice, hope, and love. Wisdom is the knowledge of what is important and how to achieve it. Moderation is the trait or habit of avoiding extremes or excess, as in eating or drinking. Courage is a proper tendency to endure in the face of pain or danger. (The word "proper" is needed here to distinguish courage from foolhardiness, on the one hand, and from cowardice on the other.) Justice is the trait or habit of giving to each person what he or she is due. It involves respecting others' rights. Hope is the opposite of despair; it is the habit of expecting realistic but positive outcomes. Love is a tendency to act in the best interests of others (as well as oneself).

Fairly obviously, some people are much more virtuous than others. NL theorists may claim that the more virtuous a person is, the more apt he is to know what is right. And they might suggest the following as helpful guidelines to identifying right and wrong acts: (1) A morally obligatory action is one that a virtuous person would characteristically perform (in the circumstances in question) and that he would feel guilty about if he did not perform. (2) A morally wrong action is one that a virtuous person characteristically would not perform (in the circumstances in question) and that he would feel guilty about if he did perform.

Furthermore, the idea that the virtues are needed for human flourishing carries with it a list of more specific moral rules: One should act charitably, one should act justly, one should act with moderation, one should act with courage, one should not act unjustly, one should not act in a cowardly way, and so on.[25] Once again, of course, such rules

144 Is God Related to Ethics?

144 *How Is God Related to Ethics?*

do not clearly indicate how one should act in every case, but they do serve as useful guidelines in many cases.

A third way of judging which acts are right and which are wrong begins with the reminder that humans do not flourish in isolation; they flourish in communities. And one of the things that binds people together in a community is a shared set of beliefs about how one ought to act and how one ought not to act. Thus, a generally respectful attitude toward the shared moral beliefs of a community is an important tie that binds it together. And such a respectful attitude is appropriate from the perspective of NL theory. But of course, a *generally* respectful attitude is compatible with rejecting and protesting against any rules that plainly undermine flourishing for many, such as rules that permit racial and sexual discrimination.

Now we must consider an important complication. One objection to utilitarianism runs as follows: Suppose that five people need organ transplants *very* soon or else they will die. One of them needs a new heart, two need one kidney each, and two need one lung each. And suppose, for the sake of the argument, that a surgeon can provide these transplants only by removing the relevant organs from one healthy person (call him "Sam") who has the right blood type. (No other viable organs are known to be available, and time is of the essence.) The surgeon asks Sam if he's willing to donate his organs. Not surprisingly, Sam replies, "No way," since donating his organs would clearly result in his death. But from a utilitarian perspective, it seems that the surgeon should go ahead with the transplants, assuming that he can. (Perhaps he can put Sam to sleep with an injection.) Five people will die if the surgeon doesn't proceed with the transplants, and the happiness of five people adds up to a lot more than the happiness of one person. The problem is this: It seems clear to most everyone that it would be very wrong for the surgeon to go ahead with the transplants. And many philosophers think that this type of case is a powerful objection to utilitarianism.[26]

The problem seems to be that the utilitarian view of the case overlooks or leaves out Sam's rights as an individual. Sam has a very strong right to life, and that right is not overridden by the interests or preferences of those needing the transplants. Furthermore, the five persons needing transplants do not have a right to Sam's organs. We must ask, however, does the case pose a similar problem for NL theory? If the surgeon does not perform the transplants, won't he be acting contrary to the flourishing of five people and in favor of the flourishing of just one person? First, let's recall that NL theory, unlike utilitarianism, does not require that the agent maximize the good in every case. And the transplant case seems to be one in which the good should not be maximized. But obviously, more needs to be said. The NL theorist can admit that NL theory, as stated here, is incomplete and needs to be supplemented by a theory of individual rights *while claiming that NL theory nevertheless captures a very important part of the foundations of ethics.* In short, we ought to promote human flourishing but within the limits set by individual rights. Even granting this qualification, however, note that if we accept that individuals have such rights as a right to life, a right to liberty, and a right not to be caused bodily harm, *those rights protect the individual's flourishing.* So those rights may be at least partly grounded in human flourishing.[27]

Space does not permit the development of a theory of rights here. But whenever we wrong someone, we arguably violate his or her rights. For example, murder violates the victim's right to life, unjust imprisonment violates the right to liberty, assault violates the right not to be caused bodily harm, stealing violates the victim's right to property, and so on. When we violate a person's rights, we demean that person, we treat her as having less value than she in fact has, and surely that is not a loving way to act.[28] So a theory of rights is apparently a vital feature of a complete ethical theory and a needed supplement to NL theory as stated here.[29]

OBJECTIONS TO NATURAL LAW THEORY

Whatever its strengths, NL theory has been criticized in many different ways. Let us now consider some of the main objections to it.

First, defenders of TV often claim that NL theory sets up a moral standard independent of God's will, and thus a standard by which God may be judged. And this, they claim, is theologically unacceptable. Now, it is true that NL theory posits a moral standard independent of God's will. God cannot make just any act right (e.g., child abuse) simply by willing that it be performed. But it is by no means obvious that this is theologically problematic. (a) Note that DCT also posits a moral standard independent of God's will, namely, God's love. Love is a character trait, a *tendency* to act, think, and regard others in a certain way. And a person's character traits—such as being wise, being fair, or being cowardly—are not identical with a person's will. For example, it is possible for a person to act *out of character* by willing to do so. Is DCT theologically unacceptable because it proposes God's love as the ultimate ethical standard? Not many theologians would answer "Yes" to that question. (b) Furthermore, since love involves caring about the good for others, *God's love itself ensures the importance of human flourishing*. You cannot love a human being if you do not care about his or her true fulfillment. Thus God's love and human flourishing are intimately linked. Why must we place God's will above love as a moral standard? There is no good reason to do so, and in fact our discussion of TV shows that there are good reasons not to do so.

Second, it seems that both DCT and NL theory are driven to claim that "Love is good" is a necessary truth—it cannot be false under any circumstances. But this means that God cannot make "Love is good" false; moreover, *if God were to act in an unloving way*, he would be in violation of a moral standard ("Love is good") that would hold independently of his character (which would be flawed if he acted in an unloving way) as well as independently of his will.

Now, this objection moves us into highly abstract metaphysical territory and into the question of God's relationship to necessary truths. Space does not permit a thorough exploration of this topic, but I think the following relatively simple points largely defuse the issue: (1) Most theistic philosophers would agree that divine omnipotence, as best understood, does not extend to making necessary truths false. Making a necessary truth false is like drawing a circular square or creating an even whole number between two and four. (2) Many theistic philosophers hold that it is simply not possible for God, the greatest possible being, to act in an unloving way. From this perspective, the proposed scenario ("if God were to act in an unloving way . . .") can be dismissed as impossible.

Third, defenders of TV and DCT often claim that NL theory makes God dispensable to ethics, for atheists can accept the NL view.

Now, it is true that non-theists can endorse a version of NL theory, but it is not clear why this should lead anyone to reject a theistic version of NL theory, especially given the objections to TV and DCT. The real issues here are "Does God exist?" and "Do human beings need a right relationship with God?" Traditional theists answer both questions in the affirmative, of course. And so they will hold that non-theistic forms of NL theory are incomplete and flawed. But even if we grant that there are incomplete and flawed versions of the NL view, this does not give us a good reason to reject every version of it.

Fourth, the defenders of TV and DCT may claim that NL theory renders divine commands superfluous. We humans can figure out which acts promote flourishing on our own; we don't need divine commands or instruction. Here the NL theorist may respond in several ways: (a) Since humans sometimes disagree about which acts promote flourishing, it would help to have an explicit command from God. (b) Even if we humans *can* figure out what promotes flourishing, doing so might take a long time. So again it would help to have clear instruction from God. (c) Having divine commands is a bit like having an answer key in a textbook on mathematics. I may think my answer is correct, but my confidence increases substantially if my answer is the same as the one in the answer key. (d) As we have already seen, there are cases in which the command of a person in authority, such as a parent, can create an obligation where none existed. (Recall the case of a parent commanding her children to go to bed at 9:00 p.m.) Thus, within limits, a divine command may create an obligation (e.g., to tithe or to worship weekly with fellow believers) when no such obligation existed apart from the divine command. (e) Divine commands can give us additional reasons to do what is right. Consider that a child may know that he ought to do something, say, return an item to the lost and found, but if the child's parent tells him to return the item, the child has an additional reason to do so. In the same way, divine commands can give us additional reasons to do what we know we ought to do.

Fifth, it may be claimed that NL theory, by focusing on human fulfillment, is unable to give a proper place to making great sacrifices for others. For example, if my nation is attacked, I may refuse to take part in the fighting because I might lose my life or be severely injured, thus undermining my chances of fulfillment. NL theorists can respond to this objection in three ways: (1) NL theory certainly does not tell me to focus simply on my own fulfillment. The fulfillment of others is just as important as my own, and I will often have to make sacrifices to help other people. Again, the master rule is, "Love thy neighbor as thyself." (2) Human beings cannot flourish in isolation; they must live in community if they are to flourish. But there can be no well-functioning community unless most of the members have a significant degree of moral virtue. Paradoxically, then, we must be prepared to make sacrifices for the sake of the community if we are to flourish as individuals. (3) Theistic NL theorists will emphasize that ultimate fulfillment cannot be achieved in this earthly life; it can be achieved only in the life after death. Depending on the circumstances, one may need to make great sacrifices or even lay down one's life for others, thus losing out on earthly fulfillment at least in part, but doing the right thing will never come at the cost of one's ultimate fulfillment in the life after death.

Sixth, some may claim that even if NL theory tells us to do the right thing, it tells us to do it for the wrong reason; *for even if we make sacrifices for others, the sacrifices are temporary and will help to secure our ultimate fulfillment in the life after death.* Now, given NL theory, it is true that doing the right thing will never cause us to lose out on our ultimate fulfillment in the life after death. But it does not follow that we should constantly be thinking about our ultimate fulfillment as we make ethical decisions. Loving others involves caring about what is good for them because *their* flourishing matters just as much as our own. If we are often helping others but only because we think that doing so will "get us into heaven," our moral motivation is indeed flawed. We should help others simply because doing so is loving and right. On the other hand, would God be a God of love if he allowed those who make sacrifices for others to be cut off from their ultimate fulfillment precisely because they've made such sacrifices? "No" seems to be the obviously correct answer. So, according to the NL view, we live in a world in which being moral will never *in the long run* penalize us; we have that assurance, but on a daily basis we need to think about the needs of others, not simply about our own ultimate fulfillment.

Seventh, there is a problem with any system of ethics that tells us to promote some end. We cannot know the long-term effects of our actions, and sometimes we seriously miscalculate even the short-term effects of our actions. Perhaps I save a child's life, but he grows up to become a vicious criminal. I thought I was promoting human flourishing, but really my act was on balance destructive of it. This objection may force a refinement in the NL view. We can certainly distinguish the intended (and reasonably expected) consequences of our actions from the actual consequences. And so NL theorists might hold that, other things being equal, we should perform acts whose *intended (and reasonably expected)* outcomes contribute positively to fulfillment for all those affected (insofar as possible).[30] We cannot be held responsible for the completely unpredictable and unintended consequences of our actions.

Eighth, defenders of TV often appeal to certain Bible passages to support their view. These are Bible passages in which acts we normally think of as wrong are given divine approval. For example, in Genesis 22 God reportedly commands Abraham to sacrifice his son Isaac. We would normally consider such an act an extreme form of child abuse. Defenders of TV often claim that their view is the only one that can make sense of such Bible passages: "Yes, human sacrifice is normally wrong, but if God wills such things on occasion, they are on that occasion right. No other ethical theory can accommodate these passages." NL theorists may respond in a number of ways:

a. As we noted previously, the worst things we can imagine an evil deity doing would in fact be right or good, according to the logic of TV, as long as the deity approves of his own acts. So TV's way of accommodating these rather disturbing Bible passages only underscores the implausibility of TV.

b. Some NL theorists may argue that, surprisingly, the acts in question could be morally permissible under special circumstances. Take the case of Abraham and Isaac. Suppose that Abraham had faith that God would keep his promise that *through Isaac* Abraham would be the father of many nations. And suppose that Abraham believed that God was able to raise Isaac from the dead. With these givens, the case of Abraham and Isaac is a very special one; would human sacrifice clearly be wrong in such a case?[31]

c. Some NL theorists may simply suggest that it would be a mistake to let admittedly disturbing and perplexing Bible passages govern one's view of ethics. Given that certain Bible passages are hard for everyone to understand, why should they be allowed to dictate our thinking about the foundations of ethics? As the old saying goes, "Hard cases do not make good law."

If one or more of these responses is reasonable, the objection does not seem to have much force.

To sum up, NL theory provides an intriguing view of the relationship between God and ethics. It also occupies an interesting middle ground between deontological and consequentialist theories of ethics. Furthermore, NL theory provides a rational alternative to moral skepticism, moral relativism, and moral subjectivism. Finally, as we have just seen, NL theorists are able to provide plausible responses to many standard objections.

EIGHT

Is Divine Foreknowledge Compatible with Human Free Will?

Part I

Suppose that, prior to creating the universe, God believed that you will drink a cup of tea tomorrow at 9:01 a.m. When that time arrives, will you have the *power to refrain* from drinking the tea? You must answer yes or no. If you answer "No," you are denying that you will drink the tea *freely*. But if you answer "Yes," you are affirming that at 9:01 tomorrow morning it will really be possible for you to refrain from drinking the tea. But if you *can* refrain, then you *can* make a belief God had long, long ago false. Alternatively, it will be possible for you to do something that changes the past by changing what God believed long, long ago. But given that God is infallible, you cannot make a belief of God's false. And no one can change the past, so you cannot change what God believed long ago. This is the problem of divine foreknowledge and human free will, in a nutshell. Responses to this problem force theists to work out their views of free will, of God's relation to time, and of divine omniscience.

KEY CONCEPTS

Let's back up and try to get a clearer understanding of the key concepts underlying the problem of divine foreknowledge and human free will: knowledge, omniscience, free will, and determinism.

What is knowledge? According to a traditional analysis, *if one knows that X (e.g., Mars is the fourth planet from the sun), then (A) one believes that X, (B) X is true, and (C) one is justified in believing that X.* Let us briefly consider each of the three clauses of this analysis. First, clause B: Why can one know only truths? Answer: Because knowledge is success in the cognitive realm, and success in the cognitive realm involves mentally grasping reality—the way things really are. When you believe something true, your belief reflects or matches the way things really are. (Of course, we sometimes think we know something when we actually don't. Jane thinks she knows that Ben Franklin was the third president of the United States, but she doesn't really know this because it isn't true; in fact, Franklin was never president.) Second, clause A: Why is belief a component of knowledge? Because the mere fact that something is true doesn't mean anyone knows it. To know something, one must grasp it mentally and have a certain confidence in it. And that's what believing is.[1] Finally, clause C: why must one's belief be justified? In part, because knowing is different from taking a lucky guess. To have knowledge, one must have a belief that is based on good evidence or is well grounded.[2] Of course, knowing is also different from believing something for inadequate or irrelevant reasons. For example, suppose that I believe that Mars is the fourth planet from the sun, but I believe this only because the tooth fairy told me so in a dream. In that case, my reason for believing is inadequate; it does not justify or warrant my belief and so I don't actually *know* that Mars is the fourth planet from the sun.

Theists claim that God is omniscient, or all-knowing. As we shall see, there is some disagreement about how best to understand the claim that God is omniscient. On one understanding, "God is omniscient" means "God knows every truth, and God believes no falsehoods." But some define "God is omniscient" as "God knows all the truths that can be known, and God believes no falsehoods." This second definition is apt to be puzzling. How could there be truths that cannot be known? We'll return to this issue later on. But for now, just keep in mind that there is some disagreement about how best to understand God's omniscience.

What do we mean when we say that someone has free will or acts freely? This question forces us into one of the greatest philosophical controversies. There are two main views of human freedom, the compatibilist view and the incompatibilist view. Compatibilists hold that an action can be both free and determined. Determinism is the view that, given the past, only one future is possible. When we deliberate, we normally assume that more than one future is open to us. For example, suppose that you go to an Italian restaurant, look at the menu, and make a selection. You opt for the spaghetti. Looking back at your decision, you assume that you might have chosen lasagna instead. But if determinism is true, spaghetti was the only thing you could have ordered. The "lasagna option" was an illusion. What, then, is a free action according to compatibilists? *One performs an act freely if and only if one performs the act because one wants to (all things considered).* The basic idea here is that one acts freely as long as one is not coerced. The "all things considered" qualifier is needed because we often have multiple "wants" or desires. At the restaurant, you might have wanted both spaghetti and lasagna, but you knew you couldn't eat (or afford) both. You chose the spaghetti because you wanted it more than you wanted the lasagna; given that you couldn't have both, the spaghetti is what you wanted *all things considered.*

If we combine the compatibilist view of free will with determinism, we get what philosophers call *soft determinism.* (It's called "soft" because it affirms determinism without denying that we have free will.) Now, suppose we ask, "Why did you want spaghetti more than you wanted lasagna?" According to the soft determinist, this feature of your psychology was fully determined. It was fully *necessitated* by the past and whatever causal factors led to your present mental states: biological, environmental, social, and so on. Nevertheless, when you ordered spaghetti you did so freely because you wanted to order spaghetti.

According to incompatibilists, free will is logically incompatible with determinism. If an act is determined, it is not free, and if an act is free, it is not determined. When is an act free, according to incompatibilists? *One performs an act A freely at time T only if one performs A at T but at T one could have refrained from performing A.* A free action is undetermined, but it is not a random event; it is "up to" the agent, and refraining from the act is genuinely possible.[3] If we combine the incompatibilist view of free will with the denial of determinism, we have what philosophers call *libertarianism.* (If we combine the incompatibilist view of free will with determinism, we get what philosophers call *hard determinism* — "hard" because it denies that we have free will.)

Libertarians deny that we are determined, but they do not deny that many different causal factors influence our choices and actions: biological factors, psychological factors, social factors, environmental factors, and so on. Often our choices may be quite limited; for example, I may simply choose to satisfy one desire rather than another, such as the desire for spaghetti rather than the desire for lasagna, and the two desires themselves may not be chosen at all—I just find that I have them.

Why does it matter if we are free? First, most people assume that a person is morally responsible only if he or she acts freely. And so we cannot hold people accountable for their good or bad actions if they are not free. Second, as noted above, whenever we deliberate, we assume that we can choose between multiple possible futures. And if we make real choices, our lives seem much more significant than if the apparent choices are illusory. If we are not free, we are like puppets or robots—or at least we are a lot more like them than we want to be or (normally) take ourselves to be. Finally, from a theological point of view, free will seems important for at least two reasons: (a) If a human being's response to God's love is not free, the response is apparently manipulated by God (either directly or indirectly). But a God of love surely would not wish to manipulate persons in this way. (b) Theists commonly appeal to human free will in explaining the presence of evil in the world. And the appeal to free will is arguably an essential element in any plausible explanation of the presence of evil—given that God is both wholly loving and almighty.

The Foreknowledge Argument

Let's now consider a more formal statement of the problem of divine foreknowledge and human free will. A more formal statement will give us a better understanding of the assumptions that lie behind the problem:

1.   God's beliefs are infallible.

2. For any event X, if God believes in advance that X will occur, then no one is in a position to prevent (or avoid) X.
3. For any event X, if no one is in a position to prevent (or avoid) X, then no one is free with respect to X.
4. For every event X that ever occurs, God believes in advance that it will occur.
5. So no one is free with respect to any event (i.e., no one ever acts freely).[4]

For ease of reference, let us call this "the foreknowledge argument." Some comments on the argument are in order. Note that the argument is stated in terms of God's *beliefs*. This makes sense if we recall the traditional analysis of knowledge. Given the traditional analysis, God knows X (e.g., Eva will lie tomorrow) only if God believes that X, X is true, and God is justified in believing X.

Premise 1 expresses the claim that God cannot be mistaken. Theists generally insist on 1, and it follows from the thesis that God is not only omniscient but necessarily so. If God cannot lose his omniscience, he cannot hold any false beliefs.

Premise 2 is the heart of the problem. As noted in the opening paragraph, this premise seems true because (a) no one is in a position to make any of God's beliefs false and (b) no one is in a position to change the past; hence, no one is in a position to change what God believed in the past. Compare this: When I was four years old I believed that Santa exists. Neither I nor anyone else can now change the fact that I had that belief when I was four.

The Christian theologian Origen denied premise 2 on the grounds that knowing something is true doesn't cause it to be true. For example, if I know that a bank robbery is happening because I'm watching it happen, I am not causing the robbery to happen. Unfortunately, Origen's solution misfires, because the argument does not say that God causes our actions. Rather, it underscores our limitations as creatures. We cannot cause God's beliefs to be false, and neither can we change the past. Thus, Origen's solution fails to address the real problem.[5]

Premise 3 reflects the incompatibilist view of free will. If you perform an act A at a time T, you must be able to refrain from or avoid that action if you act freely. Clearly, compatibilists and soft determinists will deny premise 3. This is one way to solve the problem of divine foreknowledge and human freedom, but, as we shall see, it comes at a cost.

Premise 4 must be true if God has complete and detailed foreknowledge for, as we have just seen, if one knows that X, one believes that X. Thus, if God knows you will phone your mother tomorrow, he believes you will phone her tomorrow. Many have denied premise 4 on the grounds that God is timeless, outside of time. The statement "God believes *in advance*" implies that God is in time; his believing precedes or comes before the event in question. So premise 4 is false if God is timeless. We'll examine this response to the argument momentarily.

The conclusion (5) follows logically from premises 1 through 4. It tells us that no one ever acts freely. This means that free will is an illusion. We may feel we have it, but we don't. While the argument is focused on human free will, note that the premises would seem to apply to God, too. If God has *total* foreknowledge, it would include knowledge of what he will do in the future. So if the premises of the argument are all true, they seem to imply that God never acts freely.

The Compatibilist Solution

As previously noted, compatibilists deny premise 3 of the above argument: "For any event X, if no one is in a position to prevent (or avoid) X, then no one is free with respect to X." One acts freely as long as one performs the act because one wants to (all things considered). And what one wants may be fully determined. Thus, free will does not require the power to refrain from performing the act, according to compatibilists. Traditional Calvinists embrace the compatibilist solution.[6] According to Calvinists, God knows the future because he decrees it. God is sovereign in the very strong sense that he causes every event that ever occurs. "Every event" includes every human action, every human desire, every human intention, and every human thought. God does not necessarily cause every event directly, however; he may cause many or most events indirectly by way of what theologians call "secondary causes." A secondary cause is a causal factor previously created by God. So, for example, God created you by way of your parents, and God created your parents by way of your grandparents. Given that many events occur via the operation of laws of nature, the laws of nature are especially important secondary causes, frequently employed by God in bringing events about.[7]

The compatibilist solution is open to at least three theological objections. First, it makes God the cause of every wicked action. God causes people to act as they do. Doesn't this make God the author of evil? And if so, how can God be wholly good? It doesn't help to note that human agents are secondary causes. Of course, serial killers perform acts of killing, but they are caused to act as they do by God, either directly or indirectly. Consider the following hypothetical: Suppose that a mad scientist invents a special kind of computer—call it a neuro-computer—that can control the thoughts and feelings of others by manipulating their neurons. By programming the neuro-computer a certain way, the mad scientist can cause you to have all the mental states of a bank robber, such as "I desperately need money," "Robbing a bank is a good way to get money," and so on. He programs the computer in this way, activates it, and, as a result, you rob a nearby bank. Are you responsible for this act or is the mad scientist? Surely it is the mad scientist who must be held accountable, not you. You were merely a tool in his hands—the means by which he brought about the robbery. Similarly, if God, by means of secondary causes such as laws of nature, causes a human being to act, then it seems that God is accountable for the act.

Second, according to theists, God holds humans accountable for their sins. But given the compatibilist solution, God causes people to commit whatever sins they commit. And a God who causes humans to sin while holding them accountable for their sins seems unjust.

Third, what is the significance of human responses to God given the compatibilist solution? Some people worship God and devote themselves to serving him, and some do not. Some people explicitly rebel against God. But whatever one's response to God, God causes it, directly or indirectly, given the compatibilist solution. And how can one's response to God be meaningful or significant if God is causing the responses? The responses are puppet-like or robotic, it seems.

Beyond these theological objections to the compatibilist solution, there are philosophical questions about the compatibilist view of free will. The most important objection to the compatibilist view is the consequence argument.[8] This argument can be expressed simply and intuitively as follows: "If determinism is true, then our acts are the consequences of the laws of nature and events in the remote past. But it is not up to us what went on before we were born, and neither is it up to us what the laws of nature are. Therefore, the consequences of these things (including our present acts) are not up to us."[9] This brief, intuitive version of the argument may raise some questions, so let's consider a more rigorous version. First, let's assume that determinism is true and that it is true because God determines every event that ever occurs by creating a universe that is fully governed by deterministic laws of nature. A deterministic law of nature has the following form:

> *Deterministic Law*: Given initial conditions A, B, and C, event D always occurs.

In other words, once the initial conditions are met, only one result is possible; for example, if we heat water to 212 degrees Fahrenheit, it always boils. We are assuming that every event that has ever happened has resulted from initial conditions operating in accordance with deterministic laws of nature. *The history of the universe is one long chain of events tightly linked as one set of initial conditions gives rise to a result that, in turn, becomes an initial condition leading to another result, and so on.*

Now, let L stand for a conjunction of all the laws of nature. In other words, L is a proposition of the form "A and B and C . . . ," where each letter stands for a law of nature, such as the law of gravity. L includes *every* law of nature, including any that are yet to be discovered. Let **P** stand for a proposition that describes the complete state of the universe at a moment in the remote past, before humans existed. **P** gives the location of every atom, its direction of movement, the charge of each subatomic particle, and so on. Since **P** gives a complete description of the universe at a certain point in time, it gives the initial conditions for all the laws of nature at that time. Therefore, **P** and **L** together logically imply any true proposition describing a future event. To be concrete, let **F** stand for "Fran will shoot Stan tomorrow at 9:13 a.m.," and let's assume that **F** is true. Given that the universe is fully governed by deterministic laws of nature, **P** and **L** together logically imply **F**.

This is so because **P** gives us the initial conditions of all the laws at one point in time and **L** tells us what results. (Short-term results are in effect "new" initial conditions the laws apply to, yielding further results, and so on, indefinitely into the future.)

Virtually everyone agrees that we have no choice about the laws of nature; for instance, we don't get to vote on the law of gravity. And virtually everyone agrees that we have no choice about the remote past, before humans even existed. Whatever was going on, say, a billion years ago, we have no choice about it now. It seems equally clear that we have no choice about the truth of the conjunction "**P** and **L**." Furthermore, the following principle clearly seems to be true:

> *Transfer Principle*: If one has no choice about the truth of proposition **A** and **A** logically implies **B**, then one has no choice about the truth of **B**.[10]

This principle seems to be true, in part, because we have no choice about what follows *logically* from what. The rules of logic hold of necessity; we don't get to vote on them. So if **A** is true (and one has no choice about that) and **A** logically implies **B**, it seems clear that **B** is true and one has no choice about that, either. Our lack of choice about **A** transfers to a lack of choice about **B**. Putting all the pieces together, the following argument seems sound:

1. One has no choice about the truth of "**P** and **L**."
2. **P** and **L** together logically imply **F** (assuming that determinism is true).
3. If one has no choice about the truth of "**P** and **L**" and **P** and **L** together logically imply **F**, then one has no choice about the truth of **F** (by the transfer principle).
4. So if determinism is true, one has no choice about the truth of **F**.

This is the consequence argument. We made **F** stand for "Fran will shoot Stan tomorrow at 9:13 a.m." So no one, including Fran, has a choice about the truth of this proposition. Hence, Fran will not shoot Stan *freely*. And of course, this is just one example. We could have made **F** stand for any true proposition about the future. The upshot is that, if determinism is true, no one has a choice about anything; that is, we humans lack free will. Therefore, the compatibilist view of free will is mistaken.

Compatibilists might reply that it remains true that we perform some actions because we want to. But this reply is not relevant. Compatibilists agree that we have no choice about the remote past and the laws of nature. And premise 3 tells us, in effect, that our lack of choice about the past and the laws of nature transfers to the future if determinism is true. Thus, the consequence argument directly challenges the compatibilists' claim that an act is free if the agent does it because he or she wants to. Go back to the example of the mad scientist who uses the neuro-computer to control what you believe and desire, thus bringing it about that you rob a bank. In effect, the consequence argument is saying that, given determinism, nature (or God) plays a role like that of the mad scientist, controlling what we believe, desire, intend, and so on. From this perspective, *performing an act because you want to is simply not enough to make the action free.*

Although the consequence argument seems compelling to me, it remains true that philosophers are deeply divided over the nature of free will. And many hold the compatibilist view.

The Timelessness Solution

Many great theologians have held that God is not in time, among them Augustine, Boethius, Anselm, and Aquinas. And many theologians have regarded divine timelessness as a solution to the problem of divine foreknowledge and human freedom. This solution has been defended in recent times by C. S. Lewis and Paul Helm.[11] Many theists take it for granted that God is "outside of time." But the phrase "outside of time" is a metaphor, and it invites us to form a spatial image, perhaps with a circle containing things in time and God outside of the circle. Such a picture can be misleading, so we need a literal definition of divine timelessness.

To say that God is timeless is to say that there is no sequence in the divine life, no "before and after." This is a very far-reaching claim. For example, it means that there is no sequence of divine acts, with one act coming after another. God doesn't create the universe on one occasion, then later send a prophet into the world, and still later conduct the final judgment. God doesn't call one prophet at time T and then call another prophet at T + 1. If God is timeless, there is no sequence of divine "willings" or volitions. God doesn't will different things at different times. This means, in effect, that the divine will is a "package deal," covering everything in a single volition: All divine creative acts, all revelations, all answers to prayers, and all redemptive acts are included in a single divine volition. The effects of that timeless "package deal" volition are played out in time, but the volition itself does not occur in time. From this perspective, we might compare God's timeless volition to setting a thermostat. Someone sets a thermostat just once in the morning, and then it operates throughout the day, sometimes turning the furnace on, sometimes shutting it off, depending on the temperature.

How is the timelessness solution supposed to work? Lewis puts it like this:

> Another difficulty we get if we believe God to be in time is this. Everyone who believes in God at all believes that He knows what you and I are going to do tomorrow. But if He knows I am going to do so-and-so, how can I be free to do otherwise? Well, . . . the difficulty comes from thinking that God is progressing along the Time-line like us: the only difference being that He can see ahead and we cannot. Well, if that were true, if God *foresaw* our acts, it would be very hard to understand how we could be free not to do them. But suppose God is outside and above the Time-line. In that case, what we call "tomorrow" is visible to Him in just the same way as what we call "today." All the days are "Now" for him. He does not remember you doing things yesterday; He simply sees you doing them, because, though you have lost yesterday, He has not. He does not "foresee" you doing things tomorrow; He simply sees you doing them: because, though tomorrow is not yet there for you, it is for Him.[12]

Thus, the timelessness solution denies premise 4 of the foreknowledge argument: "For every event X that ever occurs, God believes *in advance* that it will occur." God doesn't literally have *fore*knowledge because his knowledge is timeless. God doesn't believe *before* Sue drinks the tea *that she will drink it.* Rather, we should say something of this sort: *God timelessly believes that Sue drinks a cup of tea on May 21, 2072, at 9:01 a.m.* And how does God come by knowledge of the future? According to Lewis, by direct awareness—just as you might know what a friend is presently doing by observing her, God, as a timeless being, is directly aware of what occurs at all times, past, present, and future. God is like a person standing on a tall tower looking down at the events below. Just as the person on the tower can observe many events at one glance, God can be directly aware of all events in the past, present, and future.[13]

The timelessness solution is creative and fascinating, but many philosophers find it problematic. First, notice that a timeless belief cannot change. In order for an entity to change, it must have a property at one time and then lack that property at a later time; for example, think of a leaf changing from green to brown in the fall. If timeless beliefs cannot change, they are fixed, just as past beliefs are fixed. So if God timelessly believes that Sue drinks a cup of tea on May 21, 2072, at 9:01 a.m., will Sue, at that date and time, have the power to refrain from drinking the tea? It seems not, since timeless beliefs cannot be changed and God's beliefs cannot be mistaken.[14]

Second, even if God's beliefs are timeless, they are related to certain facts about the past. To see this point, we need to distinguish between sentences and propositions. For example, the English sentence "It is going to rain" and the German sentence "Es wird regnen" express the same proposition. Propositions are truths (or falsehoods) that can be expressed (put into words) via sentences. Sentences belong to specific languages, such as English and German. Propositions do not belong to languages, and they may or may not be expressed in any language. Now, let's assume, for the sake of the argument, that Zoe López will buy a Maserati on January 19, 2099. Then, even if God is not in time, last year the English sentence "God timelessly believes that Zoe López buys a Maserati on January 19, 2099" expressed a true proposition. (We might even imagine that someone carved this sentence in stone a year ago.) It is a fact about the English language that this sentence expressed a true proposition one year ago. So on January 19, 2099, will Zoe have the power to refrain from buying the Maserati? It seems not, since in doing so she would have to alter a fact about the history of the English language (or else make one of God's beliefs false).

Third, divine timelessness would make it possible for God to reveal the future to human prophets. We might call this the "possible prophet" objection.[15] It runs as follows:

1. If God is timeless, he can reveal the future to human prophets.
2. Whatever God reveals cannot be false.
3. So divine timelessness would make *fore*knowledge of human free acts possible.
4. But *fore*knowledge of human free acts is not possible.
5. So God is not timeless.

Premise 4 is crucial here. Keep in mind that part of the motivation for offering the timelessness solution is precisely that *fore*knowledge of free acts seems impossible; Lewis is very explicit about this (recall the above quotation). Of course, the foreknowledge in this case would be not God's, but the prophets'. However, since the content of the prophets' beliefs about the future is revealed by God, the content cannot be false.

Fourth, the timelessness solution, as Lewis develops it, involves an implausible assumption about time, for it claims that God is directly aware of the future. But one cannot be directly aware of something unless it exists. (One cannot be directly aware of a unicorn because there are no unicorns; one can see a tree only if it exists; one cannot see or be directly aware of a non-existent tree.) But the future is the part of time that hasn't happened yet, so the future does not exist. Yet the timelessness solution states or presupposes that the future does exist. Otherwise, God could not be directly aware of it.

Now, just at this point, Lewis says something that bears close scrutiny. He says that God sees you performing future acts "because, though tomorrow is not yet there for you, it is for Him." But if God sees the future, it exists. Even God cannot be directly aware of that which does not exist. And the idea that the future exists is both implausible and a bit disturbing. If the future exists, your great-great grandchildren exist—assuming that you will have great-great grandchildren. They are not temporally present, but they really exist. And God, according to the timelessness solution, can be directly aware not only of your future acts, but also of the future acts of each of your descendants—assuming that you will have descendants. All of this is, however, contrary to common sense. From the standpoint of common sense, your great-great grandchildren do not yet exist. And your future acts don't exist, either; you know this because you have not performed them yet.

Unfortunately, this appeal to common sense isn't the end of the matter. For according to Einstein's theory of special relativity, there is no such thing as absolute simultaneity; hence, there are no objective facts of the form "Time T is present," "Time T is past," or "Time T is future."[16] What happens "now" for an observer in one frame of reference (e.g., a person standing on the ground watching a jet fly over) may be in the past (or in the future) for an observer in a different frame of reference (e.g., the pilot of the jet). And this suggests a view of time (called "eternalism" or "the block universe") according to which past and future objects exist just as much as present objects do. But if future objects exist, God could presumably be directly aware of them, as Lewis suggests. On the face of it, then, we are left with a rather shocking choice between contemporary physics (together with eternalism) and common sense. And that would not be an easy choice to make. On the one hand, the theory of relativity has been rigorously tested by many experiments and observations. And eternalism is "the majority view among physicists and philosophers of physics."[17] On the other hand, can you actually believe that your great-great grandchildren exist—not simply that they *will* exist but that they *do* exist? (It's one thing to say these words and another to understand them and accept them as true.) Many people find that they simply cannot believe that future objects exist—that future objects are just as real as present objects.

It may be, however, that the apparent clash between contemporary physics and common-sense results from a questionable interpretation of contemporary physics. A number of contemporary thinkers suggest that this is so:

A. Some have argued that although eternalism apparently fits well with relativity theory, *it does not fit well with other parts of physics*, such as quantum theory. Philosopher of science Jeffrey Koperski comments that, unlike the special theory of relativity (STR), "quantum mechanics allows for absolute simultaneity of events." So-called entangled events are simultaneous, and "this simultaneity is completely independent of how observers are moving." Quantum mechanics "entails that there is an objective fact of the matter about simultaneity regardless of whether observers agree about it. If this is correct, then something must be wrong with the notion of time presented by STR, which explicitly denies observer-independent facts about the sequence of events."[18]

B. Physicists themselves, in certain contexts, want to make a place for cosmic time so they can say such things as "Nearly 14 billion years have elapsed since the Big Bang." This cosmic time is "a universal time that is independent of moving reference frames," and "this is a very common way of understanding time in Big Bang cosmology."[19] Again, the point is that physics itself contains ideas that warn against drawing too-strong a conclusion about the metaphysics of time from relativity theory.

C. As Koperski observes, "The Hamiltonian version of GTR [the general theory of relativity] . . . has been used by physicists for decades."[20] It is "a perfectly legitimate mathematical form of GTR, even though it is fundamentally a 3 + 1 [three dimensions plus time] approach [unlike Einstein's four-dimensional approach]."[21] Moreover, "all of the models derived from the constrained Hamiltonian equations will have absolute simultaneity which can then be the basis of an objective flow of time."[22] Now, if the Hamiltonian approach is empirically equivalent to Einstein's, how confident can we be that physics has really settled the metaphysical issue of the nature of time?

D. Physicist George Ellis notes: "The time reversible picture of fundamental physics underlying the block universe viewpoint . . . does not take seriously the physics and biology of the real world but rather represents an idealized view of things which is reasonably accurate on certain (very large) scales where very simplified descriptions are successful."[23] Ellis adds that even if space-time theories do not involve an objective flow of time, other parts of science require it: "The flow of time is very apparent at some scales (that of biology, for example), and not apparent at others (e.g., that of classical fundamental physics)."[24]

E. Finally, it may be worth noting that while relativity does not single out any point in space-time as "the" time of a given event, it does not follow that there is no such time. Just consider that fundamental physics cannot "see" a distinction between such classes of things as dogs, tables, and trees. Fundamental physics makes no use of these classes or concepts, but of course it doesn't follow that there are no dogs, tables, or trees.[25]

Plainly, the metaphysics of time is a deep and complicated issue. And there can be no pretense of settling it here. But I hope I have said enough to indicate that there is a serious question about whether physics has settled the metaphysical nature of time (and, in particular, whether physics has proven that eternalism is true). And I would suggest that, as a general principle, we ought to be reluctant to depart from common sense unless we are forced to by overwhelming evidence.[26]

Some advocates of the timelessness solution do not affirm that God is directly aware of the future. But then how does the timelessness solution explain God's knowledge of future free acts? Thomas Aquinas says, "Through His essence God knows things other than Himself in so far as His essence is the likeness of the things that proceed from Him."[27] So, apparently, God somehow knows about human acts through His own essence. And this seems to imply that God knows the future as it is represented in his mind. But how can that be? Given that humans have free will in the incompatibilist sense, there is more than one possible future. And knowing all the possible futures is emphatically *not* the same thing as knowing *which one of them is the actual future*. So how could God know the future simply by knowing His own essence? The suggestion seems quite mysterious.

Given the above objections, it is far from clear that the timelessness solution works. Of course, even if timelessness does not provide a solution to the problem of divine foreknowledge and human freedom, God might still be timeless. Nevertheless, let us here note two alternative views of God's relation to time.

Some philosophers and theologians hold that God is in time—the same time we humans inhabit—but God is without beginning and without end. God existed at all past moments, exists now, and will exist at all future moments (without end). In this view, there is sequence in the divine life. God does different things at different times. One problem with this view is that, according to physicists, to be in time one must have a location in space. But according to theists, God is not located in space.[28]

Another view begins with a thought experiment: What if God hadn't created the physical universe? Might he nevertheless have created a number of (non-physical) angels, one after the other? First God created the angel Gabriel, then later he created Michael the archangel, and so on. This scenario seems logically or metaphysically possible, but in this scenario God would obviously not be in physical time, the sort of time physicists study and theorize about. And yet God would not be timeless because there would be a sequence of actions in the divine life. We might say that in this scenario, God is in *metaphysical time*: there is a sequence in the divine life, a "before and after," but God is not located in physical space and so is not in physical time. In this connection, notice that in thinking about God's creation of the physical universe, it is quite natural to suppose that God existed *before (or prior to)* physical reality. This way of thinking seems to put God in metaphysical time. One question here is "How exactly does metaphysical time relate to physical time?" Those who hold that God is in metaphysical time will want to maintain that, for any physical time that exists, God's knowledge and power extend to events occurring at that time.

This brings our discussion of the compatibilist and timelessness solutions to a close. In the next chapter we will examine two additional responses to the foreknowledge argument.

NINE

Is Divine Foreknowledge
Compatible with Human Free Will?

Part II

In this chapter we will take up two further responses to the foreknowledge argument: The middle knowledge solution and open theism. Recall that the foreknowledge argument runs as follows:

1. God's beliefs are infallible.
2. For any event X, if God believes in advance that X will occur, then no one is in a position to prevent (or avoid) X.
3. For any event X, if no one is in a position to prevent (or avoid) X, then no one is free with respect to X.
4. For every event X that ever occurs, God believes in advance that it will occur.
5. So no one is free with respect to any event (i.e., no one ever acts freely).[1]

As we saw in the previous chapter, the compatibilist solution denies premise 3 of the foreknowledge argument, while the timelessness solution denies premise 4. As we will soon see, the middle knowledge solution denies premise 2, while open theism calls premise 4 into question.

THE MIDDLE KNOWLEDGE SOLUTION

Luis de Molina, a sixteenth-century Spanish priest, suggested that God can have complete and detailed knowledge of the future, including knowledge of future free human actions, because he has middle knowledge.[2] What is middle knowledge? It is knowledge of what *every possible free creature would freely do in every possible situation*. Middle knowledge is knowledge of conditionals (if-then propositions) of the following form:

> If person P were in circumstance C, then P would freely perform act A.

Such conditionals are properly called *subjunctive conditionals of freedom*.[3] The subjunctive mood in English is used to explore hypothetical situations (e.g., "If I were rich, then I would give lots of money to charity") and to express wishes (e.g., "I wish I were rich").[4] The if-clause of a conditional is called its *antecedent*, while the then-clause is called its *consequent*, and the consequent of a subjunctive conditional of freedom concerns an action performed *freely*. Advocates of the middle knowledge solution assume that humans have free will in the incompatibilist sense; they reject the compatibilist view of free will.

Notice that middle knowledge is not the same thing as foreknowledge. Foreknowledge is knowledge of what will actually happen. If God foreknows that Velma will drink a cup of tea on April 11, 2058, at 8:03 a.m., then Velma definitely *will* drink a cup of tea on that date and at that time. But middle knowledge is knowledge of conditionals, and many of these conditional statements have false antecedents (if-clauses). For example:

> If President John F. Kennedy had not been assassinated in 1963, then he would freely have withdrawn American troops from Vietnam.

This conditional might be true, even though its antecedent is false. But notice that this conditional, even if known to be true, does not yield knowledge of the future (i.e., of events subsequent to 1963). In fact, J.F.K. was assassinated on November 22, 1963, and thus he made no subsequent decisions regarding the troops in Vietnam. How, then, does middle knowledge provide God with foreknowledge? Suppose that the following subjunctive conditional is true:

> If you were placed in a Starbucks coffee shop on June 25, 2051, at 9:01 a.m., then you would freely drink a cup of coffee at that time.

And suppose that God has middle knowledge; he knows this conditional is true. Further, suppose that God decides to place you in a Starbucks coffee shop on June 25, 2051, at 9:01 a.m. This guarantees the truth of the antecedent (if-clause) of the conditional. And given that God knows both the conditional and its antecedent, God knows you *will* freely drink a cup of coffee on June 25, 2051, at 9:01 a.m. In this way, divine middle knowledge makes divine foreknowledge of future free acts possible.

Middle knowledge is so called because Molina thought of it as lying between (a) God's knowledge of necessary truths and (b) God's *free knowledge*, that is, God's knowledge of what depends on his own will. *Necessary truths* are truths that cannot be false under any circumstances, such as no circles are squares, no forced action is free, and no person is a number. God's knowledge of necessary truths includes his knowledge of everything that is logically possible; for example, God could have created unicorns, though he did not do so. By contrast, God's *free knowledge* is his knowledge of the things that are under his volitional control. For example, God knows Mars exists because he created it and sustains it in existence. As noted above, God's middle knowledge is his knowledge of conditionals of this form "If person P were in circumstance C, then P would freely do A." These subjunctive conditionals of freedom are not necessary truths. If they were necessary truths, then the circumstances specified in the antecedent would *necessitate* the action specified in the consequent, in which case the action would not be free. Moreover, God does not cause subjunctive conditionals of freedom to be true; if he caused these conditionals to be true, then the acts specified in their consequents would not be free acts *in the incompatibilist sense*; they would be caused by God.

It is very important to understand that, according to the middle knowledge solution, God has middle knowledge regarding *merely possible* free creatures that he decides not to create. Let's name one of these non-existent free creatures "Bea Nott." According to the theory of middle knowledge, God would know what Bea Nott would freely do in every possible situation in which she might exist. For example:

a.   If Bea Nott were placed in a Starbucks coffee shop on June 25, 2051, at 7:01 a.m., then she would freely order a Caramel Cocoa Cluster Frappuccino.

b.   If Bea Nott were placed in the Garden of Eden and told not to eat of the fruit in the midst of the Garden, then Bea would freely avoid eating that fruit.

For any possible circumstance that Bea Nott might be in, God would know what she would freely do in it. And once God decides which possible free creatures to create and which circumstances they will be placed in, God knows the future.[5]

Of course, a person's total circumstances often depend to some extent on the free choices of others. For example, if someone freely offers me a bribe, then my circumstances include the offering of the bribe. But God's middle knowledge includes the knowledge of what free creatures will freely do in *every* possible circumstance, which includes circumstances that depend on the free choices of others. So God's middle knowledge is obviously extremely complex, but such complexity is no obstacle to God, who is the greatest possible knower.

Advocates of the middle knowledge solution deny premise 2 of the foreknowledge argument: "For any event X, if God believes in advance that X will occur, then no one is in a position to prevent (or avoid) X." God's foreknowledge is based on God's middle knowledge. And God's middle knowledge is knowledge of what agents would do *freely* (in the incompatibilist sense) in such-and-such circumstances. So God knows what you will *freely* do. If God knows you will freely drink a cup of coffee at time T, you *will* freely drink a cup of coffee at T, but you have the power to refrain from doing so, since you are free in the incompatibilist sense.

Molina's solution is undoubtedly subtle and ingenious, but it is by no means certain that it works. Critics have advanced a series of objections:

Objection 1: It's not clear that the middle knowledge solution actually addresses the problem. Suppose that God believed a thousand years ago that you will drink a cup of coffee on June 25, 2051, at 7:01 a.m. (We can even imagine that a thousand years ago God instructed a prophet to carve this statement in stone, replacing the word "you" with your name.) The fact that God believed this proposition a thousand years ago cannot now be changed. So how can you possibly have the power to refrain from drinking the coffee on the specified date and at the specified time? You cannot change the past, and you cannot make God's belief false.[6]

Nothing we can do now will alter the past. "No use crying over spilled milk," as the saying goes. But advocates of the middle knowledge solution may make a more subtle claim, namely, that "we do have the power to act in such a way that, were we to act that way, God would have had a different belief."[7] This alleged power is called "counterfactual power over the past." Suppose that God believes I will tell a lie tomorrow at 11:04 a.m. At 11:04 tomorrow morning I will have the power to refrain from lying and hence the power to do something such that *if I were to do it, God would not have believed that I will tell a lie tomorrow at 11:04*. That's the idea. (This is called "*counterfactual* power over the past" because the if-clause of the conditional is *contrary to fact*: "If I were to refrain from lying . . . ," but I did not in fact refrain.)

As William Hasker notes, however, this assertion regarding counterfactual power over the past begs the question.[8] It merely declares that we have free will, but the foreknowledge argument explains why we do not have free will if God has infallible beliefs about what we will do in the future. Given that God believed a thousand years ago that I will tell a lie at 11:04 a.m. tomorrow, it seems that I'm "trapped." Consider an analogy: Suppose that I fail to finish a marathon I've entered because I have a heart attack and die at mile 15. Still, it can truly be said that *if I had finished the race, then I would not have had a heart attack and died at mile 15*. But of course, the truth of this counterfactual conditional does not alter the fact that, as matters stand, I could not finish the race.[9]

Objection 2: How does God know the subjunctive conditionals of freedom? How does he know what merely possible free creatures would do in every possible situation? The middle knowledge solution does not explain how God comes by his middle knowledge; hence, it explains one puzzling form of knowledge, namely, foreknowledge, by appealing to another puzzling form of knowledge, namely, middle knowledge. Such an explanation hardly seems illuminating. To underscore this difficulty, let's think about how God might have some other forms of knowledge. (A) Necessary truths can often be known simply by understanding the concepts involved. If one understands what a free action is, then one understands that "No forced action is free" is necessarily true. But one cannot know subjunctive conditionals of freedom in this way. If one could, the antecedents would necessitate the consequents, in which case the acts specified in the consequents would not be free acts. (B) God's knowledge of present contingent events—at least many of them—seems unproblematic if we allow that God has powers of direct awareness analogous to our human senses, such as vision and audition. But how God would know what *merely possible* creatures would freely do in every possible situation is certainly a mystery. We can often make reasonable assumptions about what our friends and loved ones would do in hypothetical situations, but that's because we have knowledge of their characters and past actions. For example, you might well know whether a friend would, or would not, freely shoplift a candy bar. But merely possible free creatures do not have a "track record"—they've never *done* anything. And one's character is formed as one makes decisions over time, thus developing *tendencies* to act in certain ways. So merely possible (uncreated) free creatures do not have characters, either. Furthermore, past actions and character do not necessitate future free actions—there is always the possibility that one will act out of character if one is free (in the incompatibilist sense). Therefore, it is very hard to see how middle knowledge is possible.

Objection 3: Robert M. Adams has called attention to the so-called grounding problem for subjunctive conditionals of freedom.[10] What would make such conditionals true? If I believe that a bank robbery is now taking place, what makes the proposition I believe true? The natural suggestion is that the proposition, "A bank robbery is now taking place," is made true by its correspondence with a certain event, namely, the occurrent robbing of the bank. And many would allow that predictions about the future are true if they correspond to future events. For example, "It will rain tomorrow" is true if rain occurs tomorrow. But many subjunctive conditionals of freedom are about merely possible creatures that God never creates, so it is not clear what would make them true. Let us again consider the case of Bea Nott, by hypothesis one of the possible free creatures God decided not to create. Which of the following is true?

A. If God were to create Bea Nott and place her in the Garden of Eden, Bea would freely eat the forbidden fruit.
B. If God were to create Bea Nott and place her in the Garden of Eden, Bea would freely not eat the forbidden fruit.

There seems to be nothing that could make either of these true. Remember, Bea Nott will never exist. She will never in fact do anything. Nor will she ever in fact have any thoughts, feelings, or intentions. Bea has no track record, nor does she have a character, since one's character is formed as one makes choices over a period of time. Simply put, A has as much claim to being true as B, *and vice versa.* So it is hard to see how the conditionals needed for divine middle knowledge could be true. And of course only *truths* can be known. Even God cannot know what isn't true.[11]

Objection 4: Divine middle knowledge would apparently lead us to deny that we have free will in the incompatibilist sense. Consider the following argument:

1. If God knew the truth values (i.e., truth or falsity) of all subjunctive conditionals of freedom prior to the creation of the world, those truth values are beyond our present control.
2. The truth of a subjunctive conditional of freedom, together with the truth of its antecedent—which corresponds to factors that are beyond the control of the agent at the time of the act—necessarily implies the truth of its consequent. (For example, if God were to place Sam in circumstance C, Sam would freely perform act A at time T. God places Sam in circumstance C. Therefore, Sam will freely perform act A at T.)
3. The consequent of a subjunctive conditional of freedom specifies *a single course of action* the agent would take; it does not specify a range of options the agent might take (such as "Either perform act A or refrain from act A").
4. So if God has middle knowledge, then a human agent does not have more than one course of action open to him or her in any given set

of circumstances, and hence human agents do not have free will in the incompatibilist sense.[12]

Some comments may help to clarify this argument. In regard to premise 1, recall that God uses middle knowledge to decide which possible creatures to create and which circumstances to place them in. This being so, there is surely no way that we (humans) can now change the truth value (i.e., truth or falsity) of the subjunctive conditionals of freedom. And advocates of middle knowledge must accept premise 2, for if 2 were not true, middle knowledge would not enable God to have foreknowledge. Premise 3 simply gives an abstract description of the contents of the consequent of any subjunctive conditional of freedom. The consequent of each true subjunctive conditional of freedom specifies an action that would be performed under the specified circumstances. For example, "If you were placed in a Starbucks coffee shop at time T, you would freely drink a cup of coffee at time T." Given that this conditional is true and that you are placed in a Starbucks coffee shop at time T, you will drink a cup of coffee at time T. If you were to refrain from drinking the coffee at time T, the conditional would not be true. So it seems that divine middle knowledge would eliminate alternative courses of action, and hence eliminate free will *in the incompatibilist sense.*

Some very resourceful philosophers defend the middle knowledge solution, so it is bound to remain an option for theists.[13] But I must confess that the objections considered here, taken together, seem rather strong to me and keep me looking for an alternative solution to the problem of divine foreknowledge and human free will.[14]

OPEN THEISM

Open theists hold that God does not have infallible knowledge of the future free acts of created agents.[15] They regard the foreknowledge argument as a sound criticism of traditional theology, but their thinking is not motivated simply by the foreknowledge argument; they also stress the need for a biblical view of God's knowledge, and they think that the Bible indicates that God's knowledge of the future is partial rather than exhaustive. Traditional theology has downplayed biblical texts that support this claim.

Space does not permit a thorough exploration of the relevant biblical texts, but let's note a few passages of the type open theists appeal to:

> Exodus 13:17. When Pharaoh let the people go, God did not lead them by way of the land of the Philistines, although that was nearer; for God thought, "If the people face war, they may change their minds and return to Egypt."

This verse strongly suggests that God was not sure how the people of Israel would react under the threat of war. Why would a being with infallible foreknowledge ever be unsure of what will happen? The suggestion hardly makes sense.[16]

> Genesis 22:12. He said, "Do not lay your hand on the boy or do anything to him; for now I know that you fear God, since you have not withheld your son, your only son, from me."

This verse is taken from the famous passage in which God commands Abraham to sacrifice his son Isaac. And the verse strongly suggests that God was testing Abraham in order to know what was in Abraham's heart. Would such a test make sense if God already knew exactly what Abraham would do? It seems not.

> Deuteronomy 8:2. Remember the long way that the LORD your God has led you these forty years in the wilderness, in order to humble you, testing you to know what was in your heart, whether or not you would keep his commandments.[17]

Here God is portrayed as testing the Israelites to see if they will remain faithful to him. But a being with infallible and complete foreknowledge obviously has no need for such tests.

Why is God's knowledge of the future partial rather than exhaustive? All open theists hold that God's lack of knowledge regarding future free acts is a self-limitation brought about by his decision to create agents that are free in the incompatibilist sense. But open theists explain this in two different ways. Some open theists, such as Clark Pinnock, think that there is no truth about future free acts because there is nothing to make propositions about future free acts true. Since these thinkers deny that that there are any true propositions of the form "Person P *will* freely perform act A," I will refer to them as *truth-value* open theists. Truth-value open theists are apt to accept C. S. Peirce's view that propositions about the future are true only if there is some condition or factor in the present that fully guarantees their truth. For example, "The earth will orbit the sun tomorrow" is true if present conditions and the laws of nature guarantee that the earth will orbit the sun tomorrow. But there is never a present condition or factor that fully guarantees what an agent will do *freely* (in the incompatibilist sense) in the future—the agent might refrain from the act in question. Hence, there are no truths regarding what agents will do freely in the future. And since only truths can be known, God does not have knowledge of future free acts.

Other open theists, such as Richard Swinburne and William Hasker, allow that propositions of the form "Person P *will* freely perform act A" can be true, and often are. For example, "I will jog tomorrow" is true if sometime tomorrow I go jogging. But although these open theists hold that propositions about future free acts can be true, they maintain that there is no way for anyone, including God, to have infallible knowledge of such propositions. Just consider: When we predict how someone will act, what is the prediction based on? Answer: Their past acts (their "track record"), their character, and what we know of their inner states (thoughts, desires, intentions, etc.). Predictions based on this type of information may very likely be true, but they cannot be infallible because free agents sometimes act "out of character." They always retain the power to refrain from an act we predict they will perform. And while God's predictions would surely be far more accurate than human predictions, even God's predictions could not be infallible if persons are truly free in the incompatibilist sense. I will refer to open theists who think there are truths corresponding to future free acts as *epistemic* open theists, since the truths in question are not *known* by God, in this view.[18]

Both versions of open theism imply that God takes risks in creating free agents. Prior to creation, people have no "track records," no characters, and no mental states for God to base predictions on. And newborn babies also have no track record and no moral character (since character is formed by a pattern of actions over time). So God works with free creatures under conditions of uncertainty in regard to what they will do. But according to open theists, God is like a master chess player who can bring the game to the outcome he desires, regardless of the moves the other player makes.

Notice that open theists reject premise 4 of the foreknowledge argument: "For every event X that ever occurs, God believes in advance that it will occur." God does not believe in advance propositions of the form "Person P will perform act A at time T" when the act in question is performed freely, for if God infallibly believed that *Person P will perform act A at time T*, the act in question would not be free; P would be unable to refrain from doing A.

Open theism certainly raises many questions. First, some wonder how God can be in control of the world if he doesn't know the future in complete detail. For example, suppose that next week a tyrant will fire off a hundred nuclear missiles, thus starting a global nuclear war that results in the deaths of all human beings. Assuming that the deaths of all humans (in the next week or so) is not part of the divine plan, doesn't this sort of example show that the God of open theism is not in control of the world? No, it does not. Open theists affirm that God is almighty and that an almighty being can intervene in the course of events whenever it wants to. The tyrant who wants to press a button to launch a hundred nuclear missiles might suddenly find that he is completely paralyzed. Or he might launch the missiles only to find that they have been transported to a galaxy far, far away, where they will explode harmlessly. Or the wiring in the launch mechanism might suddenly be disconnected. Or the missiles might all be turned instantly into "duds." And so on. Thus God can be in control of the world even if he does not have exhaustive foreknowledge.

Second, aren't open theists denying that God is omniscient? The answer here depends in part on the definition of omniscience. In the traditional understanding, "God is omniscient" means "God knows every truth, and God believes no falsehoods." Notice that by this definition, *truth-value* open theists affirm that God is omniscient, for God does know all *truths*, from this perspective, but there simply are no truths corresponding to future free acts. *Epistemic* open theists, on the other hand, claim that there are truths about future free acts, but God does not know these truths. Thus they deny that God is omniscient in the traditional sense, but they offer a different definition of omniscience. They claim that God is omniscient in the sense that he knows all the truths *that can be known* (and believes no falsehoods). Given the foreknowledge argument, truths of the form "Person P *will* freely perform act A" simply cannot be known infallibly; for if God knows in advance (and infallibly) that someone will perform an act, the act is not free. Notice that this limitation on God's knowledge is self-imposed, because it is entirely up to God whether any creatures have free will in the incompatibilist sense. In deciding to create free agents, God imposed a limit on his own knowledge. And we have already seen why there is no way for even God to know infallibly what creatures will *freely* do, for the information available at any given time (the individual's track record, character, present thoughts, etc.) does not ground infallibly correct predictions regarding free acts.

In evaluating the epistemic open theist's definition of omniscience, it may be helpful to compare it with the typical definition of omnipotence used by philosophers and theologians, which is along these lines: God can do whatever is logically possible. Given this customary definition, there are some things God cannot do, such as create a colorless green frog or a person who is identical with the number 13. And most theists, on reflection, agree that there are some things God cannot do. For example, in discussions of the problem of evil, most theists will say that much of the evil in the world consists in (or stems from) wrong acts freely performed by humans. Why doesn't God cause people to always freely do right actions? Because if God causes people to do what they do, then their actions aren't free. Even God cannot *force* you to perform some act that you *freely* perform. The epistemic open theist's definition of omniscience (God knows all the truths that can be known, and God believes no falsehoods) allows for a similar logical limit on God, but with respect to his knowledge. It simply isn't logically possible for *free* actions to be infallibly foreknown, given the foreknowledge argument.

Third, aren't open theists denying that God is the greatest possible being? Isn't the God of open theism "too small"? Actually, open theists agree that God is the greatest *possible* being. But they think that infallible knowledge of future free acts is simply not possible; the foreknowledge argument shows why.

Fourth, whatever philosophical merits open theism may have, many would argue that it cannot be held consistently by those who accept the Bible as authoritative. Let us consider three objections arising from this quarter.

Objection 1: Exhaustive Foreknowledge? Doesn't the Bible clearly state that God has exhaustive (complete) knowledge of the future, including exhaustive knowledge of future free acts? Open theists deny that the Bible clearly states this. Of course, they agree that the Bible contains predictive prophecy and that it indicates that God has quite significant knowledge of the future. But as we have already seen, open theists can point to passages in the Bible that strongly suggest that God's knowledge of the future is partial rather than exhaustive. Furthermore, open theists point out that when predictions are made, *they may concern what God has already decided to do, not what free creatures will do*. To illustrate, see Isaiah 46: 9–11: "I am God, and there is no one like me, declaring the end from the beginning . . . . I have spoken, and *I will bring it to pass*; I have planned, and *I will do it*" (italics added).

Objection 2: True Prophecies. Many biblical prophecies concern the acts of free agents. To cite just one of many examples: in the book of Genesis (chapter 40), the patriarch Joseph—presumably with divine assistance— predicts that Pharaoh will give the chief butler his job back. Since truth-value open theists deny that there are any truths of the form "Person P will freely perform act A," aren't they denying that such prophecies can be true?

Truth-value open theists would deny that "Pharaoh will freely give the chief butler his job back" was true prior to Pharaoh's giving the butler his job back, but this doesn't mean they claim that the statement was false; they can claim that it was neither true nor false.[19] Also, truth-value open theists would not claim that Joseph's prophecy was unfulfilled. It was fulfilled when Pharaoh restored the chief butler to his former position. A prophecy can be fulfilled in the sense that, at some future time, a *present-tense* version of its contents is true (in this case, "Pharaoh gives the chief butler his job back"). This way of understanding predictive prophecy, however, does bring out two additional problems for truth-value open theism:

1. We commonly regard a prediction as true if the predicted event occurs at the time specified. For example, if a newscaster says, "The President will veto the bill tomorrow," we ordinarily regard the statement as true if the President does indeed veto the bill the next day. So truth-value open theism conflicts with our ordinary ways of thinking about statements concerning future acts.

Here truth-value open theists might reply that our ordinary ways of thinking about predictions are not sacrosanct. Perhaps we are speaking loosely when we speak of true statements regarding future free acts. Perhaps it would be more accurate to say that a prediction of the form "Person P will freely perform act A" is *fulfilled* when a present-tense version of its contents is true.

2. In claiming that propositions of the form "Person P will freely perform act A" are neither true nor false, truth-value open theists are committed to a departure from standard systems of logic. In standard systems, every proposition is either true or false. Truth-value open theists typically opt for a three-valued logic: A given proposition p is either true or false or neither.[20] In departing from standard two-value systems of logic, truth-value open theists take on a complication that epistemic open theists avoid.

Truth-value open theists may reply that three-valued logics seem justified independently of the foreknowledge and free will issue. Such logics provide promising ways of handling at least two metaphysical problems. (A) Consider the metaphysical problem of vagueness. For example, think of a case in which it seems impossible to say whether a person is bald. The problem doesn't seem to be a lack of information, for example, knowing the precise number of hairs on the person's head. Sometimes there just doesn't seem to be a truth of the matter.[21] (B) Three-valued logics provide one solution to the problem of logical fatalism: Suppose it is true today that either you will tell a lie at noon tomorrow or you won't. In a standard, two-valued logic, this disjunction (either-or proposition) is true because one of its disjuncts (i.e., one of the statements comprising it) is true. Suppose that "You will tell a lie at noon tomorrow" is the true disjunct. At noon tomorrow, will you have the power to refrain from lying? It seems not, since in order to have that power you would have to have the power to change the past by changing the truth value of the proposition from true to false. Armed with a three-valued logic, we can say that the disjunction "Either you will lie at noon tomorrow or you won't" is true, even though its disjuncts are neither true nor false.[22]

To sum up, perhaps the main difficulty with truth-value open theism lies in its claim that predictions are never literally true, a claim that runs contrary to our ordinary ways of thinking about predictions. Still, truth-value open theists have inventive and apparently reasonable ways of responding to this difficulty. Furthermore, truth-value open theism has at least one important merit, for in this view God is omniscient in the traditional, strong sense of knowing every truth and believing no falsehoods.

Objection 3: Divine Knowledge of the Future. There are many prophecies in the Bible that concern the acts of free human agents. These passages imply that God has knowledge of the future free acts of human agents, contrary to open theism, right?

Open theists may suggest the following ways of understanding passages involving predictions about what free human agents will do:

A. *Warnings.* Some prophecies are warnings. For example, the prophet Jonah goes to Nineveh and makes a prediction, "Forty days more, and Nineveh shall be overthrown!" (Jonah 3:4). But Ninevah was not overthrown because the Ninevites repented. The prophecy was a warning or a prediction with an unstated condition: "Ninevah will be overthrown *if the Ninevites do not repent.*" This type of prophecy obviously does not require that God possesses infallible, exhaustive foreknowledge. And perhaps many biblical prophecies are of this type.

B. *Fallible Predictions.* Consider this: A well-grounded prediction of what your best friend will do in a certain situation does not interfere with his or her free will because your prediction, even if correct, is not infallible. Similarly, some prophecies may be regarded as correct (or fulfilled) but fallible predictions. (Note: An open theist who took this approach would be calling into question the first premise of the foreknowledge argument.) *To say that a prediction is fallible is not to say that it is mistaken*, but if humans are free in the incompatibilist sense, they have the "power to do otherwise" and so any prediction *could* in principle be made false (or not be fulfilled).

C. *Divine Intervention.* More elaborately, open theists might suggest that some prophecies are predictions made with the proviso that God will override the agent's free will if he or she does not act in accord with the prediction. Given that God has a very deep understanding of people and their circumstances, he would seldom (if ever) need to intervene in this way, but if he did, the human agent would not then be morally responsible for the action.[23]

Given the above possibilities, it seems that open theists can account for many of the predictive prophecies in the Bible, and perhaps for all of them, though it is clear that open theists must deny that God's knowledge of future free acts is *infallible*. But open theists will want to emphasize three points: (1) God's knowledge of the future is infallible whenever it is grounded in divine decrees—in what God has simply decided will be the case. (2) To say that God's knowledge of future free acts is fallible is not to say that God ever has false beliefs. If God is fallible with respect to future free acts, he could make a mistake in this area, but it does not follow that God has ever made (or will ever make) a mistake. (3) While many theologians balk at the suggestion that some of God's knowledge is fallible, open theists will emphasize, once again, that infallible knowledge of future free acts simply isn't logically possible, so a being whose knowledge is fallible *in this respect* can nevertheless be the greatest possible knower.

To sum up, open theism certainly raises its share of philosophical and theological questions. But open theists seem able to respond to most, if not all, of those questions with reasonable answers. Moreover, open theism arguably faces fewer philosophical problems than the compatibilist, timelessness, and middle knowledge solutions.

In chapter 2 we considered an argument for God's existence based on the premise that humans are morally responsible and have free will in the incompatibilist sense. The argument involved the claim that it seems unlikely that we humans have free will given naturalism. If naturalism is true, all events, including human acts, are the result of the operation of laws of nature on antecedent conditions. But since we do not control the laws of nature and the past, it is hard to see how we could have "the power to do otherwise" given naturalism. Given the foreknowledge argument, however, the naturalist might reply that it is hard to see how we could have "the power to do otherwise" if God has infallible, exhaustive knowledge of the future. With this naturalistic riposte in mind, I would suggest that a noteworthy strength of open theism is that it apparently offers one clear way out of the foreknowledge problem.

TEN

Do Humans Have Souls?

Part I

We humans each have a physical body. Do we each also have a non-physical soul? And why should we care? In this chapter and the next I'll examine answers to these questions. I'll set forth the main philosophical views on the relation between the soul and the body and sort through some of the main arguments for and against each view.

WHAT'S AT STAKE?

Does it matter if we have non-physical souls? Many would claim that it does matter, for a variety of reasons. Here is a sample list:

- Having a non-physical soul distinguishes humans from non-human animals.
- Theologically speaking, to be created in the image of God is to be endowed with a non-physical soul.
- Having a non-physical soul gives human beings a special value, thus grounding their right to life.
- Having a non-physical soul makes life after death possible.
- If humans were entirely physical beings, their behavior would be determined, in which case they would be neither free nor morally responsible.

- Believing in a non-physical soul will force us to deny certain assumptions generally made in the sciences, for example, that every physical event has a physical explanation.
- Advances in neuroscience have demonstrated a tight link between the physical and the mental—so tight that it is now reasonable to identify them.
- The belief in a non-physical soul is a relic of a pre-scientific view of the world (like the belief in witches) and we ought to avoid such superstitions.

Notice that the last three reasons for thinking this issue important arise from a very different type of concern than the earlier items on the list. It is a matter of debate whether *any* of the above claims are true. But surely it is important to try to find out if they are true.

Conscious Mental States

Almost everyone will agree that human persons have *conscious mental states*, that is, people have thoughts, feelings, desires, beliefs, purposes, and so on.[1] But can we have conscious mental states if we are simply physical beings, lacking a (non-physical) soul? This is a key question we must try to answer. First, however, let's pause a moment to get clearer about what a conscious mental state is. Perhaps the best way to do this is to consider a range of examples:

1. *Sensations*. Sensations are direct awarenesses. For example, if you are normally sighted and are looking at an evergreen tree (under normal circumstances), you have a direct visual awareness of a certain green shape. The awareness is direct in the sense that its content (the green shape) is not *inferred*. And—once again assuming normal conditions—if you plunge your hand into water cooled to 35 degrees Fahrenheit, you'll have a direct awareness of severe coldness. The felt experience of pain, as when you stub your toe on a hard object, is another example of a sensation (as the term is here employed).

2. *Thoughts and beliefs.* Thoughts and beliefs are mental states that can be expressed as statements. For example, you might entertain the proposition that *unicorns exist* without believing it, in which case you are merely having the thought that unicorns exist. By contrast, when you believe something, for instance, that *trees exist*, you are confident that it is so.

3. *Desires.* A desire is a felt inclination to act or to have an experience of some sort. For example, you might have a desire to phone a friend or a desire to experience the taste of chocolate.

4. *Intentions.* An intention is one's purpose in performing an action, one's goal or aim. For example, you may form an intention to drive to the supermarket. When an intention is effective, it results in behavior. Sometimes, however, we intend to do something but ineffectually; thus one might say, "I intended to do fifty pushups but was unable to do so."

On the face of it, mental states are strikingly different from physical states. For example, a neuroscientist can identify portions of the brain that are active at a given time, providing us with precise locations and measurements. But we cannot *in the same way* measure thoughts, feelings, desires, beliefs, hopes, and so on. In addition, most mental states seem to be *about* something, for instance, a thought *about* triangles, the fear *of* snakes, or a desire *for* coffee. But physical states don't seem to be *about* anything—a ball rolls down an inclined plane, a helium-filled balloon rises when released, molecules move in set patterns, a neuron emits an electrical charge, and so on. Furthermore, we have a kind of direct access to many of our mental states—you can know via introspection when you are sad, when you are worrying about something, when you are thinking about philosophy, and so on. But introspection does not tell you anything about which of your neurons are firing—it doesn't even tell you that you have neurons. Finally, some mental states have phenomenal qualities. Consider, for example, what it feels like to be in pain or what it is like to experience the taste of salt; physical states apparently have no such phenomenal qualities. Physical entities have properties such as location, size, shape, solidity, weight, electrical charge, and motion, and a physical state or event consists in a physical entity having such properties or changing with respect to such properties over time.[2]

THREE MAIN VIEWS

Philosophers have proposed numerous views of the relation between the soul (or mind) and the body. (Philosophers generally treat "soul" and "mind" as synonyms.) Here we shall focus on three main views.

Substance Dualism. According to substance dualists, such as René Descartes, each human being has both a physical body and a non-physical soul. Moreover, there is *causal interaction* between the soul and the body.[3] For example, your *decision* to raise your arm (a mental state or event) causes your arm to rise (a physical state or event). Stubbing your toe (a physical state or event) may cause you to experience a sharp *pain* (a mental state or event). And your *desire* to go downtown combined with your *belief* that the number 13 bus is the fastest way to get there (mental states or events) may cause you to get on the 13 bus (a physical state or event).

To understand substance dualism, we need to understand the technical philosophical meaning of the word "substance." The technical use of this term — or, rather, the use of its Greek and Latin equivalents — has a long history in philosophy going all the way back to the Greek philosopher Aristotle. The "basic idea is that an individual substance is that which has properties and stands in relations, rather than being itself a property or a relation of something(s) else."[4] For Aristotle, an individual horse or dog would be a good example of a substance. An individual dog, such as Lassie, has properties, such as *being brown*, *being a collie, weighing sixty pounds*, and *being alive*. But Lassie is not herself a property of some object. Aristotle employed the distinction between substances and properties partly as a way of clarifying the phenomena of identity and change. A substance may lose some properties and gain others over time while remaining one and the same individual. For example, Lassie (a substance) can remain herself over time while changing with respect to some of her properties; thus she may get stronger, she may learn new tricks, and she may lose weight or become ill.

Could we say simply that a substance is an entity that bears properties? No, that won't work because properties can have properties. For example, the property of *being red* has the property of *being a color*. But a *substance* has properties without itself being a property.

In modern English use, "substance" sometimes means something like "stuff"—as in, "Can you identify the gray substance in the test tube?" But a closer (albeit rough) modern equivalent to "substance" *in the technical philosophical sense* would be simply "individual thing."

For Descartes, there are just two basic kinds of substances, physical substances and mental ones. Each kind of substance possesses a distinctive property or attribute. Physical substances possess *extension*; they are extended in space or have volume. By contrast, souls or minds are *thinking things*, according to Descartes, but "thinking" here is used very broadly: Descartes meant that souls (or minds) have conscious mental states—*that* is their distinctive property or attribute. And each human being is composed of two substances—a non-physical mental substance (i.e., a soul) and a physical substance (i.e., a body).

The Greek philosopher Plato was a substance dualist, but unlike Descartes, Plato believed that the soul exists *prior* to the body. Plato also believed that the body is inferior to the soul and that the soul is better off when liberated from the body, as it will be at death.[5] In what follows, I shall not regard these specifically Platonic claims as part of substance dualism. Thus, I shall assume that the substance dualist claims that the soul comes into being at some point during the development of the fetus. And I shall assume that the substance dualist does not denigrate or devalue the body. (After all, there is no apparent *logical* connection between "The soul is non-physical" and "The body is inferior to the soul.") Many traditional theists who are substance dualists believe in the resurrection of the body; accordingly, they would deny that unembodied existence is better than embodied existence.[6]

Reductive Physicalism. Reductive physicalists claim that there is no non-physical soul. Furthermore, in spite of the apparent differences between mental and physical states, reductive physicalists claim that mental states are wholly *reducible* to physical states. This means that mental states are (in the final analysis) nothing over and above physical states. These philosophers may claim, for example, that mental states are identical to brain states. Compare: For thousands of years humans did not know that water is H_2O, but now they do; water is nothing over and above H_2O.

Here it should be noted that substance dualists fully accept that there are *correlations* between mental states and physical states. A neuroscientist might establish many such correlations by observing a series of your brain states, B1, B2, B3, and so on, and asking you what mental state you are in in each case. For example, when you are in brain state B1 (such and such neurons are firing), perhaps you are thinking that $1 + 1 = 2$; when you are in brain state B2, you are experiencing a desire for chocolate, and when in B3, you have a feeling of joy. However, the substance dualist would insist that correlations are no proof of identity. To take a simple example, we might find a perfect correlation between the movements of the hands of your wristwatch and the movements of the hands of a grandfather clock. But the two time-keeping devices (and their hands) nevertheless remain distinct.

The reductive physicalist, then, is not merely claiming that there is a correlation between mental states and physical (brain) states. A much stronger claim is being made, namely, that mental states are nothing over and above physical states. As we've just seen, the reductive physicalist may claim that mental states are identical with brain states. This view is called the *mind-brain identity theory.*[7] But many reductive physicalists make more subtle claims. Currently, perhaps the leading form of reductive physicalism is a version of *functionalism.*[8] According to functionalists, a given mental state can be defined as an *internal state* of a person that serves as the causal link between inputs (stimuli) from the environment and outputs in the form of behaviors and other mental states. For example, pain can be defined as an internal state that serves as the causal link between tissue damage (e.g., from a dog bite), certain behaviors (e.g., screaming, running away), and other mental states (e.g., fear or anger). Functionalists who are reductive physicalists would of course insist that the relevant internal states turn out to be physical states, such as brain states.

To see the difference between the mind-brain identity theory and reductive functionalism, consider the possibility that doctors may someday be able to replace parts of the brain with artificial components, say, silicon components. Such artificial components might play the same causal role as the brain parts they replace, in which case, according to functionalism, the person would be able to have the same mental states without having the same brain states as before. This possibility is ruled out by the mind-brain identity theory since it claims that mental states are just brain states; from this perspective, a mental state that is not a brain state is no more possible than is a unit of water that is not a unit of H_2O.

Non-reductive Physicalism. Non-reductive physicalism involves four theses.[9] (A) Like reductive physicalists, non-reductive physicalists insist that humans are entirely physical entities. Humans do *not* have non-physical souls. (B) But mental states (beliefs, desires, sensations, etc.) are not wholly reducible to physical states; they are not identical with physical states, nor are they states that can be wholly reduced to physical states via functionalist analyses of mental states (i.e., as whatever internal states of the person play certain causal roles). (C) Mental states *strongly depend* on physical states. Non-reductive physicalists do not all agree on the precise nature of this dependence, but the most common position is that mental states *supervene* on physical states. That is, if one is in a mental state M, one is in that state by virtue of the fact that one is in a certain physical state P, and "anything that has P at any time necessarily has M at the same time."[10] (D) Mental states (or events) are causes; they can cause both physical states (or events) and mental states (or events). For example, a decision (mental event) can cause my hand to close into a fist (physical event). And the desire for food (a mental event) can cause the thought, "I'd better go to the supermarket" (another mental event).

Note that theses B and D are shared with substance dualists. Thesis B merits further comment. It says that mental states are unique states not wholly reducible to physical states. Thus, non-reductive physicalists hold a kind of dualism, a dualism of states or events: There are physical states (or events), and there are mental states (or events), and neither type of state (or event) is wholly reducible to the other. It's important not to confuse this dualism of states (or events) with substance dualism, for non-reductive physicalists reject substance dualism — they emphatically deny the existence of non-physical souls. Thus, to understand non-reductive physicalism, it is important to distinguish between an individual and its states. For example, an individual person can be in various states—happy or sad, healthy or sick, calm or agitated. The non-reductive physicalist holds that a given brain can be in both physical and mental states.

Thesis C emphasizes the dependence of the mental on the physical. Many non-reductive physicalists hold that if two worlds were exact physical duplicates (including exactly duplicate brain states), the two worlds would also be mental (or psychological) duplicates containing precisely the same mental states.

To clarify the concept of supervenience, it may help to consider the example of a beautiful painting. The beauty of the painting supervenes on the shapes and colors the painter has brushed onto the canvas. Given the shapes and colors, the aesthetic properties of the painting must be as they are. If you want to change the aesthetic properties, you must change the shapes and/or the colors. Similarly, if mental states supervene on physical states (e.g., brain states), there can be no change in mental states apart from a change in physical states.

Naturalists are philosophers who deny the existence of God and affirm that physical reality is the ultimate reality. Most naturalists are either reductive physicalists or non-reductive physicalists. (A few naturalists, the so-called eliminative materialists, take neither position but deny the very existence of mental states; see endnote 1.) Perhaps surprisingly, many contemporary theistic philosophers, scientists, and theologians are physicalists. So, while substance dualism has traditionally been the dominant theistic view of the human person, many theistic philosophers, scientists, and theologians nowadays reject substance dualism.[11]

Let us now consider some standard arguments in favor of physicalism.

Arguments in Favor of Physicalism

Problems for substance dualism provide partial support for physicalist views. Let's begin by considering an argument that has convinced many philosophers that substance dualism is false.

The Causation Argument. The causation argument may be summarized as follows:

1. There is no conceivable way non-physical souls and physical bodies can interact causally.
2. So, they do not interact causally, contrary to what Descartes claims.

Note: Given 2, Descartes' view forces us to deny common sense, for, in Descartes' view, if the soul and body cannot interact causally, mental states cannot cause physical states (and vice versa).

Premise 1 seems to be true. A non-physical soul has no shape, no size, no weight, no electrical charge, and so on. So how could the soul possibly cause anything to happen in the body or the brain? How could the soul make a neuron fire, stimulate a nerve, or cause a muscle to move? Here it might help to try a rather bizarre thought experiment: Try to conceive of a cowboy who uses a non-physical "rope" to lasso a horse. Since the "rope" is non-physical, it has no thickness. The cowboy can't even get hold of it, can he? And if we try to conceive of a non-physical rope being pulled tight around the neck of a horse, what happens? Wouldn't such a rope pass right through the horse's neck? There just doesn't seem to be any way for a non-physical thing to causally interact with a physical thing.

But is the inference from 1 to 2 a good one? There are at least two reasons to question this inference. First, is it safe to assume that what we humans cannot conceive cannot occur or exist? Prior to the rise of science, could humans *conceive* of the causal relation between a magnet and small bits of iron? It seems not. Of course, prior to the rise of science, humans were *familiar* with the phenomenon of magnetism, but they had no understanding of the underlying mechanisms. Magnets were utterly mysterious. Nevertheless, this fact clearly would *not* have provided a good reason to deny that magnets attract iron filings.

Second, in general, we learn about causal connections from experience. We know that if we roll billiard ball A into billiard ball B, B will roll away at a certain speed and in a certain direction. Why doesn't B explode, vanish, or shoot five hundred miles into the air? Well, we've

196 Do Humans Have Souls? Part I

learned over time that these things just don't happen. It seems we can conceive of worlds in which such things do happen, worlds with laws of nature very different from our own. The point is that the behavior of billiard balls (and of physical objects in general) is not something we can predict just by examining the relevant concepts. To learn "what causes what" we have to *observe* things carefully over time.

Now suppose, just for the sake of the argument, that Descartes was right—the soul is not physical. Nevertheless, it seems apparent that a decision (a mental event) can cause a bodily movement, such as standing up. And it seems obvious that damage to one's body (a physical event) can cause pain (a mental event). So Descartes might have claimed that we have plenty of evidence, based on introspection (which tells us what's going on in our souls) and empirical observation (which tells us what bodily movements occur), of causal interactions between non-physical souls and physical bodies.

One more point about the causation argument is of theological interest. If the argument is a good one, a very similar argument would show that a non-physical God cannot create a physical world, sustain a physical world, or work miracles such as healing a person who is physically ill. In short, if the causation argument is sound, traditional theism is false. On the other hand, if traditional theism is true, then there must be something wrong with the causation argument.[12]

The Evolution Argument. The evolution argument may be outlined as follows:

1. Some animals, such as dogs, cats, and chimps, have conscious mental states (for example, they feel pain, and they experience desire).
2. Animals are entirely physical entities; they do not have non-physical souls.
3. Humans, like animals, are products of an entirely physical evolutionary process.
4. So humans are probably entirely physical entities.

Premise 1 of this argument is hard to deny, but some have denied it, among them Descartes. Since Descartes was confident that animals lack (non-physical) souls, he concluded that, in spite of appearances, animals have no conscious mental states. But this view has exceedingly implausible implications; for example, dogs can't be tortured if they can't feel pain.

Many people accept premise 2 of the evolution Argument. Historically, many religious people in the West have accepted premise 2 since they have believed that having a non-physical soul is what distinguishes humans from non-human animals. On the other hand, many who believe in reincarnation reject premise 2.[13]

Some people reject premise 3 because they reject the theory of evolution. For example, Creationists would deny 3 on the grounds that God created humans miraculously, not through the long, gradual processes of evolution. But this way out of the argument is problematic for at least two reasons. First, since the vast majority of scientists accept the theory of evolution, this way out of the argument apparently pits the objector against science. And historically, theologies that conflict with science eventually wind up discredited in the eyes of most people—religious as well as non-religious. Second, this objection relies on questionable theological assumptions that even many theists would deny, for many theists see no conflict between their theology and the scientific theory of evolution. These theists merely insist that evolutionary processes are created, sustained, and guided by God.[14]

The evolution argument raises questions that traditional dualists have not adequately dealt with, but substance dualists can raise interesting questions about the argument. (A) Consider premise 2. Substance dualists might ask, "How is it known that animals in general lack non-physical souls?" Since souls cannot be seen or touched, science can offer no proof that animals lack souls. Notice that the dualist need not claim that all animals have souls—only those with conscious mental states have souls. Which animals have conscious mental states? No one knows for sure. But one might well doubt that many animals (e.g., jellyfish, gnats, and earthworms) have conscious mental states while affirming that many others (e.g., dogs, cats, and chimps) do have such states. Furthermore, a dualist can suggest that animal souls have different (and lesser) capacities than human souls. Thus, there is no need to move from "Some non-human animals have souls" to "Some non-human animals have the same sort of souls humans have."

(B) With regard to the inference from the premises to the conclusion, objectors might again stress that humans have very different capacities from those of animals. Perhaps most importantly, humans have capacities that ground moral responsibility. And this may raise questions about the inference. For example, if human agents are entirely physical entities, are their so-called choices fully governed by laws of nature, over which humans have no control? In short, does physicalism lead to the denial of freedom (and hence, to the denial of moral responsibility)? We'll return to this question in chapter 11.

The Appeal to Simplicity. The appeal to simplicity may be outlined as follows:

1. Due to advances in neuroscience, whatever was assumed in the past to be due to the activity of non-physical souls can nowadays be explained in terms of brain states.
2. So the existence of a non-physical soul is an unnecessary hypothesis.
3. Unnecessary hypotheses are probably false and should be rejected.
4. So the hypothesis that humans have non-physical souls is probably false and should be rejected.

Undoubtedly, this argument has been very influential in recent years. To understand the appeal to simplicity, recall the example of engine-angels from chapter 1. Suppose that we ask a mechanic to explain how a combustion engine works. The mechanic gives an explanation in terms of pistons, cylinders, valves, spark plugs, crankshafts, and so on. We nod in approval at the detail and clarity of his explanation. But then he adds, "Of course, every engine is inhabited by an engine-angel, without which it won't run at all." No doubt we all would consider the "engine-angel hypothesis" superfluous. It is completely unnecessary, surely false, and so should be rejected.

Moreover, neuroscience has made dramatic advances in recent years. While there is much about the brain that remains unknown, there is no doubt that neuroscience will continue to make advances. For any mental state, neuroscientists are apt to discover some corresponding brain state. This being so, if the workings of the brain are understood, won't the idea of a non-physical soul be completely unnecessary? How could "There is a non-physical soul" possibly add anything useful to a neuroscientific explanation? A non-physical soul is as bogus as an engine-angel.

The appeal to simplicity is, without doubt, an important challenge to substance dualism, for most substance dualists accept the principle of simplicity: If a hypothesis contains *unnecessary* complications, it is probably false and should be rejected. But substance dualists can argue that the soul hypothesis helps to explain some things that *cannot be explained scientifically*. This may well be their most promising response to the appeal to simplicity, and we'll return to it in our discussion of an argument for substance dualism in the next chapter.

Very well. We've examined some arguments in favor of a physicalist view of the mind. And the appeal to simplicity, in particular, has considerable plausibility. Let us now consider some difficulties with one of the main varieties of physicalism, namely, reductive physicalism.

PROBLEMS FOR REDUCTIVE PHYSICALISM

There are a number of problems for reductive physicalism:

Problems for the Mind-Brain Identity Theory. Recall that, according to the mind-brain identity theory, each mental state is identical with a brain state, just as each unit of water is identical with a unit of H_2O. Critics have found the mind-brain identity theory problematic for various reasons. Here we will consider two of the supposed problems.

Problem 1: *Qualia.* One perennial objection to identity theories is that they fail to account for subjective conscious experiences (called "qualia"), such as the feeling of a sharp pain (or a dull ache), the experience of smelling gasoline, and the experience of tasting a lemon. No amount of information about the brain, neurons, dendrites, axons, and so on tells us *what it is like* to feel a sharp pain (or a dull ache), to smell gasoline, or to taste a lemon. We might put the point this way: Suppose that we could provide an extraterrestrial visitor with a complete set of biological facts about the human body, including all the neurobiological details about the workings of the human brain. If we confined ourselves to these physical facts, we would leave out something important, namely, such subjective conscious experiences as the feeling of pain, the experience of smelling gasoline, and the experience of tasting a lemon.

A common reply is that the complete physical description does not leave out these subjective conscious experiences but merely refers to them under a different (i.e., neurobiological) description. But here it seems to many philosophers that John Searle has it right: A description of the world in third-person physical terms such as scientists provide is not a complete description of the world. What is left out is precisely the subjective, first-person, conscious phenomena, for example, *what it is like* for a person to experience fear, a dull ache, or the sound of a cello.[15] And Thomas Nagel makes the same point with his famous question, "What is it like to be a bat?" Imagine a researcher who can fully describe, in neurobiological terms, the workings of a bat's brain. Her account leaves out what it is like to experience the world in the way a bat does. And thus, an interesting and important *feature of reality* has been omitted.[16] *Facts about first-person conscious experiences are not metaphysically reducible to facts about neurobiology.*

Problem 2: *Mental Causation.* Identity theories explain mental causation by reducing it to physical causation. But does this provide us with a satisfying explanation of mental causation? Consider that one mental state can apparently be causally linked to another mental state partly by virtue of their informational contents. For example, think of undergoing a sequence of thought such as the following:

It would be fun to see some football → I think I'll watch the Dallas Cowboys' game.

In such cases, one thought plausibly leads to (i.e., causes) the next. But the causal links surely somehow involve the *informational content* of the mental states. Thus, no one with a minimal knowledge of sports is apt to move from "It would be fun to see some football" to "I think I'll watch the Yankees' game." Brain states, however, are linked by neurobiological factors; the account is given in terms of axons, dendrites, chemical synapses, electrical synapses, neurotransmitters, ion channels, and so on. So we *seem* to have two very different causal chains here, one that involves the informational content of the mental states and one that involves the purely neurobiological factors.

Consider an analogy. Suppose that you plug a thumb drive into your computer so you can remind yourself of the words of a limerick:

A kite is a thing that can fly,
Possibly high in the sky.
If the wind is right,
You must hold the kite tight.
And that is not a lie!

Now, there are two sequences here. First, the words of the limerick form a sequence of thoughts involving informational content, one thought leading to the next. Second, there is a complex series of electronic events in the thumb drive involving capacitors (which store a charge) and transistors (each of which can be switched on or off, controlling the movement of electrons). The two different kinds of sequences coincide perfectly because the thumb drive is designed so that it can reproduce the words of a poem, essay, argument, and so on. But there are two *distinct* kinds of sequences here, and the thumb drive analogy strongly suggests that a thought sequence is a very different thing than any sort of causal sequence that can be described in terms of electrical events—including the electrochemical events in the brain.

Furthermore, the identity theorist insists that there are not two distinct causal chains but just one, and therefore, instead of providing a satisfying explanation of mental causation, the identity theorist simply changes the subject. The causal story becomes an entirely physical, neurobiological story. But this leaves us with an unsatisfying account of mental causation—at least in cases in which mental states are apparently causally linked (in part) by way of their informational contents. It is like trying to explain the thought sequence in the limerick, "If the wind is right → You must hold the kite tight" by producing a detailed description of the complex sequence of electronic events within the thumb drive. The informational aspect of the causal linkage is not illuminated.

Problems for Functionalism. Recall that functionalism is the view that mental states are simply internal states of a person that serve as causal links between certain inputs (stimuli) from the environment and correlative outputs in the form of behaviors and other mental states. For example, pain is an internal (physical) state that links a stimulus (e.g., a pin prick to the tip of a finger) with a behavior (e.g., yelling "Ouch!") and other mental states (e.g., thinking "That really hurt"). Let us consider three supposed problems for functionalism.

Problem 1: *Qualia.* John Heil makes the following observation about functionalism:

> Consider . . . the experience of a throbbing pain in my toe. Is this simply a matter of my being in a certain functional state (one that results in my believing that I have a pain in my toe, for instance, and disposes me to rub my toe)? If that were so, it would seem a simple matter to program a computing machine to be in a similar functional state. Yet it is odd to imagine that such a device might, solely because of the way we have programmed it, *feel pain.* What seems missing from the functionalist account is the *feeling* of pain. . . . And feelings, whatever they are, seem not to be functionally characterizable.[17]

Here the point is that the functionalist approach seems unable to capture "what it is like" to be in certain types of mental states. In short, functionalist analyses of certain mental states are deficient; this seems especially clear in the case of *qualia* (i.e., subjective conscious experiences such as the *feeling* of pain, the *taste* of coffee, or the *smell* of roses).

Problem 2: *Understanding.* A second objection to functionalism is pressed by John Searle via his famous Chinese Room argument.[18] Suppose that a computer is programmed to simulate the understanding of Chinese. If the computer is given a question in Chinese, it provides answers in Chinese. And suppose that the computer's answers are indistinguishable from those of a fluent speaker of Chinese. The computer's internal states could play the same causal role as the internal (brain) states of a fluent speaker of Chinese. Does the computer literally understand Chinese? Searle continues:

> Well, imagine that you are locked in a room, and in this room are several baskets full of Chinese symbols. Imagine that you (like me) do not understand a word of Chinese but that you are given a rule book in English for manipulating these Chinese symbols. The rules specify the manipulations of the symbols purely formally, in terms of their syntax [spelling, punctuation, and grammar], not their semantics [meaning or informational content]. So the rule might say, "Take a squiggle-squiggle sign out of basket number one and put it next to a squoggle-squoggle sign from basket number two." Now

suppose that some other Chinese symbols are passed into the room, and that you are given further rules for passing back Chinese symbols out of the room. Suppose that unknown to you the symbols passed into the room are called "questions" by the people outside the room, and the symbols you pass back out of the room are called "answers to the questions." Suppose, furthermore, that the programmers are so good at designing the programs and that you are so good at manipulating the symbols, that very soon your answers are indistinguishable from those of a native Chinese speaker. There you are locked in your room shuffling your Chinese symbols and passing out Chinese symbols in response to incoming Chinese symbols. On the basis of the situation I have described, there is no way you could learn any Chinese simply by manipulating these symbols.[19]

The point is this: The "internal states" of the Chinese room might well play the same *causal* roles as the internal (brain) states of a fluent speaker of Chinese. But neither you nor the room itself understand a word of Chinese. Thus, *there seems to be a big difference between sharing similar internal causal states and literally understanding something.* Hence, functionalism seems unable to provide a credible analysis of the important mental state of *understanding*.[20]

Problem 3: *A Moral Issue*. A third objection to functionalism concerns its moral implications. For example, consider the fact that, increasingly, bomb disposal experts use robots. The robots are not yet as smart and dexterous as a human bomb expert can be, but no doubt they will keep getting better. Does anyone think that, as the robots get more sophisticated—more and more like their human counterparts in terms of their functional states and what they can do—there will be a serious question about whether it is immoral or unethical to use them? Isn't it pretty obvious that we should go on using the robots even if their functional states become much more like ours? I think so. But there *would* be a serious moral issue here if we really believed that the more sophisticated robots could feel fear similar to the fear human bomb experts feel or if we really believed that the more sophisticated robots could feel pain similar to the pain human bomb experts can feel. Thus, it appears that functionalism would lead us to reach some very implausible moral conclusions.

So far we have examined some arguments for physicalism. The causation argument has been convincing to many, but for reasons I've provided, it does not seem very strong to me. The evolution argument is initially plausible, but, as we've seen, it has at least one questionable premise (how can we know that animals lack souls?), and the inference to the conclusion is also questionable (because humans, unlike animals, are morally responsible). The appeal to simplicity is, I believe, the strongest argument in favor of physicalism. If the soul explains nothing, why should we believe in souls? In the next chapter we'll look at one way in which the substance dualist might try to meet this challenge.

Finally, we've looked at arguments against the mind-brain identity theory and reductive functionalism. Interestingly, both of these views seem unable to provide an account of *qualia*, such as the feeling of pain. This is highly significant. Recall the comparative response to the problem of evil from chapter 3. According to the comparative response, the main alternatives to theism are like theism in that they falter in explaining a full range of evil and suffering *in terms consistent with their philosophical underpinnings*; hence, the problem of evil is not a good reason to reject theism in favor of the main alternative views, such as naturalism. Now, many naturalists are reductive physicalists. But if the reductive physicalist views fail to account for *qualia*, such as the feeling of pain, they fail to account for a major aspect of suffering. Therefore, it seems that naturalists who have reductive physicalist views of the mind face a rather serious problem of evil of their own. In the next chapter we'll examine a more complicated type of physicalism, namely, non-reductive physicalism.

ELEVEN

Do Humans Have Souls?

Part II

Physicalist views of the mind or soul all have this in common: They deny that humans have non-physical souls. In the previous chapter we examined two versions of reductive physicalism, specifically the mind-brain identity theory and reductive functionalism. We now turn to non-reductive physicalist views, which involve four theses.[1]

A. Like reductive physicalists, non-reductive physicalists insist that humans are entirely physical entities. Humans do *not* have non-physical souls.

B. But mental states (beliefs, desires, sensations, etc.) are not wholly reducible to physical states. Mental states are not identical to physical states, nor are they states that can be wholly reduced to physical states via functionalist analyses of mental states (i.e., as whatever internal states of the person play certain causal roles).

C. Mental states *strongly depend* on physical states. Non-reductive physicalists do not all agree on the precise nature of this dependence, but the most common position is that mental states *supervene* on physical states. That is, if one is in a mental state M, one is in that state by virtue of the fact that one is in a certain physical state P, and "anything that has P at any time necessarily has M at the same time."[2]

D. Mental states (or events) are causes; they can cause both physical states (or events) and mental states (or events). For example, a decision (mental event) can cause me to turn my head to the left (a physical event). And the desire for sushi (a mental state or event) can cause the thought, "I should go to a Japanese restaurant" (another mental state or event).

Obviously, non-reductive physicalism is a rather complex view. Notice that it involves a dualism of states, mental and physical, but not a dualism of substances, soul and body. The idea is basically that a human brain can be in both physical states (e.g., a sequence of neurons firing) and mental states (feelings, beliefs, desires, etc.). One of the most important objections to non-reductive physicalism is Jaegwon Kim's exclusion argument, to which we now turn.

KIM'S EXCLUSION ARGUMENT

To understand Kim's exclusion argument, keep in mind that non-reductive physicalists insist that mental states (or events) are unique states, distinct from (and not wholly reducible to) physical states (or events). And if a mental event, such as a decision, is to cause an action, such as standing up, it must do so by causing an event in the brain, such as the firing of some neurons (which in turn would cause nerves to fire and muscles to contract). Kim's argument can be outlined as follows.[3]

1. If a physical event has a cause, it has a sufficient *physical* cause.
2. So each brain event (that has a cause) has a sufficient physical cause.
3. If a given brain event has a sufficient physical cause, it does not also have a mental cause.
4. So mental events never cause brain events (and hence they never cause physical events, including bodily movements).

Premise 1 is called the causal closure of the physical domain or (the closure principle, for short). Note that it does not say that every physical event has a cause. It thus allows for the possibility that some events are uncaused flukes or random occurrences. But what premise 1 does say is that if a physical event has a cause, it has a sufficient *physical* cause. This, of course, is something that scientists (including neuroscientists) routinely assume in all their researches.

The subconclusion (2) merely applies the closure principle to brain events. The inference is valid assuming that brain events are physical events—which no one denies. At this point it may be useful to construct a sort of picture to help us think about Kim's argument:

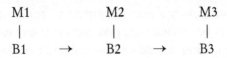

Suppose that B1, B2, and B3 are brain states and that M1, M2, and M3 are mental states. The vertical lines tell us that the mental states supervene on the brain states. For example, M1 supervenes on B1—if a person is in B1, he or she *must* be in M1. The arrows tell us that B1 is a sufficient cause of B2 and that B2 is a sufficient cause of B3. (This is just a simplified way of picturing the point that brain states have sufficient *physical* causes.) The question, in essence, is this: If B1 fully causes B2 and B2 fully causes B3, what causal role do the mental states M1, M2, and M3 play, if any?

Premise 3 gives Kim's answer: The mental states do not cause any brain states at all. How does Kim arrive at this answer? It is of course *logically possible* for an event to have two sufficient causes. For example, two assassins might strike the same person a lethal blow at the same moment. But given that B1 is a sufficient cause of B2, *what distinctive causal role does M1 play*? It seems to merely ride piggyback on B1, given that it supervenes on B1.[4] Thus, non-reductive physicalism seems, by implication, to force us to deny that there are mental causes of physical events—including actions.

An example may help to clarify Kim's point. Imagine that the functions of my smart phone supervene on the matter that constitutes it. I throw the phone at the window and the window breaks. Did my phone cause the breakage? It is natural to answer, "Yes." But obviously, any physical object with the size, shape, weight, and solidity of my phone would cause the window to break (if I threw it at the window). The information-processing functions of the smart phone make no distinctive causal contribution to the breaking of the window. They simply ride piggyback on the matter that constitutes the phone. Therefore, it seems we are speaking very loosely when we say that the smart phone caused the breakage. The true causal account has nothing to do with the distinctively smart-phone-ish aspects of the object. And Kim's point is that supervening mental states would similarly make no causal contribution to physical events in the brain.[5]

The exclusion argument also seems to force the non-reductive physicalist to deny that one mental state ever causes another mental state. For, given that mental states depend on physical (brain) states for their existence, causing a mental state requires causing the brain state it depends on. For example, in order to cause M2, M1 must cause B2. Thus, mental-mental causation presupposes mental-physical causation. But as we have just seen, the exclusion argument rules out mental-physical causation. In short, the exclusion argument seems to show that non-reductive physicalism inadvertently leads to the problematic *epiphenomenalist* thesis that mental states cause nothing. (Epiphenomenalism is the view that mental states are caused by physical states but mental states themselves cause nothing.[6])

The Exclusion Argument: Responses

There would seem to be only two points at which the exclusion argument might be called into question: Premise 1 (the closure principle) and premise 3 (might some brain events have two sufficient causes?). Let's look at each of these premises more closely.

The Closure Principle. Can non-reductive physicalists defuse the exclusion argument by denying the closure principle? For at least two reasons, most physicalists do not regard denying the closure principle as a viable option. First, to deny this principle is presumably to suggest that the sufficient cause of many brain events is not a merely physical event but *some combination* of physical and mental events. And this would imply that there is no complete natural scientific account of the brain. The laws of physics, chemistry, biology, and neurobiology would be unable to account for a vast number of brain events, namely, those caused or partly caused by mental states or events. But physicalists generally hold that a complete natural scientific account of the brain's activity is possible and may someday be achieved.

Second, how is it that mental states or events cause anything? One motive for being a physicalist is to avoid the supposed mysteries of substance dualism—how can a non-physical soul causally interact with a physical body or brain? But causal interaction between non-physical mental states and brain states would seem to be as mysterious as causal interaction between a non-physical soul and the brain. In short, physicalist views that deny the closure principle give up one of the supposedly chief advantages of physicalism over substance dualism.

Premise 3: Causal Over-Determination? Can non-reductive physicalists respond to the exclusion argument by denying premise 3, that is, by claiming that many brain events have two sufficient causes, one physical and the other mental? One problem here is that in a case of genuine causal overdetermination (when there are two sufficient causes of the same event), neither cause is necessary. For example, in the case of two assassins who shoot simultaneously (with lethal effect), neither shot is a *necessary* cause of the victim's death, for had one of the shots not been fired, the other shot would have killed the victim. But physicalists assume that the physical cause of each brain event is a necessary cause; the brain event would not have occurred without it. So physicalists apparently cannot maintain that some brain events have two sufficient causes, one physical and the other mental.[7] Moreover, if the physical causes are necessary and sufficient, why exactly should we believe that mental causes are operative? If the mental causes are not necessary (and apparently they aren't, since the physical causes are sufficient), isn't positing them contrary to the principle of simplicity? It would seem so.

Further problems with denying premise 3 arise depending on the theory of causation employed. For example, if a counterfactual theory of causation is employed (which is favored by some physicalists), event A causes event B if, had A not occurred, B would not have occurred. Example: The fire caused the smoke if, had the fire not occurred, the smoke would not have occurred. In this view, brain event B1 caused B2 if, had B1 not occurred, B2 would not have occurred, but mental event M1 also caused B2 if, had M1 not occurred, B2 would not have occurred. And M1 supervenes on B1 according to the non-reductive physicalist, so if B1 occurs, M1 *must* also occur. Hence, given that M1 supervenes on B1, it is correct to say that if M1 hadn't occurred, B2 would not have occurred. Therefore, M1 is also a cause of B2. Given the counterfactual theory of causation, then, many brain events apparently have two causes, one physical and the other mental.

Unfortunately, the counterfactual theory of causation is subject to well-known objections. Think, for example, of a person firing a pistol at a target. It is true that *had the sound of the pistol not occurred*, the hole in the target would not have occurred. Yet obviously the *sound* of the pistol is not the cause of the hole in the target.[8] From this perspective, mental states may be like the *sound* of the pistol, which *merely accompanies* the cause of the effect.

As we've just seen, while the non-reductive physicalist can raise questions about Kim's argument, each proposed response to it seems to run into immediate difficulties. Furthermore, there is no agreement even among physicalists as to whether any of the responses is adequate.[9] But if the exclusion argument is sound, it is very bad news for non-reductive physicalists; for, as noted above, this would mean that non-reductive physicalism, by implication, denies mental states any causal role at all.

To appreciate the importance of this point it will help to reconsider the comparative response to the problem of evil, which was introduced in chapter 3. There we noted that the phenomena of suffering are twofold:

A. Certain subjective conscious experiences, for example, the hurtfulness of physical pain; the feeling of being miserable; the agony of anxiety; the dreadful feeling of depression; and the raw fear of more suffering to come.
B. Cases in which pain and suffering enter into causal relations. For example: (1) A person experiencing *severe chronic pain* may opt for suicide as a means of avoiding any further feelings of an extremely unwelcome sort. Here pain and suffering seem to be among the causes of behavior. (2) The *belief* that others have been harmed or killed can cause suffering in the form of deep sadness, anxiety, or despair. Here a mental state (a belief) is apparently the cause (or among the causes) of mental pain and suffering. (3) After an earthquake, a family may sleep outside and suffer in the bitter cold because they *fear* that aftershocks will cause their house to collapse.

Here physical pain and suffering apparently result (in part) from the mental state of fear.

According to epiphenomenalism, mental events are never causes; hence, epiphenomenalism completely fails to account for the phenomena of mental causation included in B. And the same can be said for non-reductive physicalism if, in the last analysis, it implies that mental events are never causes. But the phenomena included in B are part of our common-sense understanding of the role our mental states play. It seems, then, that both epiphenomenalism and non-reductive physicalism fail to account for some important aspects of the phenomena of pain and suffering. And if so, those who adopt either of these views face a significant problem of evil (suffering).

Free Will: A Problem for All Physicalists?

Let us now consider a problem that may apply to all physicalist views, whether reductive or non-reductive. Since physicalists deny that humans have souls, they must affirm that each human being is one small part of a vast physical system. And in an entirely physical system, *all* outcomes are functions of two factors: the initial conditions and the laws of nature. Thus, given physicalism, it seems that our thoughts, feelings, desires, intentions, acts, and so on, result from past states of the physical world and the operation of the laws of nature.[10] But no human has any choice about the past and the laws of nature. Is there any room for free will in this picture?

Physicalists can answer "yes" by affirming the compatibilist view of free will: "People often perform actions because they *want* to perform them. And if the acts are not coerced, they are done freely." In the compatibilist view, free will is logically compatible with determinism. Determinism is the idea that, given the past, only one future is possible. When we deliberate, we assume that multiple options are open to us. At the next intersection, I could turn right, but I might turn left instead. At the restaurant, I might order a burger or a Caesar salad instead. And so on. But if determinism is true, the appearance of multiple options (at a given moment) is merely an illusion. *In each case,*

212 Do Humans Have Souls? Part II

given the past and the laws of nature, only one of the apparent options is possible; the other options cannot be realized. Nevertheless, in the compatibilist view of free will, one performs an act freely as long as one performs it because one wants to (or intends to)—even if the "wanting" (or intention) was itself fully necessitated by the past and the laws of nature.[11]

The most important argument against the compatibilist view is the *consequence argument*.[12] In order to state the argument succinctly, we need to consider some preliminaries. Let's assume, for the sake of the argument, that determinism is true and that it is true because the universe is governed by deterministic laws of nature. A deterministic law of nature has the following form:

> *Deterministic Law*: Given initial conditions A, B, and C, event D must occur.

In other words, *once the initial conditions are met, only one result is possible*; for instance, if we heat water to one hundred degrees centigrade (at sea level), it always boils. We are assuming that every event that has ever happened has resulted from initial conditions together with deterministic laws of nature. The history of the universe is one long chain of events tightly linked as one set of initial conditions gives rise to a result, which in turn becomes an initial condition leading to another result.

To get a firmer grip on the concept of determinism, consider a proposition of the form "L1 and L2 and L3 . . . ," where each symbol stands for a law of nature, such as the law of gravity. Call this proposition the "List of Laws." And assume that it includes *every* law of nature—even any laws that have not yet been discovered. Also consider a proposition **P** about the remote past. **P** gives a complete description of the physical universe as it was a billion years ago, including the location of every atom, its direction of movement, the charge of every subatomic particle, and so on. Since **P** gives a complete description of the physical universe, it gives the initial conditions for all of the laws of nature a billion years ago. Now, if determinism is true, the "List of Laws" together with **P** logically implies any true proposition describing a future event. Suppose, for example, that it is true that "Fiona will fly to

France next Friday." Call this statement **F**. Then the "List of Laws" together with **P** logically implies **F**.

Plainly, we have no choice about the laws of nature and the remote past, and no choice about the truth of this conjunction: The "List of Laws" and proposition **P**. Moreover, the following principle seems correct:

> *Transfer Principle*: If one has no choice about the truth of proposition **A** and **A** logically implies **B**, then one has no choice about the truth of **B**.[13]

(Example: If one has no choice about the truth of "8 is even" and "8 is even" logically implies "8 is divisible by 2," then one has no choice about the truth of "8 is divisible by 2.") The transfer principle seems to be true, in part, because we have no choice about what follows *logically* from what. The rules of logic hold of necessity; we don't get to vote on them. So if **A** is true (and one has no choice about that) and **A** logically implies **B**, it seems clear that **B** is true and one has no choice about that, either. Our lack of choice about **A** *transfers* to a lack of choice about **B**. Putting all the pieces together, then, the following argument seems sound:

1. One has no choice about the truth of the "List of Laws" and proposition **P**.
2. The "List of Laws" together with **P** logically implies **F** (assuming that determinism is true).
3. If one has no choice about the truth of the "List of Laws" and **P**, and if this conjunction logically implies **F**, then one has no choice about the truth of **F** (by application of the transfer principle).
4. So if determinism is true, one has no choice about the truth of **F**.

This is the consequence argument. We made **F** stand for "Fiona will fly to France next Friday." So the argument shows that (given determinism) neither Fiona nor anyone else has a choice about the truth of **F**. But of course, the same could be said about the truth of any proposition about the future. The upshot is that, if determinism is true, we humans have no choice about anything, that is, we lack free will. Thus, if the consequence argument is sound, the compatibilist view of free will is mistaken.

Compatibilists might reply that it remains true that we perform some actions because we want to. But this reply is not relevant. The compatibilist agrees that we have no choice about the remote past and the laws of nature. And premise 3 tells us, in effect, that our lack of choice about the past and the laws of nature transfers to the future if determinism is true. Thus, the compatibilist conception of a free act seems to be inadequate: *A free act is not simply one we do because we want to.*

Accordingly, we need a more robust understanding of what a free action is, and this is provided by the incompatibilist view of freedom. In the incompatibilist view, an agent performs an act A freely at time T only if the agent performs act A at T *but at T the agent has the power to refrain from A.* For example, Joe steals a car freely at time T only if Joe steals a car at T, but at T Joe has the power to refrain from stealing the car. Genuine free will (and moral responsibility) require the "power to do otherwise."

The point here is that the compatibilist conception of free will is flawed and inadequate; the point is not that physicalists are necessarily determinists. Some physicalists are determinists, and some are not. The issue of determinism depends (in part) on whether the laws of nature are deterministic or probabilistic. Probabilistic laws can be thought of as having a form along these lines:

Probabilistic Law: Given initial conditions A, B, and C, event D will probably occur, but E might occur instead.

Unlike deterministic laws, probabilistic laws do not always yield the same result even when the initial conditions are the same. For example, one of the laws of radioactivity is that half of the atoms in a unit of radium 226 will decay over a period of 1,602 years, but the law does not specify *which* of the atoms will decay during that period or the *precise moment* when any one of them will decay. Thus, within limits, different outcomes are possible. If some laws of nature are probabilistic—and they are according to contemporary physics—the physical world is not a deterministic system. But *regardless of whether the laws of nature are deterministic or probabilistic, it remains true that we have no choice about what the laws are and about conditions that held in the past.* And the question is "Can the physicalist give a plausible account of free will (and hence of moral responsibility)?"

It is hard to see how. In a physical system fully governed by laws of nature (whether deterministic or probabilistic), how could a "power to do otherwise," operating to some degree independently of the laws of nature, be present? Obviously the "power to do otherwise" would not be present if the laws are deterministic. But merely adding some probabilistic laws into the mix doesn't make room for free will. The clicking sounds a Geiger counter makes result from the operation of probabilistic laws governing the activity of electrons. But of course no one would suggest that a Geiger counter has free will. And while the human brain is far more complex than a Geiger counter, mere complexity is no guarantee of free will. Suppose that we had a very complicated computer that operated in part via probabilistic laws; would it have free will? I see no reason to think so. Thus, the suggestion that (incompatibilist) free will would be present in a physicalist view of the mind seems quite mysterious. Therefore, it seems that physicalist views falter in accounting for free will; hence, they also falter in accounting for moral responsibility.

Once again, this takes us back to the comparative response to the problem of evil. An adequate account of moral evil involves an account of wrong acts for which humans are *morally responsible*. But this, in turn, depends on explaining the presence of free will in the incompatibilist sense. If physicalist views falter in explaining free will, they falter in explaining moral responsibility and moral evil as well. And nearly all naturalists hold to physicalist views of the mind—either reductive or non-reductive.[14] Apparently, then, naturalism encounters difficulties in explaining the presence of moral evil in the world, and in that sense naturalism faces its own problem of evil.

By contrast, creatures endowed with free will in the incompatibilist sense are to be expected given the theistic hypothesis. As Paul Draper has remarked:

> On theism, which entails that God is morally perfect, one has reason to believe that our actions are not the inevitable consequence of natural laws and antecedent conditions chosen by God. For that would mean that God is the ultimate sufficient cause of every morally wrong action

we perform. More importantly, it would mean that any relationship we might have with God, indeed any response at all that we make to God, would be the result of divine manipulation.[15]

Thus, theists posit a God who has reasons to endow creatures with incompatibilist free will and who has the power to do so.

A "Best Explanation" Argument
for Substance Dualism

Substance dualists have offered a variety of arguments for their position. We will consider just one argument here.[16] Think back to the simplicity argument for physicalism. The crucial claim of that argument was that the "soul hypothesis" is unnecessary—all mental phenomena can be explained in terms of physical factors. But our discussion of physicalist views indicates that they falter at a number of important points. If the soul hypothesis can fill any of these explanatory gaps, substance dualists can argue that their position is probably true on the grounds that it provides the best explanation of the relevant phenomena. (Compare: Although physicists cannot see subatomic particles such as electrons and quarks, they think that electrons and quarks probably exist because theories that postulate such entities can explain phenomena that other theories cannot explain.)

What might the soul hypothesis explain? It might help to explain free will. As we have just seen, physicalist views seem to falter in explaining the presence of moral responsibility and (incompatibilist) free will. But suppose we postulate the existence of a non-physical soul having the power to form intentions and, by forming those intentions, to effect certain changes in the brain. Since the soul is a non-physical entity, mental events in the soul would not be entirely governed by laws of nature, though events in the brain—let us suppose—could affect the soul in various ways. (Example: A blow to the head would have an effect on the brain that, in turn, might cause the soul—that is, the person—to experience pain.) These considerations suggest the following argument for substance dualism:

1. Humans have the sort of free will that is needed for moral responsibility (namely, free will in the incompatibilist sense).
2. If physicalism (whether reductive or non-reductive) is true, then premise 1 seems surprising and mysterious.
3. If humans have a non-physical soul with the power to form intentions and, by forming those intentions, to effect changes in the brain, then premise 1 seems unsurprising.
4. So premise 1 seems unsurprising given substance dualism, but surprising given physicalism.
5. Therefore, the presence of free will (and moral responsibility) gives us some reason to accept substance dualism over physicalism.

Of course, physicalists are not likely to warm up to the soul hypothesis. Let's consider three objections to the "best explanation" argument for substance dualism.

The Conservation of Energy. Physicalists sometimes claim that if the soul were to effect changes in the brain, this would violate the scientific principle of the conservation of energy—namely, the principle that the energy in an isolated (or "closed") physical system remains constant. Daniel Dennett, for example, asks us to think about signals supposedly coming from a non-physical soul to the brain:

> These [signals] . . . are not physical; they are not light waves or sound waves or cosmic rays or streams of subatomic particles. No physical energy or mass is associated with them. How, then, do they get to make a difference to what happens in the brain cells they must affect, if the mind [soul] is to have any influence over the body? A fundamental principle of physics is that any change in the trajectory of any physical entity is an acceleration requiring the expenditure of energy, and where is this energy to come from? It is this principle of the conservation of energy that accounts for the physical impossibility of "perpetual motion machines," and the same principle is apparently violated by dualism. This confrontation between quite standard physics and dualism has been endlessly discussed since Descartes' own day, and is widely regarded as the inescapable and fatal flaw of dualism.[17]

As Alvin Plantinga points out, in this passage Dennett conflates two different objections to dualism. First, Dennett seems to be claiming that we cannot understand or conceive *how* a non-physical entity could have causal effects in the physical world. Now, he may be right about this, but what follows logically? Prior to the rise of science, suppose that someone had advanced this argument:

1. We (humans) cannot understand or conceive *how* magnets attract iron filings.
2. So magnets do not attract iron filings.

Prior to the rise of science, the premise of this argument was true; but the conclusion of the argument is plainly false, so the reasoning is invalid. And Dennett's argument also apparently proceeds *in part* from an alleged causal inconceivability.

Second, Dennett claims that the principle of conservation of energy somehow prevents a non-physical entity from having an effect in the physical world. But this latter point also seems to miss the mark. *If the soul causes any sort of change in the brain, the brain is not an isolated (or "closed") system, and hence the principle of conservation of energy is not violated.* Moreover, the principle of conservation of energy in no way states or implies that the brain is a closed system. In fact, even on the purely physical level, energy flows *into* the brain from other systems in the body and *from* the brain to other systems in the body.

One further observation may help to clarify the problem with Dennett's claim about the principle of conservation of energy. If Dennett's claim were correct, it would prove that God cannot work miracles. But in fact, if God works a miracle (e.g., stills a storm), this would simply show that the physical system in question is not closed: The principle of conservation of energy would not be violated.[18]

Evolution and the Soul. Another physicalist objection to the best-explanation argument is that it is implausible to suppose that non-physical souls have come into existence through the processes of evolution. After all, the processes of evolution are physical in nature, involving genes, genetic mutations, and features of the physical environment. How could physical mechanisms produce souls? This objection has some force, it seems to me, if we are thinking of evolution as naturalists do—as a process operating apart from a divine plan or divine guidance. But many theists regard evolution as a divinely designed and guided process. And given that substance dualism is logically possible, an almighty God could presumably set up and sustain evolutionary processes that give rise to creatures with both a body and a soul. Such creatures would apparently fit in well with a divine plan that includes the creation of beings with free will and moral responsibility. So the best-explanation argument, while admittedly falling well short of being conclusive, can nevertheless have a degree of plausibility, especially from a theistic perspective.[19]

Kim's Pairing Problem. A third physicalist objection to the best-explanation argument rests on Jaegwon Kim's famous pairing problem.[20] The gist of the problem is that there seems to be nothing that could link a given soul to a given body; hence, substance dualism is a fundamentally flawed hypothesis. To get a clearer grasp of the problem, consider an example of physical causation. Suppose gun A is fired, killing person X, while gun B is fired, killing person Y. What makes it the case that the firing of gun A is the cause of X's death, while the firing of gun B is the cause of Y's death? The answer seems simple enough: Gun A was within a certain distance of person X and pointed at X, while gun B was within a certain distance of person Y and pointed at Y.

Now, in the case of two non-physical souls, S1 and S2, and two bodies to which they are (supposedly) causally linked, B1 and B2, what would account for the fact that soul S1 is linked to body B1, while soul S2 is linked to body B2? Why does a choice by soul S1 affect body B1 directly and not body B2? Since souls are not physical entities, an answer in terms of spatial relationships, such as we gave in the example of the guns, is apparently not available.

To make the pairing problem clear, Kim presents us with the hypothetical case of two persons, S1 and S2, who are perfectly "psychophysically synchronized." For example, each time S1 wills to raise his right arm, S2 wills to raise her right arm; each time S1 wills to stand up, S2 wills to stand up; and so on. The question is "What makes it the case that S1's willing raises his arm? Why doesn't S2's willing raise S1's arm?"[21] Again, since souls are not physical entities, an answer in terms of spatial relationships seems out of the question. And what else is there that could serve to pair S1 to B1 and S2 to B2? It's hard to see a good answer to that question; that's the pairing problem.

But the claim that souls have no location in space has been questioned. Might souls be like the points in geometry, with no size or shape but nevertheless a location? If so, soul S1 could be located in body B1 (somewhere in the brain, presumably), while soul S2 could be located in body B2. And then dualists might suggest that soul S1 would be causally linked to body B1 (and not to B2) by virtue of its location in B1, while soul S2 would be causally linked to body B2 (and not to B1) by virtue of its location in B2. In short, perhaps each soul could have a spatial relation to a particular body, contrary to Kim's assumption. Now, Kim might reply that if souls have locations, souls must be physical entities. But a geometrical point is not a physical object. Of course, geometrical points don't move around, and if a soul is located in a person's brain, it would have to move around as the person moves around. What, then, would distinguish souls from the point particles of physics, such as quarks and electrons (which have no size but are located in space)?[22] One answer might be simply that souls, unlike the point particles of physics, are by their very nature mental, that is, capable of conscious mental states, and for this reason they do not count as physical objects. Of course, to claim this is to make a controversial claim about what counts as a physical object. But is the claim clearly wrong? Philosophers have tried to define "physical object" in a variety of ways, but all of the proposed definitions remain controversial. The main point here is that Kim's pairing problem rests on the questionable assumption that souls are not located in space.[23]

A second response to the pairing problem rests on the classical theistic view of creation. In this view, creation is regarded as having three components: (1) God creates the world ex nihilo (out of nothing), but (2) God also *conserves* it; that is, God sustains the world in existence from moment to moment, and (3) God *concurs* with the activities of each created thing, that is, he cooperates with or upholds their causal powers, which otherwise could not be exercised. (As an analogy, I might cooperate with the activity of a friend who is using a power tool by allowing him to use my electricity.[24]) Alvin Plantinga has offered a response to the pairing problem that centrally employs the concept of divine concurrence.

First, although theism involves the belief in a non-physical "soul-like" God, theism itself faces nothing like the pairing problem because, according to classical theism, it is a necessary truth that *whatever God wills, takes place*. Asking, "What makes it the case that God's volitions cause what they cause?" is like asking, "What makes it the case that eight is divisible by two?" or "What makes it the case that every blue object is non-red?" (Answer: It cannot be otherwise. End of story.) So what makes it the case that *God's willing X causes X to occur* is simply that the linkage is metaphysically necessary; it cannot be otherwise. The buck stops at necessity.

Second, God *concurs* with every genuine causal transaction. And this provides a possible solution to the pairing problem. How? Along these lines: God concurs with *Joe's willing causing Joe's arm to rise*, but God does not concur with *Pete's willing causing Joe's arm to rise*. Thus, divine concurrence serves to link Joe's soul with Joe's body, but divine concurrence does not link Pete's soul with Joe's body. And, similarly, divine concurrence links Pete's soul with Pete's body but does not link Joe's soul with Pete's body. In this way, even if souls have no location in space, divine concurrence can serve to pair a given soul with a given body.[25]

To sum up, there are a number of objections to the best-explanation argument for substance dualism, and some of the objections take us into deep metaphysical waters. But reasonable replies to the objections seem to be available. So the argument apparently gives some support, though perhaps only very modest support, to substance dualism.

THEISTIC PHYSICALISM?

To this point I've been thinking of physicalist views of the human person as views held by philosophical naturalists. But nowadays many theologians, theistic philosophers, and theistic scientists are physicalists. So let's briefly consider whether a *theistic* version of physicalism might be defensible in a way that *naturalistic* versions are not.

Everyone should agree with physicalists that human mentality is dependent on brain activity; a blow to the head may cause a loss of consciousness, and brain injury may permanently impair mental functioning. But the dependence relationship may not be as strong as physicalists claim (e.g., supervenience or identity), with physical events always "running the show." The brain might be more like a radio receiver—smash the receiver and the music stops, but the receiver is not, all by itself, the source of the music. Given theism, God creates the physical world and sets in place those regularities we call laws of nature. Might God also be able to actualize the following sorts of relations between the mental and the physical?

1. Some mental events are caused by a combination of a mental event and a physical event, *neither of which is by itself a sufficient cause.* For example, one thought—together with supporting brain activity—causes another thought.
2. Some physical events are caused by a combination of a mental event and a physical event, *neither of which is by itself a sufficient cause.* For example, a decision—in combination with supporting neural activity—causes an action, such as sitting down or standing up.

If such relationships are logically possible, almighty God could presumably actualize and sustain them, and the causal links between mental and physical states could then be accounted for. If this version of physicalism is coherent, it would escape Kim's exclusion argument for two reasons: (1) It can account for a system of mental causes that is *coordinated* with the system of physical causes. The coordination is guaranteed by an almighty, all-knowing, and good Creator whose purposes include the creation of free moral agents and who sets up laws of nature that accord with this purpose. (2) Consistent with traditional theism, this theistic version of physicalism denies the closure principle ("If a physical event has a cause, then it has a sufficient *physical* cause"). At least two kinds of physical events do not have a *sufficient* physical cause:

a. Physical events caused directly by God, such as miracles.
b. Any physical event, such as a brain event, that is at least partly caused by a mental event and not *fully* caused by any physical factors.

Finally, if mental events are not physical events, and if mental events do not supervene on physical events, then mental events (including choices and decisions) are presumably not governed by physical laws of nature. So perhaps there is room for free will in a theistic version of physicalism. But I hope it is clear that such a theistic version of physicalism is quite different from naturalistic versions. While there is no soul in either view, in the theistic version mental states or events are much less dependent on physical states or events. Such a scenario may be possible if God sustains the operation of both the mental and the physical events. But given naturalistic assumptions, it seems to me that any such scenario is very implausible.

These brief reflections are, of course, tentative. But perhaps they suggest that it would be wise for theists to keep their options open as regards the choice between substance dualism and a theistic version of physicalism.[26]

In this chapter (and the previous one) I have tried to carefully sort through the complexities of the soul-body issue. I have weighed the pros and cons regarding reductive physicalism, non-reductive physicalism, and substance dualism. I have argued that the physicalist views, at least when combined with naturalism, have significant problems. I have also argued that the standard objections to substance dualism are not conclusive. Moreover, I have argued that, assuming humans are morally responsible and have free will, we have some reason to accept substance dualism. But I have also left open the possibility that physicalism is a viable position if it is combined with theism.

TWELVE

Does Reincarnation Provide
the Best Explanation of Suffering?

According to the doctrine of karma, one always reaps what one sows. But to all appearances, the innocent often suffer—for example, babies, those with severe mental impairments, and non-human animals often suffer. So, at first glance, the doctrine of karma does not appear to be true. But if we combine the doctrines of karma and reincarnation, appearances may well be quite misleading. According to the doctrine of reincarnation, as Goldschmidt and Seacord phrase it, "Subjects undergo cycles of life and death, living as one form and dying, then living again as another form any number of times."[1] Thus, a person might live as a human, die, be born as, say, a bird, die, and be reborn as some other kind of animal or perhaps as a human again.[2] And this makes possible the view that suffering is always deserved as punishment for wrongs committed in one's previous lives (if not for wrongs committed in one's current life). Because here I am interested in karma—together with reincarnation—as an explanation of the suffering in the world. I shall understand karma to be a law, analogous to a physical law of nature, that ensures that no one suffers more than he or she deserves—no more, but also no less. Karma also ensures that a person is rewarded in accordance with what he or she deserves—no more, but also no less.

The doctrines of karma and reincarnation are logically consistent with belief in a personal God. But, as in the case of Theravada Buddhism and Advaita Vedanta (a Hindu system of thought), these doctrines can be held independently of a belief in a personal God or gods. In this chapter I ask whether the doctrines of karma and reincarnation, taken together and independently of theism, provide a satisfying explanation of the suffering in the world. But I also ask whether theism could be made more defensible if combined with the doctrines of karma and reincarnation. More specifically, would theism, if combined with the doctrines of karma and reincarnation, have a better response to the problem of evil?

It is worth noting that reincarnation is a part of many different religious traditions. Everyone knows that reincarnation is generally held among Hindus and Buddhists, but the doctrine is also featured in Druzism, Sikhism, and Jainism. In addition, it is widespread among orthodox Jews.[3] And, interestingly, over a quarter of Americans now believe in reincarnation.[4]

While the belief in reincarnation and karma is widespread, it needs to be emphasized that these beliefs come in many variations. And *my purpose here is not to evaluate the actual beliefs of any particular religion (or set of religions).* My formulation of the law of karma is meant to be one that shows promise as an explanation of suffering. It is not an attempt to provide a scholarly interpretation of that law as it appears in any historic religious text(s). And, as a matter of fact, the law of karma is often stated in rather vague or unclear ways. Here is an example taken from a Buddhist text: When a person's deeds are performed through covetousness, hatred, or infatuation, "wherever his personality may be, there those deeds ripen, there he experiences the fruition of those deeds, be it in the present life, or some subsequent life."[5] Thus stated, the doctrine of karma is obviously susceptible of multiple interpretations. So let me emphasize, once again, that I am going to examine *just one version* of the belief in karma and reincarnation—a version that is formulated for philosophical purposes—specifically for the purpose of explaining the presence of suffering in the world. And the version I'm evaluating claims that *each instance of suffering is deserved as punishment for wrongs committed by the sufferer either in the sufferer's current life or in some previous life (or lives).*

SUPPORT FOR REINCARNATION AND KARMA

Let's begin by considering some possible grounds for believing the doctrines of karma and reincarnation. One line of thinking begins with the assumption that the universe is ultimately just. But, as noted previously, there would apparently be much undeserved suffering—and hence much unjust suffering—if reincarnation does not occur. So, reincarnation seems to be a necessary postulate if one is to maintain the belief that the universe is ultimately a just moral order *in the sense of containing no undeserved suffering at all.* Let us call this the appeal to cosmic justice.[6]

A second line of thinking in support of reincarnation concerns déjà vu experiences. In such experiences one has the feeling that the situation one is currently experiencing is a situation one has experienced in the past, and yet one does not recall having ever been in such a situation. For example, one may travel to a faraway place where—as far as one knows—one has never been before, but, upon arriving, find oneself possessed of a strong feeling that one *has* been there before. Déjà vu experiences are rather common, and they are indeed puzzling. But given that reincarnation occurs, such experiences can be explained along these lines: When having a déjà vu experience, the situation one is experiencing is in fact a situation one experienced in a previous life. And in the absence of a better explanation, déjà vu experiences provide support for the belief in reincarnation. I shall refer to this type of support for reincarnation as the déjà vu argument.

A third line of thinking in support of reincarnation depends on cases of so-called past-life recall. While most people do not recall any previous lives, many cases of past-life recall have been recorded, and some of these cases have been carefully investigated. We cannot here explore the literature of past-life recall in detail, but let me characterize the type of case that seems to me most worthy of consideration. In this type of case, Ian Stevenson writes, "a child between the ages of 2 and 4 . . . begins to narrate details of a previous life that he claims to have lived before his birth."[7] Some of these children "make only three or four different statements about a previous life, but others may be credited with 60 or 70 separate items pertaining to different details in the life remembered."[8] In the majority of these cases, "the volume and clarity of the child's statements increase until at the age of 5 and [or?] 6 he usually starts to forget the memories; or, if he does not forget them, he begins to talk about them less."[9] Often "the child asks, or even clamors, to be taken to the place where he says he lived before, and shows marked concern over the people 'he' left there."[10] Not infrequently the parents take the child to the place in question, where, via details provided by the child, persons corresponding to the child's claims are found. Let us consider two representative cases.

The Case of Ravi Shankar. As Stevenson reports, in January of 1951 Ashok Kumar of Kanauj, India, the six-year-old son of Sri Jageshwar Prasad, was murdered with a knife or razor.[11] There were no witnesses to the crime, and so the suspects (two adult neighbors) were never brought to justice. "A few years later word reached Sri Jageshwar Prasad that a boy born in another district of Kanauj in July 1951 . . . had described himself as the son of Jageshwar . . . and had given details of 'his' murder, naming the murderers, the place of the crime and other circumstances of the life and death of Munna [another name for Ashok Kumar]."[12] This boy, Ravi Shankar, son of Sri Babu Ram Gupta, "kept asking his parents for various toys which he claimed he had in the house of his previous life."[13] When Ravi was four years old, Sri Jageshwar Prasad arranged a visit with him. "At this meeting, Ravi Shankar gave Sri Jageshwar Prasad an account of the murder (of Munna) which corresponded very closely with what he [Prasad] had been able to put together of the event from the retracted confession of one of the murderers, the inspection of the murder site . . . , and the mutilated body."[14] Ravi Shankar displayed fear of the persons he believed to be the murderers of Munna (Ashok Kumar) and expressed his intention to avenge the murder, though he never acted on that intention. Extensive interviews with those who knew Ravi Shankar turned up no likely explanation of how the four-year-old might have known (through ordinary means) the details of Ashok Kumar's death.

The Case of Ampan Petcherat. Ampan Petcherat was born in Thailand in 1954. When she was about one year old, Stevenson records, "she began to tell her mother that she had another mother and father at Klong Bang Chag, a town about 20 kilometers from their residence in Klong Darn."[15] Ampan claimed to have been a boy in her previous life, and she claimed that she had died by drowning. She "would cry in talking about her previous home and ask to be taken to it."[16] One day when Ampan was seven she claimed that a woman she saw on the street in Klong Darn was her aunt, specifically, her "other mother's" older sister. As it turned out, this woman was "in fact the older sister of Tong Bai Puang Pei, of Bang Chag, who had lost a son, Chuey, by drowning in 1950."[17] The "aunt" took Ampan and her mother to Klong Bang Chag to meet Chuey's family. "Ampan's statements fitted very closely facts of the life and death of Chuey Puang Pei who was a boy of about four when he drowned at Klong Bang Chag in 1950."[18]

Naturally, cases such as those summarized here raise many questions. But some of the cases cannot plausibly be dismissed as attempts at deception. They are apparently sincere, and they merit serious consideration. Let us refer to this type of support for reincarnation as the argument from past-life recall.

A fourth type of support for the belief in karma and reincarnation involves an appeal to the sacred texts of particular religious traditions, such as Hinduism and Buddhism. For example, in the *Kauṣītaki Upaniṣad* we read, "When people depart from this world, it is to the moon that they all go. . . . Now, the moon is the door to the heavenly world. It allows those who answer its question to pass. As to those who do not answer its question, after they have become rain, it rains them down here on earth, where they are born again in these various conditions—as a worm, an insect, a fish, a bird, a lion, a boar, a rhinoceros, a tiger, a man, or some other creature—each in accordance with his actions and his knowledge."[19] Or, again, in the *Kaṭha Upaniṣad*: "When a man lacks understanding, is unmindful and always impure; he does not reach that final step, but gets on the round of rebirth. But when a man has understanding, is mindful and always pure; he does reach that final step, from which he is not reborn again."[20] Turning to an example from the Buddhist Scriptures, we read:

> "Bhante Nagasena," said the king, "are there any who die without being born into another existence?"
>
> "Some are born into another existence," said the elder, "and some are not born into another existence."
>
> "Who is born into another existence, and who is not born into another existence?"

"Your majesty, he that still has the corruptions is born into another existence; he that no longer has the corruptions is not born into another existence."[21]

Here we should note that Buddhists typically speak of rebirth instead of reincarnation, since they deny that there is an enduring soul or self that can transmigrate to the next life.[22] Let us refer to this type of support for karma and reincarnation (or rebirth) as the appeal to sacred texts.

Strong Support?

How strong is the support for the doctrines of reincarnation and karma outlined above? Let us consider the arguments one by one.

The appeal to cosmic justice leans heavily on the assumption that the universe is perfectly just *in the sense of containing no undeserved suffering at all.* Obviously, this is a non-trivial assumption. Indeed, it is an assumption that runs contrary to appearances and that many people find implausible. Furthermore, it is hard to conceive of any non-question-begging support for this assumption. And in the absence of such support, the argument can hardly be considered a strong one, or so it seems to me.

The déjà vu argument depends crucially on the claim that in the absence of a better explanation, déjà vu experiences lend support to the belief in reincarnation. But, as a point of logic, the déjà vu argument is not strong unless reincarnation can be shown to be the *best* explanation of déjà vu experiences. If other explanations are *equally* good or better, the argument is weak. And there are well-known alternative explanations. For example, William James suggested that in déjà vu experiences the situation (or scenario) *resembles* a situation one has experienced before, but one fails to recognize this—one may have no memory (or no clear memory) of the earlier situation.[23] To the extent that James's explanation is plausible, the déjà vu argument is lacking in force. And many find James's relatively simple explanation quite plausible. This being so, the déjà vu argument seems to have little force. Notice also that the déjà vu argument is meant to provide support for the doctrine of reincarnation; it apparently provides no support for the doctrine of karma.

The appeal to sacred texts undoubtedly carries weight with those who accept the authority of the writings in question. But these texts do not provide arguments for the doctrines of reincarnation and karma. Rather, in these texts the doctrines are simply asserted or presupposed. Thus, for example, trying to prove the doctrines of reincarnation and/or karma by appeal to the Hindu or Buddhist Scriptures is rather like trying to prove that God exists by appealing to the Bible. The Bible doesn't give arguments for God's existence; it merely asserts or presupposes God's existence. Accordingly, "The Bible says or presupposes that God exists; hence God exists" is an argument that *should* fail to convince the non-theist (unless there are some *independent* arguments or grounds supporting the belief that the Bible is a reliable source concerning God's existence). Similarly, the appeal to sacred texts in support of reincarnation and karma apparently needs to be supported by arguments or grounds justifying belief in the reliability of these texts *as concerns the doctrines of karma and reincarnation.* What sort of argument or ground could play this role? Perhaps the best answer is along these lines: It might be claimed that the authors of these texts possessed knowledge of reincarnation because they themselves had memories of one or more past lives. But this claim naturally shifts the discussion to the issue of past-life recall.

As regards cases of past-life recall, I must first of all emphasize that there is no substitute for a detailed examination of the various reports, and such an examination would be a major undertaking, far beyond the scope of this chapter. That said, it is not difficult to outline a series of points that qualify the evidential value of the appeal to past-life recall:

1. Even if we accept all of the apparently sincere reports as true, in comparison to the total number of human lives, the number of reports is minuscule. Perhaps the vast majority of people fail to remember any past lives simply because they have had none. That seems a sensible suggestion. Thus, it is doubtful that the appeal to past-life recall supports the claim that *every person* is reincarnated—what we might call "universal reincarnation." Perhaps only a very small percentage of persons experience reincarnation.

2. As far as I can tell, the documented cases of past-life recall provide no solid evidence for the law of karma. Of course, even people who

reject the doctrine of karma often give credence to the proverb that one reaps what one sows. But they take this not as an exceptionless dictum, only as a rough generalization or approximation: "*Other things being equal*, good behavior usually pays off for the agent (in the long run); bad behavior usually doesn't." But other things aren't always equal—tragic accidents, natural disasters, and wicked acts often cause apparently undeserved suffering.

3. A theist might allow that God, for reasons of his own (e.g., so that a person can perform some special task or so that an injustice might be rectified), may occasionally grant someone a second life. This sort of possibility suggests one way in which the *reported* cases of past-life recall could fail to be representative of all lives.

4. It seems to me that many of the past-life recall cases cannot reasonably be regarded as fraudulent, but it doesn't follow that reincarnation is the best explanation of the phenomena. For example, some cases are likely cases of cryptomnesia, that is, the information reported was acquired through some ordinary means, but the reporter has forgotten how it was obtained. And some cases may be cases of mental telepathy.[24]

5. Reports of past lives are more easily obtained (and apparently much more common) in those parts of the world in which the belief in re-incarnation is widespread (such as India, Thailand, and Sri Lanka).[25] This suggests the possibility that the reports are strongly influenced by cultural factors. But I think it would be a mistake to turn this reasonable caution into a staunch skepticism. As Stevenson notes: "Children who claim to remember previous lives have been found in every part of the world where they have been looked for."[26]

These brief remarks about the cases of past-life recall certainly do not support any firm conclusions. But I suggest the following: (a) Many of the reports are not fraudulent; they are sincere and, in my view, at least some of them may rationally be believed.[27] (b) On the other hand, many of the past-life recall cases *could* be cases of cryptomnesia or telepathy. (c) Most importantly, the past-life recall cases provide no significant support for the law of karma, nor do they provide solid support for *universal* reincarnation, as far as I can see.

To sum up, it seems to me that the strongest argument for reincarnation is the argument from past-life recall. The other arguments are open to fairly strong objections—or else, as in the case of the appeal to sacred texts, seem under analysis to depend ultimately on an appeal to past-life recall. And while the appeal to past-life recall may justify the belief that reincarnation *sometimes* occurs, it seems to me that it does not justify a belief in universal reincarnation; nor does it justify a belief in the doctrine of karma.

REINCARNATION AND PERSONAL IDENTITY

A person is an entity that is capable of thinking, knowing, making choices, and acting.[28] And the doctrine of reincarnation affirms that one and the same person can have multiple lives, with each life involving a different body. But this raises a deep and controversial philosophical issue concerning the identity of persons over time: If a person X exists at a time T and something Y exists at another time T*, what must be the case in order for X to be identical with Y (or, in other words, under what conditions is X one and the same entity as Y)?[29] Depending on how one answers this question, reincarnation may seem impossible. For example, Paul Edwards argues as follows:

> Bodily continuity and memory seem to be the two major constituents of personal identity. If a later person, B, whose body is obviously not identical with that of an earlier individual, A, also fails to remember experiencing or doing anything as A, B cannot be said to be the same person as A. The total absence of memories, even of the possibility of bringing any memories back by means of hypnosis or free association, does not destroy identity if the individual has the same body. However, if we do not have the same body, and of course in putative reincarnation cases we do not, the absence of memory does destroy personal identity: nothing that could constitute identity is left.[30]

Notice that Edwards's argument leaves the possibility of reincarnation open in cases of past-life recall, for in such cases memory would apparently ground personal identity *assuming that the memories are genuine.* Note also that Edwards's argument allows that person B existing at time T can be identical with a person A existing at an earlier time T*, even if B has total amnesia and remembers nothing of her existence at T*, *provided that B has the same body as A.* But, of course, if B is a reincarnation of A, B has a different body than A. So if Edwards's argument is sound, anyone who does not remember any past life is not a reincarnation of a previously existing individual.

In order to assess Edwards's argument, we need to examine the main theories of personal identity. Let's begin by noting that statements of the form "A is identical with B" are ambiguous in ordinary English. "A is identical with B" can mean "A is one and the same individual as B." For example, in a courtroom the judge and jury need to determine whether the defendant is identical with the person who committed the crime; is he *one and the same individual* as the person who performed the deed in question? (Obviously, it wouldn't do to convict the defendant's identical twin, who is a distinct person from the defendant.) Philosophers call this *numerical identity.* On the other hand, looking at two cars of the same make, model, year, color, and so on, we might say, "They are identical." In this case we mean that the two distinct cars have all the same qualities. Philosophers call this *qualitative identity.* When we speak of identical twins, for example, we are clearly speaking of two distinct persons who are *qualitatively* identical (or nearly so), not *numerically* identical. For present purposes, our concern is with numerical identity. Even if there is a currently existing person who is *qualitatively* identical with a person who lived centuries ago, this would not necessarily be a case of reincarnation. The previously existing person might be a distinct person, like an identical twin. Person B is a reincarnation of A only if A and B are *numerically* identical—one and the same individual.

According to some philosophers, if a human person X exists at a time T, then something Y existing at another time T* is identical with X if and only if X and Y have the same body. Given the same-body view of personal identity, reincarnation is impossible. The statement, "Person X died and then some time later lived another life with a *different* body" is logically or metaphysically impossible if something must have X's body in order to be X.[31]

Of course, we do in practice identify people via their bodies. For example, in solving a crime, police will use evidence of "same body," such as fingerprints or DNA tests, as evidence of "same person." But thought experiments strongly suggest that the "same body" test could fail in conceivable cases. Take, for example, "brain switch" cases. Suppose Tom Cruise's brain is removed from his body and Matt Damon's brain is removed from his body; further suppose that subsequently Tom's brain is successfully transplanted into Matt's body and that Matt's brain is successfully transplanted into Tom's body. Tom's brain carries with it Tom's memories, knowledge, preferences, emotional tendencies, and so on, while Matt's brain carries with it Matt's memories, knowledge, preferences, emotional tendencies, and so on. With these givens, it is plausible to suppose that Tom now has Matt's body and Matt has Tom's body. Apparently, then, "same body" doesn't *necessarily* imply "same person."[32]

The "brain switch" thought experiment may suggest that if a person X exists at T, then something Y existing at another time T* is identical with X if and only if X and Y have the same brain. But the same-brain theory also seems doubtful. Try another thought experiment: Amy's heart stops beating, and her brain ceases to function; Amy is brain-dead and hence *dead*. But Amy's brain is placed in cold storage, and about a month later a mad scientist takes Amy's brain, reprograms it, and restarts it using his latest invention, called the Reanimator. The reprogramming of Amy's brain, however, is quite extensive. All of Amy's memories are erased. Whereas Amy spoke English, her brain is now programmed to speak Korean. Whereas Amy was an introvert, her brain is now programmed for extroversion. Whereas Amy loved reading, classical music, and high art, her brain is now programmed to despise these things. Whereas Amy was hard-working and honest, her brain is now programmed for laziness and dishonesty. Amy's reprogrammed brain is transplanted in the body of a person who is about to die of brain cancer. The cancerous brain is removed, discarded, and replaced with Amy's brain, which is restarted via the Reanimator. Of course, the mad scientist has done something shocking, but the question is, "Has Amy come back to life?" And that seems doubtful. Isn't it more plausible to say that Amy remains dead but her brain has been used to bring a new person into existence? If so, then the same-brain theory of personal identity does not seem to be right.

Here is another problem for the same-brain theory. We know that large portions of a person's brain can sometimes be surgically removed and yet the person survives the operation. In fact, it is even possible for a person to have one of the hemispheres of his or her brain removed (in a hemispherectomy) and to survive the operation. But after the operation, does the patient have the same brain as before—even though half of his or her original brain has been removed and discarded? If the answer is no, the same-brain theorist (by implication) denies that the person survives the operation. But in such cases, if the surgery is successful, the patient retains his or her memories, preferences, beliefs, mental skills, and character traits. This being so, it isn't plausible to say that the patient does not survive the operation. On the other hand, suppose the answer to the question is yes—the person does have the same brain after the operation. In that case, it would seem possible, in principle, to transplant the right hemisphere of a person's brain into one body (from which the brain has just been removed) and to transplant the left hemisphere of the same person's brain into another body (from which the brain has just been removed). Call the person whose brain is removed, halved, and transplanted A and the resulting two persons B and C. B and C both have the same brain that A had, but they cannot both be identical to A. For if B is identical to A and C is identical to A, then B is identical to C. (The identity relation is transitive, like the relation of equality in math: If $x = z$ and $y = z$, then $x = y$.) But B and C are not identical; for example, if B dies of a disease or is killed, C may still go on living. And B and C may perform different acts and have different experiences. So "same brain" apparently does not necessarily guarantee "same person."[33]

Given the problems with the same-body and same-brain theories of personal identity, many philosophers opt for a psychological continuity theory. In this view, if person X exists at time T and something Y exists at another time T*, then X is identical with Y if and only if X and Y are psychologically continuous to a suitable degree. Naturally, the notion of psychological continuity needs some elaboration. Consider my psychological states and characteristics of yesterday. I had certain beliefs, certain desires, certain preferences, certain emotions, certain memories, certain skills and abilities. States and characteristics of these types may stay the same over time, or they may change in familiar ways. Yesterday I believed that $2 + 2 = 4$, and I still believe that today, but as I listened to the news this morning I acquired some new beliefs about what's going on in the world. Yesterday I spoke English, and I'm still doing so today, but today I learned some new words in German. Yesterday I saw a deer; today I remember seeing that deer. Of course, I am psychologically linked to the person I was yesterday to a very high degree since I have retained most of the memories, beliefs, preferences, and skills I had yesterday. I am also psychologically linked to the ten-year-old me, but to a much lesser degree. I remember relatively few of my experiences as a ten-year-old, and my emotional life as an adult is very different from that of my ten-year-old self. In addition, my ten-year-old self had none of the philosophical training I later acquired in college and graduate school. However, in spite of the vast differences between my ten-year-old and adult selves, if we trace my life back day by day, there is very great psychological continuity from each day to the next. It is important to add that psychological continuity involves certain *causal connections* between my previous states and abilities and my current states and abilities. For example, if I had not had the ability to speak English fluently yesterday, I would not have that ability today. And if I had not seen the deer yesterday, I would not remember seeing it today.

Is reincarnation possible given psychological continuity theories? It is possible if and only if there is "a suitable degree" of psychological continuity from one life to another. In the reported cases of past-life recall, a suitable degree of psychological continuity may be present (assuming that the reports are true). But memory is one of the most important aspects of psychological continuity, and most people have no memory of any past life or lives. Even so, there could still be significant psychological continuity in terms of character traits, preferences, goals or purposes, desires, and so on, from one life to the next. (The reincarnated person would then be similar to a person with total amnesia.) Leaving aside the past-life recall cases, however, there seems to be no way to know whether there is any psychological continuity (let alone how much) between the life of a person who has died and that of any person who exists at some later time. (Keep in mind that two *distinct* persons may have similar desires, beliefs, emotional reactions, purposes, and character traits; hence, similarity of psychological states is not necessarily solid evidence of numerical identity.) More importantly, what might be the causal connection between the mental states of X, who just died, and the mental states of some person Y who exists at a later time? Believers in reincarnation might claim that the law of karma somehow provides the causal linkage. Such a claim cannot be empirically verified, of course, but if it is possibly true, then reincarnation is apparently possible given the psychological continuity theory of personal identity.

Let's now consider some objections to the psychological continuity theory. First, psychological continuity comes in degrees. Other things being equal, a person with severe amnesia has less of it than a person who is not suffering from amnesia. Similarly, a person with significant brain damage may well have a lot less psychological continuity than a person with a healthy, undamaged brain. And the fact that psychological continuity comes in degrees leads to a problem for psychological continuity theories. Suppose that Y has a very high degree of psychological continuity with X; now gradually reduce the degree of continuity. Eliminate memories; eliminate many preferences, desires, and purposes; alter character traits; and so on: Y becomes less and less psychologically continuous with X. Indeed, Y is only partially continuous with X, but person Y cannot be partially identical to person X, for identity does not come in degrees. Just consider that a defendant either is or is not the person who committed the crime. Even if the defendant has changed a lot— say, he has undergone a dramatic religious conversion—the question remains, "Is he, or is he not, the person who committed the act in question?" It would be absurd for a defense attorney to suggest that the defendant is only half (or some other fraction) of the person who committed the crime. So can we properly analyze the personal identity relation in terms of psychological continuity? Can a concept that does not come in degrees (personhood) be reduced to one that does (psychological continuity)? Not clearly.

Second, the split-brain thought experiments also lead to difficulties for psychological continuity theories. Suppose that person A's brain is removed, the right and left hemispheres are separated, and then they are transplanted into two different bodies, with the resultant persons B and C. B and C have the same memories as A, the same feelings, the same preferences, the same skills, the same emotional reactions, and so on. Thus, B and C are equally candidates for being the same person as A, according to the psychological continuity theory. But they cannot both be A. For if B is identical to A and C is identical with A, then B is identical with C. Clearly, however, B and C are not identical, for one might die while the other goes on living. Or they might both stay alive but have different experiences and perform different actions.

Here is a third problem for psychological continuity theories. Suppose that we had a device that could do two things: It could erase the mental contents of a brain, and it could transfer the mental contents of one brain to another brain. Call the device the Brain Eraser. (Think of the Brain Eraser as analogous to a device that can erase the contents of a computer drive and can also copy the contents of one computer drive to another computer drive.) Now, suppose a mad scientist uses the Brain Eraser to erase the mental contents of my brain; all of my memories, preferences, skills, knowledge, and so on are erased. (Not a good day for me!) Next, the mad scientist uses the Brain Eraser to erase the mental content of your brain and to transfer that content to my brain. Would you survive this operation? (How much are you willing to bet that you would survive it?) Not everyone responds in the same way to this thought experiment, but many think either that you would not survive the operation or that it is doubtful that you would survive it. If this response is on the right track, the psychological continuity theory seems dubious at best. Note, too, that if this objection to the psychological continuity theory is a good one, then—from the standpoint of the psychological continuity theory—the very possibility of reincarnation seems doubtful.[34]

At this point, a defender of reincarnation may claim that X is the same person as Y if and only if X and Y have the same soul, where a soul is a nonphysical entity capable of conscious mental states such as beliefs, emotions, desires, thoughts, memories, and choices. But questions also arise about the same-soul theory of personal identity. For example, in thinking about universal reincarnation, we must allow for the possibility that there will be little or no psychological continuity (at least in some cases) from one life to the next. Suppose that a soul has none of your memories, none of your distinctive character traits, none of your distinctive goals or preferences, and so on; could such a soul be you? A yes answer here seems no more plausible than it was in the case of the same-brain theory. (Recall the discussion of Amy's case.)

At this point we have briefly examined the main theories of personal identity. And they all seem to be problematic. Moreover, our discussion seems to raise doubts about the very possibility of reincarnation. However, there is an important idea we have yet to consider, an idea first articulated by the medieval philosopher John Duns Scotus. Scotus argued for a distinction between qualitative properties, which can be shared by individuals (e.g., having preferences, desires, or neurons) and non-qualitative properties, which can be possessed by only one individual, such as *being Abraham Lincoln* or *being identical to Cleopatra*. Philosophers call these non-qualitative properties *haecceities* (hex-ay-uh-tees), a technical term based on the Latin word "haec" for "this." A haecceity is a "this-ness," the property of being *this* particular individual.

Some philosophers reject the idea that there are such properties as haecceities, but others think the idea makes sense and helps us understand the issue of identity. For example, if a soul, body, or brain can possess the property of *being Abraham Lincoln*, it could presumably possess that property over time, in spite of undergoing many changes, even dramatic changes. And if the property of *being Abraham Lincoln* can be transferred from one life form to another, Abraham Lincoln could be reincarnated, at least in principle. Such a transfer might be most plausible on the assumption that each person has a soul that can be transferred from one body to another; if each soul has a haecceity, reincarnation would seem to be possible. At any rate, Edwards's argument against the possibility of reincarnation does not take account of the possibility that each person has a soul with its own haecceity.

Would the concept of a haecceity help in split-brain cases? Maybe. Suppose that A's brain is halved, the right hemisphere is transplanted in the body of B (whose brain has been removed and discarded), and the left hemisphere is transplanted into the body of C (whose brain has been removed and discarded). Perhaps one of the resulting persons has the haecceity of *being A*. Of course, we would not *know* whether B has that property; nor would we *know* whether C has it. But in spite of the limitations on our knowledge, perhaps B has inherited the property of *being A*; if so, B is identical with A. And perhaps C has become an entirely new person through the transplant process, with his or her own haecceity, in which case C is a distinct person from A (and B).

At this point, we've seen that the standard theories of personal identity are problematic. And some of the problems raise questions about the very possibility of reincarnation. But let me offer two observations at this point. First, in spite of the difficulties with the standard theories of personal identity, I think it would be a serious mistake to jettison the concept of personhood, for this concept plays a key role in our thinking about morality. For example, if I am to praise or blame someone for doing something, I must assume that the person I'm praising or blaming is *the very same one* who performed the act in question. Second, while the concept of a haecceity may seem strange, we may be driven to it by the hard questions about personal identity. And the concept of a haecceity, as applied to the issue of personal identity, seems to leave open the possibility of reincarnation.

KARMA AND REINCARNATION: CRITICAL QUESTIONS

Let us now consider whether the doctrines of karma and reincarnation, taken together, provide a plausible explanation of the suffering in the world. To what extent can suffering be explained as punishment the sufferer deserves for wrong acts she has performed, either in her current life or in a previous life? First, some have questioned whether punishment is just if the wrongdoer has no memory of her wrong acts.[35] And clearly many people have no memory of committing any wrong acts in a previous life So, is reincarnation irrelevant to an explanation of the suffering of such people? I don't think so, because not remembering an act does not necessarily eliminate responsibility for it. Goldschmidt and Seacord give this example: "Consider a war criminal who has escaped detection until the end of his life, at which point he has such advanced Alzheimer's disease that not only has he no memory of his crimes but he cannot even be made to understand that he is guilty. Nevertheless, punishing the war criminal is just."[36] Or at least arguably just. In this type of case, the punishment would not serve a rehabilitative function, of course, but it could still serve the purpose of retribution — giving the wrongdoer his just deserts. To press the point a bit further, a person driving while intoxicated might harm or kill a pedestrian but not remember the incident. And clearly, "I don't remember" is not a cogent defense; punishment would still be justified.

Second, does the combination of karma and reincarnation lead to an infinite regress of explanation? John Hick has argued that it does:

> Either there is a first life, characterized by initial human differences, or else (as in the Vedāntic philosophy) there is no first life but a beginningless regress of incarnations. In the latter case the explanation of the inequalities of our present life is endlessly postponed and never achieved, for we are no nearer to an ultimate explanation of the circumstances of our present birth when we are told that they are consequences of a previous life, if that previous life has in turn to be explained by reference to a yet previous life, and that by reference to another, and so on to an infinite regress. One can affirm the beginningless character of the soul's existence in this way, but one cannot then claim that it renders either intelligible or morally acceptable the inequalities found in our present human lot. The solution has not been produced but only postponed to infinity. If instead we were to postulate a first life (as Hinduism does not), we should then have to hold either that souls are created as identical psychic atoms or else as embodying, at least in germ, the differences that have subsequently developed. If the latter, the problem of human equality arises in full force at the point of initial creation; if the former, it arises as forcefully with regard to the environment that has produced all the manifold differences that have subsequently arisen between initially identical units.[37]

But Roy Perrett claims that Hick's argument is flawed: "Of course it is conceded that my previous life situation is to be explained by reference to my life before that, and so on. It is also true that the Indians believe this cycle of rebirths to be beginningless (*anadi*) and thus there is an infinite regress. But it is not a vicious one, for there is no particular instance of suffering that is inexplicable."[38] This reply to Hick, however, seems less than adequate. One cannot provide an illuminating explanation of the suffering of a person's present life simply by postulating more instances of the same sort of thing (i.e., prior lives that contain suffering and lead causally to the present suffering). Nevertheless, I think Hick's argument fails. The karmic theorist explains the present suffering as punishment for some past wrong action, and that wrong action is assumed to be due to a free choice *that is not itself fully caused by some previous event.* So the karmic theorist appeals to a prior free choice and is not simply postulating more instances of the type of suffering that needs to be explained.

That said, we need to ask why the karmic theorist usually does not postulate a first life. Simply put, if one postulates a first life, one needs to explain how it originated, but no such explanation is needed if the cycle of births and deaths is beginningless. From this perspective, reincarnationists view the cycle of births and deaths rather in the way that theists view God's existence, as without a beginning.

Third, it does seem to me that the claim that each human has already had infinitely many past lives is problematic. According to contemporary science, our universe began (with a "Big Bang") about 13.7 billion years ago. And life has been present on earth for about 3.5 billion years. These are big numbers, of course, but they are finite. So to defend the claim that each human person has had infinitely many past lives, it seems that the reincarnationist is forced to postulate lives existing in some state of affairs that obtained (without beginning) prior to the existence of our universe—such as an infinite series of previous universes. But such a postulate is speculative, and speculative add-ons decrease the plausibility of a hypothesis.

Fourth, given the combination of karma and reincarnation, can't those bent on harming others (such as terrorists) reasonably see themselves as the agents of karma, and so reasonably see their actions as just? There are at least two replies to this objection: (1) Suppose a murderer is about to receive the death penalty, and suppose for the sake of the argument that he fully deserves the death penalty—it is a just punishment. But as the prison guards are leading the murderer to the gallows, a vigilante rushes forward and shoots him. The murderer dies immediately, thus receiving his just deserts. But in a standard view, the vigilante has no right to administer this punishment; it is not his role. That role must be assigned to someone by the appropriate authorities.[39] Now, this reply raises the question "How does karma assign the role of punisher (when the cause of suffering is a person, as opposed to, say, a natural disaster)?" Perhaps the answer is that karma never assigns this role to anyone. Of course, punishments are often delivered by persons, given the doctrine of karma. But the human punishers are like the vigilante in the above case, without a right to administer the punishment, even though it is just. (Exceptions could be made here for cases in which harm is morally justified—for example, in protecting the innocent or in self-defense.) (2) Terrorists (and, more generally, those bent on harming others) usually do not have the intention of administering just punishment. Terrorists, in fact, deliberately harm *innocent* people for a political purpose. (Even if the terrorists are seeking to correct an injustice, they are not intending to treat their *victims* justly.) And to be morally justified, a human punisher must have the right intention.[40] These claims about intention seem right, but they point to a further problem. Suppose that someone has the right intention. He thinks that many humans deserve punishment because they are immoral. He intends to punish as many as he can. Moreover, he reasons as follows: "If I try to punish anyone who doesn't deserve it, the law of karma will ensure that I do not succeed. So I will go ahead and punish as many as I can." Now, this reasoning is surely perverse, but where does it go wrong given the doctrines of karma and reincarnation? As far as I can see, the only available reply is a return to the claim that such a punisher is a vigilante, taking on a role he has not been assigned by the proper moral authority. So the point about having a properly assigned role seems the crucial one here.

Fifth, does the combination of karma and reincarnation have implausible implications about free will or human agency?[41] Suppose that Bloggs wishes to inflict harm on someone, perhaps for revenge. The law of karma may allow Bloggs to inflict the harm if it is deserved (using Bloggs as an instrument of justice), but if the harm isn't deserved, Bloggs will be prevented (one way or another) from inflicting the harm. I submit, however, that it is very implausible to suggest that human free will (or human agency) is limited in this way—that is, that something will always interfere with anyone's attempt to inflict undeserved harm.

Sixth, does the combination of karma and reincarnation lead logically to some serious distortions of our moral attitudes toward suffering? Suppose we look back at a historical example of great suffering, say, of many children dying of starvation in a famine. There is nothing we can do about it now, of course, but how should we view the suffering of the children? Well, how should we view the suffering of a vicious criminal whose punishment is exactly what he deserves? We generally don't lament such suffering, *assuming it is truly deserved*. Of course, we wish the criminal had never violated the law in the first place, but given that he did, it is good that he hasn't gone scot-free. Justice is served, and that's a good thing. So isn't that how we should view the suffering of the children who starved to death, given the doctrines of karma and reincarnation? If the law of karma ensures that each instance of suffering is deserved by the sufferer, the children got exactly what they deserved. But surely this is a terrible distortion of moral thinking. The starvation and deaths of the children ought to be lamented and seen as tragic. And if the combination of karma and reincarnation leads logically to viewing the starvation and deaths of the children as we view the punishment of criminals, can we reasonably and in good conscience endorse this combination? It seems to me that we cannot.

Seventh, the combination of karma and reincarnation requires us to accept some rather shocking claims regarding just punishments, among them, for example:

a. All the prisoners in Auschwitz deserved the suffering inflicted on them.
b. Everyone who has ever been burned at the stake deserved being so treated.
c. All persons who have been raped deserved being raped.
d. All children who have ever been abused deserved the abusive treatment they received.

Claims such as these give rise to what Kaufman has called the *proportionality problem*.[42] Just punishments must be proportional to the crimes. But can you believe that the victims of Auschwitz all committed some wrong act—possibly in another life, of course—*equivalent in gravity* to confining someone to a Nazi death camp? Can you believe that everyone who was ever burned at the stake committed some wrong act (possibly in another life) morally equivalent to burning someone at the stake? Can you believe that every rape victim has committed some act (possibly in another life) as wicked as rape? Can you believe that every victim of child abuse has committed an act (possibly in another life) as heinous as child abuse? If you answer "No" to these questions, you are in effect saying that the law of karma does not uphold justice; in fact, it inflicts serious injustices. The punishments are not proportional; they are beyond what the recipients deserve.

Goldschmidt and Seacord, however, offer the following reply to the problem of proportionality: "There are powerful arguments for the view that we are much more morally culpable than we take ourselves to be. For instance, someone who prefers to watch a child drown in a shallow nearby pond than to get his pants wet is a monster, but if the arguments of Peter Singer and Peter Unger have any force, then we are all very much like that person in allowing the starvation of very many children in Africa instead of donating some—indeed, a large proportion—of our income to them."[43] Now, a person who lets a child drown because saving her would involve getting some of his clothing wet is, by his inaction, highly blameworthy. And if we are all on that level, morally speaking, we all deserve to be punished—rather severely, I would assume. I suspect that this is the best response karmic theorists can give to the proportionality problem. But it depends on the Singer-Unger assessment of human depravity, which is highly controversial. Our ordinary, common-sense view of morality is not nearly so harsh in its evaluation of persons. And since it is highly implausible to claim that all who suffer horribly have done something horrible in their current lives—think of children who suffer horribly, for example—the doctrine of karma forces us to postulate vast numbers of acts of great wickedness *for which we have no independent evidence.* That seems to me a questionable way to proceed. In any case, I submit that it remains difficult to believe that *everyone*—not just many or even most—who has suffered horribly has done something to deserve it in another life (if not in his or her current life).

Eighth, even if we set aside the proportionality problem, there is another problem—a very serious one—lurking in the same vicinity. We might call it the problem of cruel and wicked punishments. Just punishments must not only be proportional; they must also not be "cruel and unusual," as the saying goes. I take this to mean that certain punishments, even if arguably proportional to the crimes, are themselves very cruel and wicked and so cannot serve the end of justice. Moreover, burning someone at the stake, confining someone to a death camp, raping someone, and abusing a child all count as "cruel and unusual" punishments. These are cruel and wicked acts that cannot, as punishments, serve the end of justice. The point here, put bluntly, is that the law of karma (as here formulated) dishes out a lot of punishments that cannot serve the end of justice. In fact, it dishes out a lot of cruel and wicked punishments, for the law of karma is a law that employs a vast number of extremely wicked acts to deliver punishment. Remember, all suffering is deserved, according to the law of karma (as I have formulated it), including all suffering caused by the most cruel and wicked acts in human history.[44] Far from being a correct law of retributive justice, then, the law of karma (as here formulated) appears to be a terribly unjust law.

Now let us consider one last problem with the combination of karma and reincarnation, taken as an alternative metaphysic to theism.[45] Given that karma and reincarnation hold in the absence of any personal God, the universe is governed not only by a complex of physical laws (such as the law of gravity, the laws of electromagnetism, and so on), but also by the impersonal moral law of karma. And think of all the factors the law of karma must coordinate or organize. It must take into account every act, every intention, and every choice of every moral agent. It must *correctly* categorize each act, each intention, each attitude, each character trait, and so on, as morally right (or good), morally wrong (or evil), or morally neutral. In addition, it must assess each agent's overall moral record and accurately determine the rewards and punishments he or she deserves. Then it must link each soul (or person) up with the appropriate body (i.e., the body it deserves) for its next life. Furthermore, the law of karma must ensure that the embodied agent is placed in the right set of circumstances so that it will receive exactly what it deserves and justice will be served. It is, I suggest, literally incredible to suppose that an impersonal law, analogous to a law of nature, can perform all these functions. Such a complex organization of factors *serving a moral end* cries out for explanation in terms of an extremely knowledgeable and powerful Intelligence, that is, a personal God. In short, the moral order postulated by non-theistic reincarnation would (if it existed) paradoxically provide evidence for theism — or at least for a personal God of exceptional knowledge and power who guarantees justice.

But if God exists, there is no need for the law of karma. A just, loving, omnipotent, and omniscient God can establish an appropriate moral order without the assistance of any independent, impersonal law of karma. Moreover, if God is omnipotent, there can be no law of karma that is independent in the sense of operating beyond God's control. So if one believes that God exists, one should reject belief in the law of karma for two reasons: (1) It is an unnecessary complication to one's system of beliefs, and (2) it is inconsistent with one's beliefs about God's power.

Let's now take stock. Does the combination of karma and reincarnation (minus a personal God) provide us with a better metaphysic than theism does? That seems doubtful. First, as we've seen, the arguments in favor of karma and *universal* reincarnation are not strong. Second, the moral order postulated by the karma-plus-reincarnation view would in fact provide strong evidence for a personal God. Third, the karma-plus-reincarnation view is fraught with serious problems:

a.   The claim—made by most who believe in reincarnation—that we have all already had an infinite number of lives, comports poorly with the scientific evidence that our universe has a temporally finite history tracing back to the "Big Bang."
b.   Given the law of karma, there are mysterious and implausible limitations on human free will or agency; namely, we can never inflict undeserved suffering, try as we might.
c.   The karma-plus-reincarnation view leads to morally wrong attitudes toward apparently morally decent people who have suffered horribly in the past—and even toward children who have suffered horribly. Instead of regarding these instances of suffering as lamentable tragedies, we should view them as we view instances of criminal punishment in which criminals receive the punishment they fully deserve.
d.   The karma-plus-reincarnation view faces the problem of proportionality. Can we really believe that everyone who has suffered horribly has done something horrible enough to deserve that suffering?
e.   The karma-plus-reincarnation view faces the problem of cruel and wicked punishments. Given the law of karma, the cruelest acts in history, such as torture, child abuse, and rape, are entirely appropriate ways of administering justice.

Given these problems, I submit that the reincarnation-plus-karma view provides an implausible explanation of much of the suffering in the world. I grant that traditional theism fails to explain significant amounts and kinds of suffering, but it is not clear that the reincarnation-plus-karma view is better.

Would theism have a better response to the problem of evil and suffering if it were combined with reincarnation and karma? For the reasons I've just given, it seems to me that the answer is "Apparently not." In addition, I've argued that karma and reincarnation are unnecessary postulates if there is a just God fully capable of establishing a moral order in accordance with his own will and plan. Furthermore, a law of karma existing independently of God (and out of his control) is inconsistent with the idea of an all-powerful God.

The problem of evil and suffering is indeed a problem for theism. I have said what I could about this problem in chapter 3 of this book. But part of what I argued there (and in chapter 11) is that theism isn't the only worldview that struggles to account for the phenomena of evil and suffering; so does naturalism, for example. And we are now in a position to see that the karma-plus-reincarnation view also comes up short as an explanation of these phenomena. Yes, the karma-plus-reincarnation view, in one sense, has a ready answer for certain tough questions, such as "Why do little children suffer?" But the answer is "They deserve it," and I have argued that this answer does not hold up well under scrutiny. In closing, may I suggest that the comparative response to the problem of evil is on the right track? Theism falters in explaining a full range of evil and suffering, but so do alternative metaphysical schemes such as naturalism and the karma-plus-reincarnation view.

EPILOGUE

Let's take stock. This book provides tools for constructing a theistic worldview. Chapter 1 contrasts theism with its main contemporary rival, naturalism. The overarching claim in chapters 1 and 2 is that naturalism is too simple; it leaves too much unexplained or inadequately explained—for example, the existence of physical reality, the fine-tuning of the universe, free will (and hence moral responsibility), and the overriding reasons thesis (i.e., if an act is one's moral duty, one has an overriding reason to perform the act, and if an act is morally wrong, one has an overriding reason not to perform it). I have argued that theism provides a better explanation of these phenomena.

Critics of theism claim that it has serious problems of its own, of course. First, the problem of evil: can theism account for the amounts and kinds of evil and suffering we find in the world? The main thesis of chapter 3 is that much evil and suffering can be accounted for by means of a soul-making theodicy. It is admitted, however, that the soul-making theodicy leaves much suffering unexplained, for example, the suffering of those who die at a young age and the suffering of those with very severe mental impairments.

Chapter 3 also introduces the comparative response to the problem of evil. According to the comparative response, while theism admittedly fails to explain *all* of the evil and suffering in the world, the main alternatives to theism (such as naturalism) falter in explaining evil and suffering *in terms consistent with their philosophical underpinnings*; hence, the problem of evil is not a good reason to reject theism in favor of the main alternative views. The comparative response is briefly illustrated in chapter 3 but worked out in detail in chapters 10, 11, and 12. Throughout the book I have emphasized that philosophy is fundamentally a comparative enterprise; one needs constantly to compare alternative views and to assess their strengths and weaknesses.

Chapter 4 develops another idea relevant to the problem of evil: Given that an almighty, all-knowing being exists, there are strong reasons to suppose that such a being would also be thoroughly good. For such a being would know that the overriding reasons thesis is true. Therefore, such a being would know that the strongest reasons always support doing what is morally required. And an almighty being can do what is morally required simply by willing to do so. Hence, the suggestion that such a being would will to do wrong is mystifying. Why act on weaker reasons when one knows that stronger reasons apply and one can act on the stronger reasons simply by willing to do so? Here some have suggested that an evil God might be irrational. But the hypothesis of an irrational God compares poorly with traditional theism because *there's no telling what an irrational God might do*; hence, the hypothesis of an irrational God fails to provide a plausible explanation of the phenomena involved in the cumulative case for traditional theism (such as contingent beings, the fine-tuning of the universe, and the free will required for moral responsibility). Furthermore, the hypothesis of an evil God is self-defeating, for on this hypothesis, all our beliefs would come to us through channels created and controlled by an evil being. On this assumption, there would be strong reason to doubt that our cognitive faculties are reliable, for an evil being might well wish to systematically deceive us about important things. But then, if we believe an evil God exists, we have reason to doubt this very belief.

Chapters 5 and 6 take up the problem of divine hiddenness: If a God of love exists, why doesn't he make his existence clear to everyone? I have linked the problem of divine hiddenness to the problem of evil and suffering. There is a general problem of ignorance. There are many things we humans do not know. The relevant evidence may be very hard or even impossible to obtain. And in many cases knowledge would be beneficial—for example, knowing the cure for a disease, knowing whether (or when) war is justified, or knowing whether (and whom) to marry. Why would a loving God leave us in such ignorance? This, it seems to me, is just one aspect of the problem of evil and suffering. I have suggested that a soul-making theodicy can account for much human ignorance, because coping with ignorance requires many virtues: patience, hope, diligence, modesty, the willingness to cooperate, humility, tolerance of disagreement, and so on. Beyond this I have suggested that the belief that God exists is not necessarily a blessing. Religious convictions can have negative effects; for example, the belief that God exists causes some to live in fear of judgment, it apparently makes some people self-righteous and intolerant, it can play havoc with moral motivation, and so on. Finally, I have claimed that via divine hiddenness, God can avoid making the choice between devotion to holy love and its alternatives (e.g., love of self), the choice between being reasonable and being unreasonable; this leaves those who live in opposition to holy love free of one kind of strong pressure to conform to God's will. And a loving God might very well want created agents to follow the way of holy love simply or primarily because they see that love is good.

Many religious believers assume that there would be no objective right and wrong if there were no God who issues commands. In chapter 7 I have claimed that this assumption is mistaken. It seems to me that certain moral claims, if true, are necessarily true. They cannot be false under any circumstance; for example, if human beings exist, it is wrong to torture them just for sadistic pleasure. I have suggested that morality is, at least in large part, about human fulfillment or flourishing. Thus I have provided a natural law theory of ethics. From this perspective, it is a basic moral principle that we should promote human flourishing. (I have, however, acknowledged that this principle needs to be restricted in its application in cases in which individual rights would be violated.) Given the natural law view, "Love your neighbor as yourself" is an entirely sensible principle because one who loves cares about the best interests of the one loved. Furthermore, I have suggested that a natural law theory provides a viable alternative to the two best-known ethical theories: Kant's deontological view and utilitarianism.

Chapters 8 and 9 concern the issue of divine foreknowledge and human free will. Earlier I argued that naturalism has difficulty accounting for free will, specifically, for free will in the incompatibilist sense. If theism leads us to deny that humans have free will (in this sense), theism has a quite serious flaw, in my opinion.

Of course, the issue of free will is one of the most hotly disputed philosophical issues. Many deny that we humans have free will in the incompatibilist sense. But it seems to me that moral responsibility requires free will in this sense. If we blame a person for some wrong act, say, robbing a bank, aren't we assuming that a genuine alternative was open to him? Unfortunately, many philosophers answer this question negatively, citing so-called Frankfurt cases, but (in chapter 2) I have explained why I think these cases do not prove the intended point.

If an infallible God believes I'll do X at time T, can I refrain from doing X at time T? Many theologians and philosophers have answered this question affirmatively, but I have tried to explain why I think their views do not hold up under scrutiny. In short, it seems to me that the idea of an infallible God who has *exhaustive* knowledge of the future is an idea that leads to determinism. Fortunately, however, theists do not have to claim that God has *exhaustive* knowledge of the future. From the perspective of open theism, simply by creating humans and endowing them with incompatibilist free will, God makes the future to some extent unknowable (even for himself). Of course, given that God knows each person's history, character traits, and current thoughts, he may often have true beliefs about what someone will *probably* do. But free creatures have "the power to refrain." Nevertheless, God remains sovereign because an almighty being has the power to interfere in human life, including the power to temporarily suspend a person's free will. Furthermore, an almighty God can know as much of the future as suits his purposes simply by deciding that certain things *will* take place.

No worldview is complete without a theory of the mind (or soul). And advances in neuroscience have convinced many (including many learned theists) that humans do not have a soul (that is, a non-physical soul). Chapters 10 and 11 explore the main theories of the mind or soul. In these chapters I summarize standard objections to physicalist views of the mind and suggest that, on the assumption that humans have (incompatibilist) free will, there is some reason to suppose that humans have a soul.

Chapters 10 and 11 also develop the comparative response to the problem of evil by arguing that naturalism, with its physicalist theories of the mind, runs into difficulties in accounting for the phenomena of evil and suffering. Here again I have argued that naturalism fails to account for the kind of free will needed for moral responsibility. And assuming that the phenomena of evil include wrong acts for which people are *morally responsible*, this is a noteworthy failing. But beyond this, I have argued that naturalistic theories of the mind leave significant parts of the phenomenon of suffering unexplained. The story here is unavoidably complex because there are many different naturalistic theories of the mind. But in chapter 10 I explained that reductive physicalism has well-known problems accounting for qualia, such as the feeling of pain or the feeling of great fear. In chapter 11 I argued that non-reductive physicalism seems unable to explain certain apparent relevant facts about mental causation, for example, that chronic *pain* can cause a person to despair or even to commit suicide. Or that the *belief* that a loved one has died can cause one to feel miserable. The point here is that while the phenomena of evil and suffering undoubtedly pose problems for theism, they pose important problems for naturalism, too. Thus, it is not clear that the problem of evil and suffering gives us a strong reason to prefer naturalism to theism.

Chapter 12 returns to the problem of evil and suffering but looks at it from a radically different perspective. The question is "Can a metaphysical view combining karma and reincarnation provide a better explanation of suffering than traditional theism can?" For example, could the suffering of young children and animals be explained as *deserved punishment* for wrongs committed in a previous life? I argued that an attempt to employ the ideas of karma and reincarnation *in this way* would lead to many difficulties. For one thing, it would commit us to some very implausible limitations on free will. (One could not inflict suffering unless it was deserved, assuming that all suffering is deserved as punishment for something the sufferer has done.) It would also lead to some distortions in our moral thinking, for example, instead of taking pity on those who suffer, we would view them as we view criminals who are getting their just deserts. A series of such implausible implications leads me to conclude that combining karma and reincarnation *for the purpose of explaining all suffering* yields no clear net advantage over traditional theism. (Of course, one need not combine the ideas of karma and reincarnation *for this purpose*; there are other ways of understanding karma and reincarnation; therefore, I have not claimed that these ideas are problematic regardless of how they are formulated.)

All in all, then, it seems to me that there is much to be said for a theistic worldview. Theism is not, of course, a popular position in the current philosophical community. But it is my hope that those who have found my arguments on the whole unconvincing may nevertheless come away from reading this book with a better understanding of the issues, and especially with a better understanding of the questions that both theism and naturalism must face.

NOTES

INTRODUCTION

1. I am not here assuming that all our beliefs can or should be based on evidence, where "evidence" takes the form of arguments. Like most philosophers, I take some beliefs to be properly basic, that is, rational (or known) without needing to be based on other beliefs. To take a simple example, I believe that trees exist, but I do not base this belief on an argument; nevertheless, my belief that trees exist is rational. (In this case, my belief is presumably grounded in sense experience, though not based on an argument.) Some philosophers hold that the belief that God exists can be properly basic. See, for example, Plantinga, *Warranted Christian Belief*, 167–98.

2. The evidence or grounds can include various types of religious experiences as well as philosophical and historical considerations.

ONE   Does God Exist? PART I

1. This definition paraphrases one offered by Wielenberg, "Omnipotence Again," 42.

2. It is important not to confuse the laws of nature with the laws of logic. For example, it is not a logical contradiction to say that a person died, was buried for a week, and then came back to life. But of course, such an event cannot happen if only natural causes are at work. Only a supernatural cause could raise someone from the dead. And laws of nature describe what happens when only natural causes are operative.

3. It has proven difficult for philosophers to produce an uncontroversial characterization of what it is to be physical. For an insightful discussion of this issue, see Markosian, "What Are Physical Objects?"

4. Theists typically claim that God is omnipresent. But this is not best understood as the claim that God is literally located everywhere; rather it should be understood as the claim that God knows what is going on at every location and God can bring about effects in every location.

5. Accounts of religious experience may in some sense locate God and even associate God with sensory images. For example, in Exodus 3 God reportedly speaks to Moses out of a burning bush. But I certainly don't think we are meant to suppose that God is a physical object located in the bush. I think we are rather meant to suppose that God caused sounds to come from within the bush.

6. Misunderstandings about the *quantum vacuum* of physical theory have led some to suppose that contemporary physics denies the principle that "nothing comes from nothing." (According to modern physics, virtual particles can "pop" into temporary existence in the quantum vacuum.) The word "vacuum" may suggest nothingness, but the quantum vacuum is not nothing; it is the lowest energy state of the quantum field. And the quantum field is a physical entity.

7. The example of utilitarianism is merely illustrative; naturalists have multiple options as regards ethical theories. We will consider some additional ethical theories in chapter 7.

8. Schellenberg, "What Divine Hiddenness Reveals." My outline of the hiddenness argument is a paraphrase. For a detailed presentation of the hiddenness argument, see Schellenberg, *Divine Hiddenness and Human Reason* and *Wisdom to Doubt*.

9. If you doubt this, it might be helpful to ask yourself what your religious views might have been had you been brought up in a culture in which the belief in God was lacking.

10. Cited in James, *Varieties of Religious Experience*, 68.

11. Brother Lawrence, *The Practice of the Presence of God*, 17.

12. Cited in Beardsworth, *A Sense of Presence*, 121.

13. Underhill, *Mysticism*, 242–43.

14. Cited in James, *Varieties of Religious Experience*, 67.

15. Underhill, *Mysticism*, 242.

16. Weil, *Waiting for God*, 24.

17. Ibid., 69.

18. My formulation of the principle of credulity is borrowed from Alston, "Religious Experience." For Alston's masterful, detailed discussion of religious experience, see Alston, *Perceiving God*.

19. I am not suggesting that the belief that trees exist is typically (if ever) based on an argument. I think that, for most or all of us, the belief that trees exist is a "starting point," that is, a basic belief (one not based on other beliefs). But I am suggesting that if the belief is challenged, it can be justified or defended along the lines I've outlined.

20. Webb, "Religious Experience."

21. Ibid.

22. My responses to objections B, C, D, and E owe a heavy debt to Alston, "Religious Experience," section 3.

23. To cite one specific case, Edmund Creffield, the leader of a small religious group in the state of Washington, claimed that God had ordered him to commit adultery. See Baldasty, *Vigilante Newspapers*, 61.

24. Not all scientists agree that the universe had a beginning. The noted physicist Stephen Hawking has argued for "the possibility that space-time was

finite but had no boundary, which means that it had no beginning." See *A Brief History of Time*, 116. For interesting critical comments on Hawking's view, see W. L. Craig, "Theism and Physical Cosmology," 419–22. For a more extended (and I think powerful) critique of Hawking's view, see Craig's "'What Place, Then, for a Creator?'" 288–300.

25. Hume, *Dialogues Concerning Natural Religion*, 55.

26. The main point of this paragraph is borrowed from Kripke, *Naming and Necessity*, 116–29. Before Kripke's work became well known, most philosophers denied that "Water is H_2O" is a necessary truth and that "Water is not H_2O" is a necessary falsehood. But if something is water, it must be H_2O, and if it is not H_2O, it cannot be water. Suppose we visited another planet and found something that looked, smelled, and tasted like water, but wasn't H_2O. Would we claim it was water? Surely not, though we might call it "fool's water" as we refer to "fool's gold."

27. For insightful discussions of the principle of sufficient reason, see Wainwright, *Philosophy of Religion*, 44–47, and Rowe, *Philosophy of Religion*, 19–28.

28. To put the point more technically, an explanation is complete when any attempt to go further "would result in no gain of explanatory power or prior probability." Swinburne, *Existence of God*, 86. We can assess the explanatory power of a hypothesis by asking, "*Assuming* the hypothesis is true, to what extent does it make the phenomenon (whatever we're trying to explain) likely, or unsurprising?" We can assess the prior probability of a hypothesis by asking (roughly) this question: "Without considering the phenomenon ('prior' to considering it), how plausible is the hypothesis?" For more on the distinction between explanatory power and prior probability, see chapter 4, under "Preliminaries."

29. This is just an illustration. Whether humans evolved from previously existing life forms or were specially created by God, the earliest humans were not begotten by human parents. The illustration is borrowed from Wainwright, *Philosophy of Religion*, 43.

30. This raises the question of "scientism," the philosophical view that we should believe only what is established via the scientific method. Scientism, though popular in some quarters, is self-defeating since it cannot be established via the scientific method. And in fact, anyone who wants a comprehensive worldview, including a plausible view of morality and moral responsibility, will be forced to employ philosophical arguments that do not exemplify the scientific method.

TWO   DOES GOD EXIST? PART II

1. Davies, *The Accidental Universe*, 89–91. Note: $1/10^{60}$ may also be written 10^{-60}.

2. Davies, *Superforce*, 242.

3. This point and the next are borrowed from McMullin, "Fine-Tuning the Universe?" 113.

4. Tegmark, "Parallel Universes," 46.

5. McMullin, "Fine-Tuning the Universe?" 113.

6. Koperski, *The Physics of Theism*, 59–60.

7. Ibid., 61.

8. "According to the Standard Model of particle physics, there are 20 or so free parameters whose values must be determined by experiment. . . . These parameters might just have well taken some other value." Ibid. For a more rigorous and detailed discussion of fine-tuning, see Leslie, *Universes*, esp. chapters 2 and 3.

9. This example is inspired by one provided by van Inwagen, *Metaphysics*, 135.

10. The basic idea here is borrowed from van Inwagen, though he states it differently and perhaps more cautiously: "Suppose that there is a certain fact that has no known explanation; suppose that one can think of a possible explanation of that fact, an explanation that (if only it were true) would be a very *good* explanation; then it is wrong to say that that event stands in no more need of an explanation than an otherwise similar event for which no such explanation is available." Ibid.

11. Craig, W. L., "Theism and Physical Cosmology," 423.

12. Polkinghorne, *Science and Theology*, 39. In some versions of the multiverse hypothesis, the universes are regarded as coexisting, isolated sub-regions in a greater physical reality.

13. The argument of this paragraph is borrowed from White, "Fine-Tuning and Multiple Universes," 260–76.

14. These types of cases owe a major debt to Frankfurt, "Alternate Possibilities and Moral Responsibility," 829–39.

15. This second point summarizes a response to the Frankfurt cases offered by Widerker, "Frankfurt's Attack on the Principle of Alternative Possibilities," 247–61.

16. Hasker, "The Foreknowledge Conundrum," 107.

17. van Inwagen, *An Essay on Free Will*, 56. We will examine a more rigorous version of the consequence argument in chapter 8 ("Is Divine Foreknowledge Compatible with Human Free Will? Part I").

18. Compatibilists may point out that, in a given case, the agent could have done otherwise if he had wanted to do otherwise. But could the agent have wanted to do otherwise? Not if his wants or desires were necessitated by the laws of nature operating on past conditions.

19. Draper, "Seeking But Not Believing," 201.

20. A famous example is the Harvard psychologist B. F. Skinner's *Beyond Freedom and Dignity*.

21. Might there be another possibility? We'll consider that question in chapter 11.

22. Does God make necessary truths true? That seems very doubtful. If God makes them true, then he could presumably make them false. But then

there is a circumstance in which they would be false (namely, one in which God decides to make them false), and so they aren't necessary truths after all. If a truth is not necessary, it is contingent, that is, it's true but could be false under different circumstances. Examples of contingent truths include "I exist," "Leo Tolstoy wrote *War and Peace*," and "The capital of Ohio is Columbus."

23. The case is borrowed from Layman, "God and the Moral Order," 307.

24. My argument here owes a debt to Swinburne, *The Existence of God*, 97–102.

THREE   Why Does God Permit Evil?

1. Rowe, "The Problem of Evil and Some Varieties of Atheism," 336.
2. Ibid., 337.
3. This point is borrowed from Hasker, *Providence*, 53–54.
4. This objection is borrowed from Schellenberg, *Wisdom to Doubt*, 301.
5. Ibid., 301–2.
6. For a defense of skeptical theism, see Daniel Howard-Snyder, "The Argument from Inscrutable Evil," 286–310.
7. Can we conceive of a world containing only physical entities? Many would say no, because in a world containing physical entities, there must be some number of them, and numbers do not seem to be physical entities. For example, it seems one could not eliminate the numbers by destroying physical objects.
8. The PT is especially problematic for those theists who accept the Bible as an authoritative text. For example, the main point of the book of Job in the Old Testament is that it is wrong to infer that those who suffer always deserve to suffer because of sins they have committed. Job suffers terribly, but within the biblical story it is made clear that his suffering is not punishment for sin.
9. "The son shall not suffer for the iniquity of the father, nor the father suffer for the iniquity of the son; the righteousness of the righteous shall be upon himself, and the wickedness of the wicked shall be upon himself" (Ezekiel 18:20).
10. See chapter 2 under "A Design Argument" for more details about what is involved in the claim that the universe is fine-tuned.
11. Hick, *Philosophy of Religion*, 45–46.
12. Ibid., 46. I am here loosely paraphrasing Hick.
13. Hasker, *Providence*, 33.
14. Ibid., 39.
15. Ibid.
16. Hasker, "Theism and Evolutionary Biology," 428.
17. van Lawick-Goodall, *Innocent Killers*, 13. Italics added.
18. A Creator may, of course, bring animals into existence via the long, slow processes of evolution.

19. It is interesting to note that, in a famous sermon, John Wesley, the founder of Methodism, speculated that God would provide animals with a life after death but with enhanced intelligence. See Wesley, "The General Deliverance."

20. I've omitted the last clause of Rowe's premise for the sake of brevity, but the argument that follows in no way exploits this omission.

21. Hasker, *Providence*, 58–75.

22. Ibid., 68 and 71.

23. I am indebted to Hugh McCann for the idea that the defeat of evil is itself part of the original divine plan—one of God's primary purposes, not merely a "backup" plan. See McCann, "Pointless Suffering?"

24. The shadow analogy is borrowed from Kim, *The Philosophy of Mind*, 179.

25. For a defense of epiphenomenalism, see Huxley, "On the Hypothesis That Animals Are Automata, and Its History."

26. Searle, *Mind*, 97–98.

27. Nagel, "What Is It Like to be a Bat?" 435–50.

28. In chapter 12 we will consider whether a metaphysical view involving karma and reincarnation (without the belief in a personal God) can account for suffering and evil better than traditional theism can.

FOUR   Why Think God Is Good?

1. Law, "The Evil-God Challenge," 353–73.

2. A universe is fine-tuned if (a) its most basic physical structures support life and if (b) it would not support life if slight changes were made in those basic structures. See chapter 2 for a presentation of a fine-tuning design argument for God's existence.

3. Law, "The Evil-God Challenge," 360.

4. The soul-making theodicy is the idea that God permits evil and suffering because confronting these challenges well requires human beings to develop their most admirable and valuable character traits, namely, virtues such as hope, courage, patience, compassion, wisdom, and love. See chapter 3 for an elaboration of the soul-making theodicy.

5. Law, "The Evil-God Challenge," 357.

6. Ibid., 358.

7. Ibid.

8. Ibid., 363.

9. Ibid.

10. Ibid., 364.

11. Ibid., 365.

12. Ibid. See chapter 7 for a thorough exploration of the relationship between God and ethics.

13. Ibid., 368.

14. Ibid.

15. Ibid. Of course, theists do typically claim or assume that God permits or causes suffering as the necessary means to some greater good.

16. Ibid. By "evil" here Law does not mean *moral* evil; rather, he simply means "something bad" as in "Bad things happen to good people."

17. Some may question this claim by pointing to biblical passages in which God commands a person or group to do something we would normally consider morally wrong, for example, Genesis 22 (wherein God commands Abraham to sacrifice his son, Isaac). But two points need to be kept in mind: (a) The claim that any given case of apparent wrongdoing has a good God's approval is rightfully assigned a very low probability unless there is specific evidence pointing to divine approval. (b) Even if God on rare occasions commands people to do things we normally consider to be morally wrong, in cases of wrongdoing in general it remains highly unlikely that a good God helps someone perform them; otherwise the phrase "good God" lacks significant content.

18. (a) Some people doubt the principle of simplicity because they think it implies that we should reject complicated hypotheses in general. This is a misunderstanding. For example, contemporary physics endorses very complicated hypotheses regarding the subatomic realm. But these hypotheses are not thought to contain *unnecessary* complications; the complications are needed to explain the phenomena. (b) Some philosophers question whether (relative) simplicity is evidence of truth, though they may regard it as a legitimate reason to *prefer* one hypothesis over another—after all, a (relatively) simple hypothesis is easier to grasp and to work with than its more complex rivals. In practice, however, it seems to me that when people compare two hypotheses that are equal in explanatory power, and one is plainly more complicated than the other, they usually view the more complicated hypothesis as less likely to be true. (c) I should add that there is much debate among philosophers about the *facets* of simplicity—what makes one hypothesis simpler than another—and about the extent to which we can judge (objectively) that one hypothesis is simpler than another.

19. When employing a reductio ad absurdum argument, one refutes a claim by reducing it to absurdity, that is, by showing that it implies something that is clearly false. The underlying principle is this: *whatever implies a falsehood is itself false.*

20. Ward, "The Evil God Challenge: A Response," 46.

21. Ibid.

22. According to many philosophical theologians, there are additional problems with regarding the greatest possible being as a physical entity. First, a physical entity must have a location in space. And where would a greatest possible being be located? If we answer, "Everywhere," we are implying that the greatest possible being is like a gas spread out through the entire universe—surely an odd notion. (Note: Divine omnipresence is better analyzed as a *derivative* of omniscience and omnipotence—God knows what is going on everywhere, and

he can bring about effects in every location.) Second, the greatest possible being, God, is regarded as the Creator of physical reality, but not creator of himself.

23. Ward, "The Evil-God Challenge: A Response," 44.

24. Ibid.

25. Ibid.

26. There may, of course, be cases in which an agent has strong reasons to do A but equally strong reasons to do B (and there is no other act he has stronger reasons to perform). To take a mundane case, suppose one has strong reasons to go jogging but equally strong reasons to go cycling (and no stronger reason to perform some other action). In such a case, I assume that the agent can perform either act just by willing to do so. The agent can, as it were, mentally "flip a coin" to select one of the two actions.

27. My argument here owes a debt to Swinburne, *The Existence of God*, 97–102.

FIVE   Why Is God Hidden? Part I

1. See Schellenberg, *Divine Hiddenness and Human Reason*, 83.

2. Ibid., 3n.

3. This formulation does not exclude the possibility that belief in God can be properly basic, i.e., reasonably held but not on the basis of an argument (or arguments). For example, according to some philosophers, one's belief that God exists may be grounded in religious experience (and be reasonable by virtue of being so grounded). But even if one's belief is grounded in experience, it can still be unreasonable if defeaters (i.e., grounds for doubt) are available but they are not dealt with responsibly. (For example, in the case of belief in God, some philosophers consider the problem of evil a defeater.) The main point here is simply that to maintain a properly (i.e., reasonable) basic belief, one must respond to apparent defeaters in a responsible manner.

4. Schellenberg, *Divine Hiddenness and Human Reason*, 58.

5. Of course, a person's "honest assessment" can be marred or distorted by unconscious bias. But is it plausible to suppose that *every* non-theist's assessment of the evidence for God's existence is so marred or distorted by unconscious bias that his or her non-belief is unreasonable? Such a sweeping generalization seems dubious to me.

6. One can exercise some degree of *indirect* control over one's beliefs. For example, one might choose to read a book on a subject about which one is largely ignorant and by reading the book one is apt to form many new beliefs on the subject in question. But one cannot, for example, simply choose to believe that unicorns exist if one thinks there is no good evidence for their existence. And one cannot simply choose to believe that the number of rocks on the surface of Mars is odd if one thinks there is no way to determine whether that number is odd.

7. Schellenberg, *Wisdom to Doubt*, 236.

8. Schellenberg, *Divine Hiddenness and Human Reason*, 18. Italics Schellenberg's.

9. Ibid., 20.

10. Ibid., 22–23.

11. Ibid., 32–33.

12. Ibid., 48–57.

13. This characterization of God's power is a paraphrase of one offered by Wielenberg, "Omnipotence Again," 42. See chapter 1 for some clarification of this characterization.

14. See chapters 1 and 2 for a cumulative case for theism. Although I think this cumulative case supports theism, I must also acknowledge that reasonable questions can be raised about the premises (or inferences) in each of the arguments.

15. I am not here endorsing agnosticism or atheism. Nor am I denying that belief in God can be reasonably held. But I *am* suggesting that agnosticism and atheism can be reasonable positions. Bear in mind that a belief can be mistaken and yet be reasonably held. For example, in controversies about moral issues (e.g., abortion, euthanasia, affirmative action, the death penalty, etc.), people on both sides of an issue may have well-argued, defensible, reasonable views. Yet presumably, given that there is disagreement, someone is in error.

16. Maybe it's possible to conceive of evidence (or experiences) God could supply that would exclude reasonable non-theism entirely, but it would have to be evidence (or experiential grounds) far more powerful than Schellenberg has suggested; it would have to be strong enough to *clearly* outweigh or override—in everyone's judgment—the evidence of evil and suffering.

17. Schellenberg, *Divine Hiddenness and Human Reason*, 82.

18. Some scholars claim that Buddhism is agnostic rather than atheistic, but this claim is open to question: "A careful examination of both the implications of Buddhist metaphysics and Buddhist texts themselves indicate that Buddhism is more than merely agnostic on the question of a Creator God; it rules out the possibility of there being such a God," Yandell and Netland, *Buddhism*, 183. These authors cite a number of Buddhist thinkers, including the Dalai Lama, who state that Buddhism rules out the existence of a Creator God.

19. Philosophical naturalism is roughly the view that there is no God or anything like God (such as angels or souls); everything is physical with the possible exception of so-called abstract entities such as numbers.

20. Andrew Cullison, "Two Solutions to the Problem of Divine Hiddenness," 121.

21. Schellenberg himself does not analyze "belief" in terms of confidence. According to him, a belief is a disposition "to apprehend the state of affairs reported by a certain proposition, when the state of affairs comes to mind, under the concept *reality*." *Wisdom to Doubt*, 2. In other words, if one believes that P, one takes it that the content of P describes things as they really are. In merely hoping that P, one allows that the content of P may not (or even probably does not) describe things as they really are.

22. Kierkegaard's works are famously difficult to interpret, in part be-

cause he wrote under various pseudonyms. So I may here be ascribing a view to Kierkegaard that he did not actually hold. My concern in this chapter, however, is not to settle a question of Kierkegaard scholarship but to consider a representative range of attempted solutions to the problem of divine hiddenness. For Kierkegaard's view of faith, see Kierkegaard, *Concluding Unscientific Postscript*, 182. I should add that Kierkegaard's works provide more than one approach to the problem of divine hiddenness. His famous story of the king and the peasant maiden suggests that God remains hidden to avoid overwhelming us; see Kierkegaard, *Philosophical Fragments*, 32–43. We will consider a response of this sort to the hiddenness problem momentarily.

23. Kierkegaard, *Concluding Unscientific Postscript*, 182. In context, it seems clear that an "objective uncertainty" is a proposition that is improbable on the evidence.

24. This summary of Kierkegaard's view is borrowed from Schellenberg, *Divine Hiddenness and Human Reason*, 159–60. For Kierkegaard's own wording, see Kierkegaard, *Concluding Unscientific Postscript*, 218–20.

25. Swinburne, *The Existence of God*, 212.

26. I am not here appealing to the Bible as an authoritative or inspired document. I am merely assuming that the picture of faith given in the story of the Exodus provides a plausible account of human religious psychology.

27. Again I'm using illustrations from the Bible simply because they are relatively well known and provide plausible accounts of human religious psychology. I am making no assumption about the authority or inspiration of the Bible.

28. In the biblical story, the prophet Nathan confronted David in order to make him realize that he had sinned—and sinned greatly (2 Samuel 12: 1–15). This may suggest that David had been engaging in self-deception.

29. Of course I have already questioned whether even vivid religious experiences would remove all reasonable doubt about God's existence *given the problem of evil and suffering*.

30. Schellenberg, *Wisdom to Doubt*, 301–2. In this connection it is worth mentioning that in conversations I have often heard believers use skeptical theism to defend the claim that some people will suffer eternally in hell: "We can't see how God would be justified in making someone suffer forever, but so what? We humans shouldn't expect to know what God's reasons are." This has always seemed to me a rather glib response to a very difficult question.

31. Ibid., 302. Paul Draper made the same point in his essay "The Skeptical Theist," 188.

32. Ibid., 304.

33. It could also include reasons to doubt the veridicality of any religious experiences that seem to indicate that ultimate reality is not personal (or not almighty, not wholly good, and so on). For example, some Hindu mystics claim that reality is non-differenced (or distinction-less) in spite of appearances; and it might be argued that such a claim fails to give sufficient weight to sense experience (which presents us with a world containing many different things). But I doubt that such criticisms of non-theistic religious experiences will always be

available or always be strong enough to undermine the veridicality of the experience in question.

34. Ontological arguments do not involve claims regarding what God would have reason to do. But the best version of the ontological argument has at least one premise that is arguably not "better known" than the conclusion of the argument, in which case the argument is of no value as evidence for theism. See van Inwagen, *Metaphysics*, 75–99.

SIX   Why Is God Hidden? Part II

1. Schellenberg, *Divine Hiddenness and Human Reason*, 83.
2. This point is borrowed from Hasker, *Providence*, 33.
3. Here it may be of interest to note that the Bible often speaks of the "living God," but of course God is not a form of biological life, so "living" in this context is a metaphor. And I believe this metaphor is intended to suggest the praiseworthiness of a God who is active—who is at work in the world. See Deuteronomy 5:26, Joshua 3:10, 1 Samuel 17:26, 2 Kings 19:4, Psalms 42:2 and 84:2, Isaiah 37:4, Jeremiah 10:10, Hosea 1:10, Matthew 16:16 and 26:63, John 6:69, Acts 14:15, Romans 9:26, 2 Corinthians 3:3, 1 Timothy 3:15, and Hebrews 3:12.
4. My use of the word "prior" here assumes that there is a sequence in the divine life and hence that God is not timeless. But on the view that God is timeless, one can still make a distinction between God's mostly merely dispositional goodness *independent of* creation (and the presence of evil) and God's much less merely dispositional goodness given creation (and the presence of evil). For more on God's relation to time, see chapter 8.
5. If God is triune, as Christian theology teaches, there can be relations of love between the persons of the Trinity prior to (or independent of) creation. For a discussion of theories of the Trinity, see Layman, *Philosophical Approaches*, 123–73.
6. I am indebted to Hugh McCann for the idea that the defeat of evil is itself part of the original divine plan—one of God's primary purposes, not merely a "back up" plan. I am, however, working these ideas out in my own way, so I must take responsibility for any errors in the presentation. See McCann, "Pointless Suffering?" 161–84.
7. While I assume that a perfectly good God will defeat evil via "soft" power *insofar as possible*, it may well be that the final defeat of evil will require some dramatic miraculous activity in which the power of evil is sharply restricted or eliminated. Also, if natural evils are to be eliminated, this will surely involve some miracles.
8. Here is one way to argue that ignorance itself can be an evil (i.e., a bad thing): Suppose that someone suggests that there is a rather easy solution to the problem of suffering, namely, that suffering is an illusion. But if suffering is an illusion, the vast majority of humans are ignorant of this "fact." And wouldn't

it be a *bad thing* to be "clued out" about a salient aspect of the human condition such as suffering? Thus, the suffering-is-an-illusion "solution" in fact posits the evil (badness) of ignorance about something of great spiritual importance.

9. Schellenberg, *Wisdom to Doubt*, 244.

10. Ibid., 204.

11. Here it is interesting to note that in one passage of the Christian Scriptures people are judged, not on the basis of what they believe but on how they treat the needy — *and how a person treats the needy is equated with how one treats the Lord*: "Then the King will say . . . , 'Come, O blessed of my Father, inherit the kingdom prepared for you . . . ; for I was hungry and you gave me food, I was thirsty and you gave me drink, . . . I was naked and you clothed me, . . . Then the righteous will answer him, 'Lord, when did we see thee hungry and feed thee, or thirsty and give thee drink? . . . or naked and clothe thee? . . . And the King will answer them, 'Truly, I say to you, as you did it to one of the least of these . . . , you did it to me'" (Matthew 25:34–40).

12. Schellenberg, *Wisdom to Doubt*, 207, 218, and 288–89.

13. Howard-Snyder, "Divine Openness and Creaturely Non-Resistant Non-Belief," 130.

14. The word "epistemic" is an adjective derived from one of the ancient Greek terms for knowledge: *episteme* (ee-pis-tuh-may). It means "of or related to knowledge."

15. Exclusivists also face the problem of specifying exactly which beliefs are necessary for salvation; obviously, the more beliefs that are required for salvation, the greater the number of persons that would be excluded from salvation.

16. Maitzen, "Divine Hiddenness and the Demographics of Theism," 179.

17. Marsh, "Darwin and the Problem of Natural Nonbelief," 358. Marsh is summarizing material in Stark, *Discovering God*.

18. Marsh, "Darwin and the Problem of Natural Nonbelief," 359.

SEVEN   How Is God Related to Ethics?

1. Boyd and VanArragon, "Ethics Is Based on Natural Law," 305–6.

2. This point is borrowed from Murphy, "The Natural Law Tradition."

3. One well-known NL theorist provides the following list of basic forms of good: life (which includes health), knowledge, play, aesthetic experience, sociability (friendship), practical reasonableness (being able to bring a reasonable order into one's actions and attitudes), and religion (roughly, being able to establish and maintain proper relations between oneself and the divine). See Finnis, *Natural Law and Human Rights*, 85–90.

4. Murphy, "The Natural Law Tradition."

5. Ibid.

6. Arguably also John Duns Scotus, Francisco Suarez, and Thomas Hobbes,

but NL theory is defined in different ways by different authors. See Murphy, "The Natural Law Tradition."

7. For a defense of theological voluntarism, see Henry, "The Good as the Will of God," 95–99.

8. Here are some examples of contingent truths: *J. W. Booth shot Abraham Lincoln, Helena is the capital of Montana, Some cars are red,* and *Frogs exist.* Some moral truths are contingent, such as *Many murders (unjustified or wrongful killings) occur every year in the United States.*

9. The argument of this paragraph is borrowed in its essentials from Swinburne, "What Difference Does God Make to Morality?" 151–55.

10. Thomson, *The Realm of Rights*, 15–16.

11. The best-known proponent of DCT is Adams; see his *Finite and Infinite Goods*, 231–91.

12. Non-theists can in principle take this position, but many philosophical naturalists cannot because either (a) they deny that there are any necessary truths at all or (b) they deny that there are any necessary truths about morality.

13. Or, more generally, one ought to obey the reasonable commands of those who are legitimately in authority over one.

14. As we saw in chapter 6, however, the comparison between God and a human parent can easily be taken too far. See the reflections under "The General Problem of Ignorance."

15. Many Bible passages enjoin tithing, for example, Malachi 3:8–12.

16. My reasoning in this paragraph owes a debt to Swinburne, *The Coherence of Theism*, 203–9. Here is another example of a divine command in which a degree of arbitrariness could enter the picture: Suppose that God commands a certain group of people to worship him on Friday or on Saturday. Presumably God might have chosen some other day—there is nothing inherent in either Friday or Saturday to make it a better choice than, say, Tuesday.

17. I am not here claiming that there are no exceptions to any of these principles. For example, some would argue that mercy killing (which involves killing the innocent) is permissible in exceptional cases. My point is just that, exceptional cases aside, there is good reason to think the actions listed here are right (or wrong) whether or not God has issued a relevant command.

18. Murphy, "The Natural Law Tradition."

19. "Act only on that maxim through which you can at the same time will that it should become a universal law." Kant, *Groundwork of the Metaphysic of Morals*, 88.

20. Floyd, "Thomas Aquinas: Moral Philosophy."

21. The most famous utilitarian is John Stuart Mill. See Mill, *Utilitarianism*.

22. In some cases, we are forced to choose between acts each of which will produce more dissatisfaction than satisfaction. In such cases we should choose the act that will produce the smallest (net) amount of dissatisfaction. In case of "ties," we may perform any of the acts for which no alternative has greater utility.

23. Murphy, "The Natural Law Tradition." It may be of interest to know

that this rule appears in Leviticus 19:18 as well as in some other passages of the Bible (e.g., Mark 12:31).

24. Floyd, "Thomas Aquinas: Moral Philosophy."

25. This point is borrowed from Hursthouse, "Virtue Theory and Abortion," 220–21.

26. This objection is borrowed from Thomson, *The Realm of Rights*, 135.

27. Two things: (a) Notice that rights are linked to goods, for example, the right to life protects the good of being alive, the right to liberty protects the good of not being interfered with in certain ways (e.g., by being unjustly imprisoned), and so on. (b) In speaking of individual rights, I do not assume that such rights are absolute. For example, I may forfeit my right to liberty by committing a violent crime (and thus wind up in prison).

28. For the perspective expressed in this paragraph I am indebted to Nicholas Wolterstorff. See Wolterstorff, *Justice: Rights and Wrongs*, esp. 285–310 and also Wolterstorff, *Justice in Love*, esp. 101–9. In *Justice: Rights and Wrongs*, Wolterstorff defends this *principle of correlatives*, linking rights and obligations: "If Y belongs to the sort of entity that can have rights, then X has a right against Y to Y's doing A if and only if Y has an obligation toward X to do A" (8). Example: Bob has a right against Joe to Joe's refraining from assaulting him if and only if Joe has an obligation toward Bob to refrain from assaulting him.

29. For insightful and detailed theories of rights, see Thomson, *The Realm of Rights*, 205–373 and Wolterstorff, *Justice: Rights and Wrongs*, 241–384.

30. The "other things being equal" qualification is included to allow for cases in which promoting (reasonably expected) flourishing would involve a violation of someone's rights.

31. I am not endorsing this argument; I am simply noting that it is open to NL theorists to employ such arguments. For a concerted attempt to reconcile problematic Old Testament passages with a God of love, see Copan, *Is God a Moral Monster?*

EIGHT   Is Divine Foreknowledge Compatible
with Human Free Will? Part I

1. Alternatively, if one believes that P (e.g., Bats are mammals), one takes it that the content of P describes things as they really are. Compare believing to hoping: If one merely hopes that P (e.g., I passed the exam), one allows that the content of P may not (or even probably does not) describe things as they are.

2. Since one's thinking must apparently start somewhere, one's knowledge of the "starting points" in one's system of beliefs—what philosophers call one's "basic beliefs"—is an important topic in philosophy. For example, suppose that "Trees exist" is a basic belief for you—you have no argument for it. Still, the belief is surely an item of knowledge, presumably grounded in your sense experience.

3. Some philosophers use so-called Frankfurt cases to challenge the claim

that an agent acts freely only if he could have done otherwise than he in fact did. This type of challenge is discussed in chapter 2 under the heading "The Argument from Free Will and Moral Responsibility."

4. This statement of the problem is borrowed from Morris, *Our Idea of God*, 91. I have added the words in parentheses to premises 2 and 3 and modified step 5 slightly.

5. Furthermore, Origen did not explain *how* God knows the future. For this reason, his "solution" is arguably incomplete. After all, many theologians have held that God can know the future only if it is determined. And if our actions are determined (necessitated), they are ultimately determined by God, if God exists, for all the causal factors in the world, such as the laws of nature and the physical constants, are created by God.

6. For a contemporary defense of the compatibilist or Calvinist solution, see Helm, "The Augustinian-Calvinist View," 161–89.

7. Admittedly, my wording is a bit loose here. The causes in question are presumably the propensities of physical entities that account for the regularities in the way the physical world behaves.

8. The argument has been stated rigorously by van Inwagen in *An Essay on Free Will*, 55–105.

9. Ibid., 56.

10. Principles similar to this have been discussed extensively by philosophers, and some have been shown to be flawed. My version is a paraphrase of one defended by Finch and Warfield in "The *Mind* Argument and Libertarianism," 515–28. These authors state their principle as follows: "One has no choice about the logical consequences of those truths about which one has no choice" (522). As far as I know, no one has refuted this principle.

11. Lewis, *Mere Christianity*, 130–33. Helm, "Divine Timeless Eternity," 28–60.

12. Lewis, *Mere Christianity*, 133. Lewis's italics.

13. Paul Helm also seems to regard God's knowledge of future free acts as a kind of direct awareness. The temporal ("before and after") order is one in which "every moment is also eternally present to God." See Helm, "Divine Timeless Eternity," 58.

14. This objection and the next are borrowed from Plantinga, "On Ockham's Way Out," 239–40.

15. This objection is borrowed from Morris, *Our Idea of God*, 98–99.

16. As Stephen Hawking remarks: Einstein's "theory of relativity put an end to the idea of absolute time! It appeared that each observer must have his own measure of time, as recorded by a clock carried with him . . . ." See Hawking, *A Brief History of Time*, 21. But W. L. Craig comments: "Einstein did not eliminate absolute simultaneity: he merely redefined simultaneity." See Craig and Smith, *Theism, Atheism, and Big Bang Cosmology*, 297.

17. Koperski, *The Physics of Theism*, 131.

18. Ibid., 122 (all quotations are from this paragraph). In a similar vein, Michael Tooley states: "What the Einstein-Poldolsky-Rosen thought experiment shows . . . is this. Either particles have determinate states prior to measurement,

in which case quantum mechanics does not provide a complete description of physical reality, or else correlated particles must acquire corresponding determinate properties simultaneously, in the absolute sense—or at least without there being an intervening temporal gap—in which case the Special Theory of Relativity does not provide a complete description of the spatiotemporal relations between events." See Tooley, *Time, Tense, and Causation*, 361.

19. Koperski, *The Physics of Theism*, 126.

20. Ibid., 130.

21. Ibid.

22. Ibid., 131.

23. Ellis, "Physics in the Real Universe: Time and Space-Time," 74 (as quoted in Koperski, *The Physics of Theism*, 137).

24. Ibid., 52–53 (as quoted in Koperski, *The Physics of Theism*, 137).

25. This point is borrowed from Zimmerman, "The Privileged Present," 219.

26. Some philosophers are presentists, holding that only present objects exist. Others hold the "growing universe" theory, that both past and present objects exist. Still others, as we've seen, hold the block universe theory (or eternalism), that the future exists just as much as the present and the past. For a summary of the key issues involved, see Savitt, "Being and Becoming in Modern Physics."

27. Aquinas, *Summa Contra Gentiles*, 217.

28. If soul-body dualism is logically or metaphysically possible, however, then the non-physical soul may be an entity that could be in time while lacking a location in space. Since souls (by hypothesis) undergo a temporal sequence of conscious experiences (thoughts, sensations, feelings, volitions, etc.)—a sequence that can be dated and measured—souls would be in physical time. Since souls are non-physical, however, they may have no location in space. As we shall see in chapter 11, however, it is a matter of debate whether the soul has a location.

NINE   Is Divine Foreknowledge Compatible
with Human Free Will? Part II

1. Morris, *Our Idea of God*, 91. I have added the words in parentheses to premises 2 and 3 and modified step 5 slightly.

2. Molina, *On Divine Foreknowledge*. For a contemporary defense of the middle knowledge solution, see Craig, "The Middle Knowledge View."

3. These conditionals are also referred to as *counterfactuals* of freedom, but this is a misnomer, since a counterfactual conditional has an antecedent (if clause) that is contrary to fact, and many subjunctive conditionals of freedom do not have this feature.

4. The subjunctive mood contrasts with the indicative mood, for instance, "I am rich." The indicative mood is used to state a fact, express an opinion, or ask a question.

5. The word "once" here is not to be taken literally. To take it literally is to assume that God did not have knowledge of the future *from all eternity*. God's decision to create (including whom to create) is not *temporally* prior to his knowledge of the future but *prior in the order of explanation*, that is, there is a logical order in the divine decrees. God's decision about whom to create (and which circumstances to put them in) is logically prior to his knowing the future.

6. This point is borrowed from Swinburne, *Providence and the Problem of Evil*, 133.

7. Hasker, "The Foreknowledge Conundrum," 103. Hasker isn't endorsing this claim; he is merely explaining that advocates of the middle knowledge solution make it.

8. Ibid., 104.

9. This analogy is inspired by one offered by Hunt in "The Simple Foreknowledge View," 85.

10. Adams, "Middle Knowledge and the Problem of Evil."

11. Material conditionals, which are the focus of beginning courses in symbolic logic, are truth-functional. And a material conditional is true if its antecedent is false. But subjunctive conditionals are not truth-functional. If they were, both of the following conditionals would be true:

a. If President John F. Kennedy had not been assassinated in 1963, he would have freely withdrawn American troops from Vietnam.
b. If President John F. Kennedy had not been assassinated in 1963, he would *not* have freely withdrawn American troops from Vietnam.

It's hard to see how both of these conditionals could be true.

12. The argument is borrowed in its essentials from Adams, "An Anti-Molinist Argument." I am, however, putting the argument in my own words, so I must take responsibility for any errors in the presentation.

13. For example, Flint, *Divine Providence*, and W. L. Craig, "The Middle Knowledge View."

14. There are some passages in the Bible that apparently ascribe knowledge of subjunctive conditionals of freedom to God. For example, a story in 1 Samuel 22 apparently ascribes knowledge of a subjunctive conditional along the following lines to God: "If David were to stay in the town of Keilah, then the people of Keilah would surrender him to King Saul." Given this conditional information, David left the town of Keilah and so was not surrendered to King Saul. Is this an example of middle knowledge? Not clearly. There is no hint in the biblical story that God knew this conditional "from all eternity." The people of Keilah had moral track records, and (theists assume) God knew their innermost thoughts. In short, we can locate possible grounds that would make the conditional true (or at least probably true), but these grounds were not present before the creation of the world.

15. G. Boyd, "The Open-Theism View"; Hasker, *God, Time, and Knowledge*; Pinnock, *Most Moved Mover*; and Swinburne, *The Coherence of Theism*.

16. Similarly, the following passage seems to suggest uncertainty on the part of God: "If they will not believe you," God said [to Moses], "or heed the first sign, they may believe the latter sign" (Exodus 4:8).

17. In a similar vein, consider this passage from the book of Judges: "Now these are the nations that the LORD left to test all those in Israel who had no experience of any war in Canaan: the five lords of the Philistines, and all the Canaanites, and the Sidonians, and the Hivites who lived on Mount Lebanon, from Mount Baal-hermon as far as Lebo-hamath. They were for the testing of Israel, to know whether Israel would obey the commandments of the LORD, which he commanded their ancestors by Moses" (Judges 3:1, 3–4).

18. The word "epistemic" is an adjective derived from one of the ancient Greek terms for knowledge, *episteme* (ee-pis-tuh-may). It means "of or related to knowledge."

19. If the statements are neither true nor false, can they have meaningful content? Yes. For example, imperatives, such as "Shut the door" obviously have meaningful content, but they are neither true nor false.

20. Truth-value open theists need not deny the law of the excluded middle, namely, that for every proposition P, either P or not-P. The disjunction (either-or proposition) is true, but neither P nor not-P is true in some cases.

21. Similar cases to consider include cases in which it does not seem quite true to say that a person is old (or tall) but also not quite true to say that he or she is not old (or not tall); cases in which it does not seem quite correct to say that an object is red (or blue), but also not quite correct to deny that it is red (or blue).

22. Many philosophers think there are better solutions to the problem of logical fatalism. Suppose that "Eve will freely lie" was true long ago. This is said to be a "soft fact" about the past because it is wholly parasitic on the future. If "Eve will freely lie" was true long ago, in virtue of what was it true? "It was a fact simply in virtue of its then being the case that *x* [Eve's freely lying] *will happen.*" See Hunt, "The Simple Foreknowledge View," 150–51. Soft facts about the past do not deprive us of our free will. By way of contrast, "God believed long ago that Eve will freely lie" is a so-called hard fact. Since it is about what God believed in the past, Eve cannot change it, just as I cannot now change the fact that I believed in Santa when I was four.

23. This third possibility would not work, I take it, in the case of cruel acts, such as torture. The human agent would not be responsible, but God would.

TEN   Do Humans Have Souls? Part I

1. The so-called eliminative materialists deny that humans have conscious mental states. See Churchland, "Eliminative Materialism and the Propositional Attitudes," and Dennett, "Quining Qualia."

2. For a highly regarded discussion of phenomenal qualities, see Chalmers, *The Conscious Mind.*

3. Descartes, *Meditations on First Philosophy.* Some substance dualists

have denied that there is causal interaction between the soul and the body, but such denials fly in the face of common sense. Accordingly, I shall ignore these versions of substance dualism.

4. Alston, "Substance and the Trinity," 181. This definition isn't *exactly* right, but it will serve for our present purposes. It isn't exactly right for at least two reasons: (1) Consider a specific event, such as John Wilkes Booth's shooting of Abraham Lincoln on April 14, 1865. Such an event has properties (e.g., *being tragic*) but is not itself a property. Yet philosophers don't count events as substances. (2) Consider numbers, such as the number thirteen. They also seem to have properties (e.g., *being odd*) and yet they don't seem to be properties. Many philosophers regard numbers as abstract entities. (A key feature of abstract entities is their lack of causal powers.) So events and certain abstract entities complicate our effort to define "substance," but we can proceed simply by noting that events and abstract entities don't count as substances in the relevant sense.

5. Plato, "Phaedo."

6. Traditionally, Christians have believed that the soul exists in an unembodied state from death until the Day of Judgment, when it will be united with a resurrected body. But they have not held that the soul would be better off to stay in this unembodied state for all eternity.

7. Smart, "Sensations and Brain Processes."

8. Putnam, "Psychological Predicates." While Putnam formulated early versions of functionalism, he has since produced important criticisms of it.

9. My characterization of non-reductive physicalism is substantially borrowed from Kim, *Philosophy of Mind*, 290–91. My characterization differs at point (c), however, in that Kim assigns the supervenience thesis to all non-reductive physicalists. But some non-reductive physicalists characterize the relation of strong dependence in alternate ways. For example, some say that mental states are *constituted* by physical states, and others say that mental states *emerge* from physical states. And the relation of supervenience is itself understood in different ways. For some discussion of these issues, see N. Murphy, "Nonreductive Physicalism," 127–48.

10. Kim, *Philosophy of Mind*, 198.

11. See, for example, the essays by biologists, neuroscientists, psychologists, philosophers, biblical scholars, and theologians in Brown, Murphy, and Maloney, eds., *Whatever Happened to the Soul?*, and also in Jeeves, ed., *From Cells to Souls—and Beyond*. We will consider the possibility of combining theism and physicalism in chapter 11.

12. In a celebrated correspondence with Princess Elizabeth of Bohemia, Descartes discussed the causal relationship between the soul and the body. See Anscombe and Geach, trans., *Descartes: Philosophical Writings*, 274–86.

13. While many who believe in reincarnation think that humans and animals have souls, a great many do not. For example, Buddhists in general deny that there is any enduring self or soul. We will discuss the issue of reincarnation in chapter 12.

14. For an informative discussion of evolution as it relates to issues in the philosophy of mind, see Ayala, "Human Nature." For insightful philosophical

reflections on evolution and theism, see van Inwagen, "Genesis and Evolution," 128–62.

15. Searle, *Mind*, 97–98.
16. Nagel, "What Is It Like to Be a Bat?"
17. Heil, "Philosophy of Mind," 177.
18. Searle, *Minds, Brains, and Science*, 31–33.
19. Ibid., 32.
20. For a discussion of the Chinese Room argument, see Kim, *Philosophy of Mind*, 145–49.

ELEVEN   DO HUMANS HAVE SOULS? PART II

1. My characterization of non-reductive physicalism is substantially borrowed from Kim, *Philosophy of Mind*, 290–91. My characterization differs at point C, however, in that Kim assigns the supervenience thesis to all non-reductive physicalists. But some non-reductive physicalists characterize the relation of strong dependence in alternate ways, for instance, some say that mental states are *constituted* by physical states. And the relation of supervenience is itself understood in different ways.

2. Ibid., 198.
3. Ibid., 194–97.
4. I am here paraphrasing Kim, *Physicalism*, 48. I have borrowed the phrase "ride piggyback" from Kim.
5. The smart phone example is borrowed from Jennifer Corns via email correspondence (November 23, 2015), but the analysis of the example is mine and I must take responsibility for it.
6. See chapter 3 under "The Comparative Response" for a brief elaboration of epiphenomenalism.
7. The "necessity argument" is borrowed from Moore, "Mind and the Causal Exclusion Problem."
8. Ibid., under the heading "Metaphysics of Causation," 14. A thorough discussion of the exclusion argument would require an examination of the various philosophical theories of causation, but space does not permit me to explore this complicated philosophical territory here. As a response to the exclusion argument, however, the counterfactual theory of causation is one that is particularly advantageous for the non-reductive physicalist.
9. For an overview of attempts to respond to the exclusion argument, see Moore, "Mind and the Causal Exclusion Problem." See also Robb and Heil, "Mental Causation."
10. Here I am considering the physicalist position as one aspect of naturalism, where naturalism is the view that there is no God or anything like God (e.g., no angels, no souls) and only physical entities exist. In a later section of this chapter (titled "Theistic Physicalism?") I briefly consider whether a theistic version of physicalism might be able to make room for free will.

11. Some compatibilists point out that, in any given case, one can do otherwise in the sense that *if one had wanted to do otherwise, one would have done otherwise*. But this way of defining "can do otherwise" essentially empties the concept of meaning. As Alvin Plantinga observes, "One might as well claim that being in jail doesn't really limit one's freedom on the grounds that if one were not in jail, he'd be free to come and go as he pleased." See Plantinga, *God, Freedom, and Evil*, 32. Given determinism, one's "wantings" or desires are necessitated by the past and the laws of nature.

12. The consequence argument has been developed and stated rigorously by van Inwagen in *An Essay on Free Will*.

13. My transfer principle is a paraphrase of one defended in Finch and Warfield, "The *Mind* Argument and Libertarianism." These authors state their principle as follows: "One has no choice about the logical consequences of those truths about which one has no choice" (522). There has been much discussion of principles of this type, but as far as I know, no one has refuted this principle.

14. A few (not many) naturalists are eliminative materialists, who hold that the mental states (beliefs, desires, intentions, etc.) posited by common sense do not actually exist. See, for example, Churchland, "Eliminative Materialism and the Propositional Attitudes."

15. Draper, "Seeking But Not Believing," 201.

16. For a defense of substance dualism, see Dilley, "Taking Consciousness Seriously," and also Plantinga, "Materialism and Christian Belief."

17. Dennett, *Consciousness Explained* (as quoted in Plantinga, "Materialism and Christian Belief," 125).

18. My responses to Dennett are borrowed in their essentials from Plantinga, "Materialism and Christian Belief," 125–27.

19. According to some theists, one's body is generated by one's parents, but each soul is directly created by God (and linked to one's body). This view is called *creationism*. In the alternative view, both body and soul are generated by one's parents—though of course all such natural processes are created and sustained by God. This view is called *traducianism*.

20. Kim, *Physicalism*, 76–90.

21. We cannot solve the pairing problem by claiming that S1 wills *his body* to move while S2 wills *her body* to move; for what makes a given body B the body of a given person S is (at least in part) that S can cause some changes in B *directly*, simply by willing to do so. So how can we speak sensibly of "S1's body" if we can identify nothing that would make it the case that S1 is causally linked to B1 *and not to B2*?

22. By definition, the point particles of physics have no spatial extension—they do not take up any space.

23. For a careful discussion of the idea that souls might be located in space, see Bailey, Rasmussen, and Van Horn, "No Pairing Problem." I am indebted to these authors for the suggestion that souls might count as non-physical, since, unlike the point particles of physics, souls are fundamentally mental in nature. For an insightful essay that examines the various proposed definitions of "physical object," see Markosian, "What Are Physical Objects?"

24. The analogy is borrowed from Davison, "Divine Providence and Human Freedom," 225.

25. Plantinga, "Materialism and Christian Belief," 130–33.

26. At this juncture some readers may wonder whether the Bible teaches that people have souls. This is not the place for a discussion of an issue of biblical interpretation, but perhaps it is appropriate to note one important fact that complicates this issue. The Hebrew and Greek words translated by the English word "soul" do not have "non-physical" built into their meaning. For example, the Hebrew word *nephesh* can mean "living being" or "self." Similarly, the Greek word *psyche* may mean "life" or "self." Where the word "soul" appears in English translations of the Bible, the meaning is often something like "my innermost self or being." Thus it would be an error to assume that a Bible verse such as "Praise the Lord, O my soul!" (Psalm 146:1) is referring to a non-physical soul. For an exploration of the biblical teaching about the soul, see Green, *Body, Soul, and Human Life.*

TWELVE   Does Reincarnation Provide
the Best Explanation of Suffering?

1. Goldschmidt and Seacord, "Judaism, Reincarnation, and Theodicy," 395.

2. Some reincarnationists think that a human person can be reincarnated only in a human body, but as "the Hindu scriptural commentator Louis Renou points out, a *jīva* (life force) is said to be granted a human life only after going through 8,400,000 previous incarnations of lower forms of life—2,000,000 as a plant, 900,000 as an aquatic animal, 100,000 as an insect, 100,000 as a bird, 300,000 as a cow, and 400,000 as a monkey." See Chadha and Trakakis, "Karma and the Problem of Evil," 546.

3. Goldschmidt and Seacord, "Judaism, Reincarnation, and Theodicy," 394.

4. Ibid., 393.

5. Warren, *Buddhism in Translations,* 215.

6. According to Stuart C. Hackett, "It is not difficult to sketch the grounds which make . . . [reincarnation] all but universally plausible among Indian thinkers." The doctrine of reincarnation provides "a basis for reconciling the concept of moral order embodied in the principle of *karma* with the empirical facts about the human situation. The circumstances and native endowments of different human individuals . . . are so strikingly various, and apparently at least, so uncorrelated with the moral state of these individuals in the present life that, if we confine our attention to this context, it seems extremely difficult to suppose that the distribution of privileges and powers is expressive of any sort of principle of reasonable and proportionate justice." Hackett, *Oriental Philosophy,* 201.

7. Stevenson, "Reincarnation," 207.

8. Ibid.

9. Ibid.
10. Ibid., 208.
11. Stevenson, *Twenty Cases Suggestive of Reincarnation*, 91–105.
12. Ibid., 91.
13. Ibid.
14. Ibid., 92.
15. Stevenson, "Some New Cases Suggestive of Reincarnation: The Case of Ampan Petcherat: 1973," in Kelly, ed., *Science, the Self, and Survival after Death*, 230.
16. Ibid.
17. Ibid.
18. Ibid.
19. *Upaniṣads*, trans. Olivelle, 202.
20. Ibid., 239.
21. Warren, *Buddhism in Translations*, 232.
22. Said the king: "Bhante Nâgasena, does rebirth take place without anything transmigrating [passing over]?"—"Yes, your majesty. Rebirth takes place without anything transmigrating."—"How, bhante Nâgasena, does rebirth take place without anything transmigrating? Give an illustration."—"Suppose, your majesty, a man were to light a light from another light; pray, would the one light have passed over [transmigrated] to the other light?"—"Nay, verily, bhante."—"In exactly the same way, your majesty, does rebirth take place without anything transmigrating." Ibid., 234. For a careful examination of Buddhist metaphysics, see Yandell and Netland, *Buddhism*. These authors state: "For Buddhism, no soul travels from life to life, or even exists within a single lifetime. . . . If there is a cycle of rebirth, *something* or other must be reborn. The most straightforward Buddhist answer is that what you are is simply a collection of momentary states. Over time, you are simply a series of these collections, each collection causing the next" (120).
23. James, *Principles of Psychology*, vol. 1, 675–76.
24. For a careful discussion of a range of possible explanations of cases of past-life recall, see Stevenson, "Reincarnation," 201–27. The famous case of Bridey Murphy was apparently a case of cryptomnesia: In 1952 Morey Bernstein, an amateur hypnotist, put Virginia Tighe, a Colorado homemaker, through hypnotic regression, during which she claimed to have been Bridey Murphy, a nineteenth-century Irishwoman, in a previous life. The case became a sensation, and Bernstein's book, *The Search for Bridey Murphy*, sold over a million copies. A thorough investigation of the case, however, revealed that Tighe's claims were probably best explained as forgotten memories from her childhood; see Edwards, *Reincarnation*, 59–79.
25. Stevenson, *Twenty Cases Suggestive of Reincarnation*, 2.
26. Stevenson, "Birthmarks and Birth Defects Corresponding to Wounds on Deceased Persons: 1993." In Kelly, ed., *Science, the Self, and Survival after Death*, 264.
27. That a proposition can be rationally believed is not, of course, a guarantee that it is true. For example, based on the available evidence, a jury might rationally believe that a defendant is guilty, but at a later time further relevant

evidence (such as DNA evidence) might become available and might indicate that the defendant is not guilty.

28. The word "capable" is important here. For a person might temporarily be unable to think or make choices due to being drugged or due to a severe head injury, while the underlying capacity for thinking and choosing remains in place; it is merely temporarily blocked from being expressed.

29. I say "one and the same entity" here and not "one and the same person" because there is a question whether being a person is an essential property. For example, if I suffer a sufficiently severe brain injury, might I still exist but be incapable of having mental states, and thus no longer be a person?

30. Edwards, *Reincarnation*, 235.

31. Something is logically impossible if its description involves an explicit *or implicit* logical inconsistency, for instance, "Rembrandt drew a circular square." Metaphysical impossibilities are difficult to characterize, but examples include "Abe Lincoln was the number 13" and "On my car there is a patch of blue that has no size at all."

32. Cases of this type were introduced into the literature by Sydney Shoemaker in *Self-Knowledge and Self-Identity*, 22–25.

33. One philosopher who has drawn attention to the importance of the split-brain cases is David Wiggins, in *Identity and Spatio-Temporal Continuity*, 50.

34. I am assuming here, of course, that if B is a reincarnation of A, B has a different body—including a different brain—than A.

35. Kaufman, "Karma, Rebirth, and the Problem of Evil," 19–20.

36. Goldschmidt and Seacord, "Judaism, Reincarnation, and Theodicy," 401.

37. Hick, *Philosophy of Religion*, 139–40.

38. Perrett, "Karma and the Problem of Suffering," 5.

39. This reply is borrowed in its essentials from Chadha and Trakakis, "Karma and the Problem of Evil," 547.

40. This reply is borrowed from Goldschmidt and Seacord, "Judaism, Reincarnation, and Theodicy," 408.

41. My argument in this paragraph is inspired by Kaufman, "Karma, Rebirth, and the Problem of Evil," 24–27; however, I'm developing the argument in my own way and must take responsibility for any mistakes in the reasoning.

42. Ibid., 21–22.

43. Goldschmidt and Seacord, "Judaism, Reincarnation, and Theodicy," 404. See Singer, "Famine, Affluence, and Morality," and Unger, *Living High and Letting Die*.

44. If some suffering is not deserved *according to the law of karma*, it is unclear to me how that law would explain the undeserved suffering. Remember, I've tried to formulate a version of the doctrine of karma that purports to give us a better explanation of suffering than traditional theism can provide.

45. The argument of this paragraph is borrowed in its essentials from Collins, "Eastern Religions," 206.

Adams, Robert Merrihew. "An Anti-Molinist Argument." *Philosophical Perspectives* 5, Philosophy of Religion (1991): 343–53.

——. *Finite and Infinite Goods: A Framework for Ethics.* Oxford: Oxford University Press, 1999.

——. "Middle Knowledge and the Problem of Evil." *American Philosophical Quarterly* 14 (April 1977): 109–17.

Alston, William. *Perceiving God: The Epistemology of Religious Experience.* Ithaca, NY: Cornell University Press, 1991.

——. "Religious Experience." In E. Craig, ed., *Routledge Encyclopedia of Philosophy.* London: Routledge (1998). http://0-www.rep.routledge.com.

——. "Substance and the Trinity." In Stephen T. Davis, Daniel Kendall, S.J., and Gerald O'Collins, S.J., eds., *The Trinity: An Interdisciplinary Symposium on the Trinity.* New York: Oxford University Press, (1999): 179–202.

Anscombe, Elizabeth, and Peter Thomas Geach, trans. *Descartes: Philosophical Writings.* Indianapolis, IN: Bobbs-Merrill, 1971.

Aquinas, Thomas. *Summa Contra Gentiles*, Book One, chapter 66, trans. Anton C. Pegis, F.R.S.C. (Notre Dame, IN: University of Notre Dame Press, 1975).

Ayala, Francisco J. "Human Nature: One Evolutionist's View." In Warren S. Brown, Nancey Murphy, and H. Newton Maloney, eds., *Whatever Happened to the Soul? Scientific and Theological Portraits of Human Nature.* Minneapolis, MN: Fortress Press, 1998, 31–48.

Bailey, Andrew M., Joshua Rasmussen, and Luke Van Horn. "No Pairing Problem." *Philosophical Studies* 154 (2011): 349–60.

Baldasty, Gerald J. *Vigilante Newspapers: A Tale of Sex, Religion, and Murder in the Northwest.* Seattle: University of Washington Press, 2005.

Beardsworth, Timothy. *A Sense of Presence.* Oxford: Religious Experience Research Unit, 1977.

Bernstein, Morey. *The Search for Bridey Murphy.* New York: Doubleday, 1956.

Boyd, Craig A., and Raymond J. VanArragon. "Ethics Is Based on Natural Law." In Michael L. Peterson and Raymond J. VanArragon, eds., *Contemporary Debates in Philosophy of Religion.* Maldon, MA: Blackwell, 2004, 299–310.

Boyd, Gregory. "The Open-Theism View." In James K. Beilby and Paul R. Eddy, eds., *Divine Foreknowledge: Four Views.* Downers Grove, IL: IVP Academic, 2001, 13–47.

Brother Lawrence. *The Practice of the Presence of God.* Springdale, PA: Whitaker House, 1982.

Brown, Warren S., Nancey Murphy, and H. Newton Maloney, eds., *Whatever Happened to the Soul? Scientific and Theological Portraits of Human Nature.* Minneapolis, MN: Fortress Press, 1998.

Chadha, Monima, and Nick Trakakis. "Karma and the Problem of Evil: A Response to Kaufman." *Philosophy East and West* 57, no. 4 (October, 2007): 533–56.

Chalmers, David J. *The Conscious Mind: In Search of a Fundamental Theory.* New York: Oxford University Press, 1996.

Churchland, Paul M. "Eliminative Materialism and the Propositional Attitudes." *Journal of Philosophy* 78 (1981): 67–90.

Collins, Robin. "Eastern Religions." In Michael J. Murray, ed., *Reason for the Hope Within.* Grand Rapids, MI: Eerdmans (1999): 182–216.

Copan, Paul. *Is God a Moral Monster? Making Sense of the Old Testament God.* Grand Rapids, MI: Baker Books, 2011.

Craig, William Lane. "The Middle Knowledge View." In James K. Beilby and Paul R. Eddy, eds., *Divine Foreknowledge: Four Views.* Downers Grove, IL: IVP Academic (2001): 119–43.

——. "Theism and Physical Cosmology." In Philip L. Quinn and Charles Taliaferro, eds., *A Companion to the Philosophy of Religion.* Oxford: Blackwell (2000): 419–22.

——. "'What Place, Then, for a Creator?': Hawking on God and Creation." In William Lane Craig and Quentin Smith, *Theism, Atheism, and Big Bang Cosmology.* Oxford: Clarendon Press (1993): 288–300.

Craig, William Lane, and Quentin Smith. *Theism, Atheism, and Big Bang Cosmology*. Oxford: Clarendon Press, 1993.

Cullison, Andrew. "Two Solutions to the Problem of Divine Hiddenness." *American Philosophical Quarterly* 47, no. 2 (2010): 119–34.

Davies, Paul. *The Accidental Universe*. Cambridge: Cambridge University Press, 1982.

——. *Superforce: The Search for a Grand Unified Theory of Nature*. New York: Simon and Schuster, 1984.

Davison, Scott A. "Divine Providence and Human Freedom." In Michael J. Murray, ed., *Reason for the Hope Within*. Grand Rapids, MI: Eerdmans (1999): 217–37.

Dennett, Daniel C. *Consciousness Explained*. Boston: Little, Brown, and Co., 1991.

——. "Quining Qualia." In A. Marcel and E. Bisiach, eds., *Consciousness in Contemporary Science*. New York: Oxford University Press (1988): 42–77.

Descartes, René. *Meditations on First Philosophy*. In *The Philosophical Works of Descartes*, vol. I, trans. Elizabeth S. Haldane and C.R.T. Ross. London: Cambridge University Press, 1977, 131–99.

Dilley, Frank B. "Taking Consciousness Seriously: A Defense of Cartesian Dualism." *International Journal for Philosophy of Religion* 55 (2004): 135–53.

Draper, Paul. "Seeking But Not Believing: Confessions of a Practicing Agnostic." In Daniel Howard–Snyder and Paul Moser, eds., *Divine Hiddenness: New Essays*. Cambridge University Press, 2001, 197–214.

——. "The Skeptical Theist." In Daniel Howard-Snyder, ed., *The Evidential Argument from Evil*. Bloomington and Indianapolis: Indiana University Press (1996): 175–92.

Edwards, Paul. *Reincarnation: A Critical Examination*. Amherst, NY: Prometheus Books, 1996.

Ellis, George F. R. "Physics in the Real Universe: Time and Space-Time." In Vesselin Petkov, ed., *Relativity and the Dimensionality of the World*. Montreal: Springer, 2007, 49–80.

Finch, Alicia, and Ted A. Warfield. "The *Mind* Argument and Libertarianism." *Mind* 107, no. 427 (July, 1998): 515–28.

Finnis, John. *Natural Law and Human Rights*, 2nd ed. Oxford: Oxford University Press, 2011.

Flint, Thomas P. *Divine Providence: The Molinist Account*. Ithaca, NY: Cornell University Press, 1998.

Floyd, Shawn. "Thomas Aquinas: Moral Philosophy." In James Fieser and Bradley Dowden, general editors, *Internet Encyclopedia of Philosophy*. http://www.iep.utm.edu/.

Frankfurt, Harry. "Alternate Possibilities and Moral Responsibility." *Journal of Philosophy*, 66, no. 23 (December 4, 1969): 829–39.

Goldschmidt, Tyron, and Beth Seacord. "Judaism, Reincarnation, and Theodicy." *Faith and Philosophy* 30, no. 4 (October 2013): 393–417.

Green, Joel B. *Body, Soul, and Human Life: The Nature of Humanity in the Bible*. Grand Rapids, MI: Baker Academic, 2008.

Hackett, Stuart C. *Oriental Philosophy: A Westerner's Guide to Eastern Thought*. Madison: University of Wisconsin Press, 1979.

Hasker, William. *God, Time, and Knowledge*. Ithaca, NY: Cornell University Press, 1989.

———. "The Foreknowledge Conundrum." *International Journal for Philosophy of Religion* 50, no. 1/3 (December 2001): 97–114.

———. *Providence, Evil, and the Openness of God*. New York: Routledge, 2004.

———. "Theism and Evolutionary Biology." In Philip Quinn and Charles Taliaferro, eds., *A Companion to Philosophy of Religion*. Oxford: Blackwell, 2000: 426–32.

Hawking, Stephen. *A Brief History of Time: From the Big Bang to Black Holes*. NY: Bantam Books, 1988.

Heil, John. "Philosophy of Mind." In Leemon McHenry and Frederick Adams, eds., *Reflections on Philosophy: Introductory Essays*. New York: St. Martin's Press (1993): 165–85.

Helm, Paul. "The Augustinian-Calvinist View." In James K. Beilby and Paul R. Eddy, eds., *Divine Foreknowledge: Four Views*. Downers Grove, IL: IVP Academic, 2001: 161–89.

———. "Divine Timeless Eternity." In Gregory E. Ganssle, ed., *God and Time*. Downers Grove, IL: IVP Academic, 2001: 28–60.

Henry, C. F. "The Good as the Will of God." In William K. Frankena and John T. Granrose, eds., *Introductory Readings in Ethics*. Englewood Cliffs, NJ: Prentice-Hall, 1974, 95–99.

Hick, John. *Philosophy of Religion*, 4th ed. Englewood Cliffs, NJ: Prentice-Hall, 1990.

Howard-Snyder, Daniel. "The Argument from Inscrutable Evil." In Daniel Howard-Snyder, ed., *The Evidential Argument from Evil*. Bloomington: Indiana University Press, 1996: 286–310.

———. "Divine Openness and Creaturely Non-Resistant Non-Belief." In Adam Green and Eleonore Stump, eds., *Hidden Divinity and Religious Belief: New Perspectives*. Cambridge: Cambridge University Press, 2015, 126–38.

Hume, David. *Dialogues Concerning Natural Religion*, ed. Richard H. Popkin. Indianapolis, IN: Hackett, 1980.

Hunt, David. "The Simple Foreknowledge View." In James K. Beilby and Paul R. Eddy, eds., *Divine Foreknowledge: Four Views*. Downers Grove, IL, IVP Academic, 2001: 65–103.

Hursthouse, Rosalind. "Virtue Theory and Abortion." In Roger Crisp and Michael Slote, eds., *Virtue Ethics*. Oxford: Oxford University Press, 1997, 217–38.

Huxley, Thomas H. "On the Hypothesis That Animals Are Automata, and Its History." *Fortnightly Review* 22 (1874): 555–80.

James, William. *Principles of Psychology*, vol. 1. New York: Henry Holt, 1890.

———. *The Varieties of Religious Experience*. New York: New American Library, 1958.

Jeeves, Malcolm, ed. *From Cells to Souls—And Beyond: Changing Portraits of Human Nature*. Grand Rapids, MI: Eerdmans, 2004.

Kant, Immanuel. *Groundwork of the Metaphysic of Morals*, trans., H.J. Paton. New York: Harper and Row, 1964.

Kaufman, Whitely R.P. "Karma, Rebirth, and the Problem of Evil." *Philosophy East and West* 55, no. 1 (January 2005): 15–32.

Kelly, Emily Williams, ed. *Science, the Self, and Survival after Death: Selected Writings of Ian Stevenson*. New York: Rowman and Littlefield, 2013.

Kierkegaard, Søren. *Concluding Unscientific Postscript*, trans. David F. Swenson and Walter Lowrie. Princeton, NJ: Princeton University Press, 1941.

———. *Philosophical Fragments*, trans David Swenson. Princeton, NJ: Princeton University Press, 1936.

Kim, Jaegwon. *The Philosophy of Mind*, 2nd ed. Cambridge, MA: Westview Press, 2006.

———. *Physicalism; or Something Near Enough*. Princeton, NJ: Princeton University Press, 2005.

Koperski, Jeffrey. *The Physics of Theism: God, Physics, and the Philosophy of Science*. Oxford: Wiley Blackwell, 2015.

Kripke, Saul. *Naming and Necessity*. Cambridge, MA: Harvard University Press, 1972.

Law, Stephen. "The Evil-God Challenge." *Religious Studies* 46, no. 3 (September 2010): 353–73.

Layman, C. Stephen. "God and the Moral Order." *Faith and Philosophy* 19, no. 3 (July 2002): 304–16.

———. *Philosophical Approaches to Atonement, Incarnation, and the Trinity.* New York: Palgrave Macmillan, 2016.

Leslie, John. *Universes.* New York: Routledge, 1989.

Lewis, C. S. *Mere Christianity.* New York: Macmillan, 1958.

Maitzen, Stephen. "Divine Hiddenness and the Demographics of Theism." *Religious Studies* 42 (2006): 177–91.

Markosian, Ned. "What Are Physical Objects?" *Philosophy and Phenomenological Research* 61 (2000): 375–95.

Marsh, Jason. "Darwin and the Problem of Natural Nonbelief." *Monist* 96, no. 3 (2013): 349–76.

McCann, Hugh J. "Pointless Suffering? How to Make the Problem of Evil Sufficiently Serious." In Jonathan Kvanvig, ed., *Oxford Studies in Philosophy of Religion*, vol. 2. Oxford: Oxford University Press, 2009: 161–84.

McMullin, Ernan. "Fine-Tuning the Universe?" In Mark H. Shale and George W. Shields, eds., *Science, Technology, and Religious Ideas.* New York: University Press of America, 1994: 97–125.

Mill, John Stuart. *Utilitarianism.* New York: Bobbs-Merrill, 1957.

Molina, Luis de. *On Divine Foreknowledge: Part IV of the Concordia*, trans. with introduction by Alfred J. Freddoso. Ithaca, NY: Cornell University Press, 1988.

Moore, Dwayne. "Mind and the Causal Exclusion Problem." In *Internet Encyclopedia of Philosophy.* https://www.iep.utm.edu/causal-e/.

Morris, Thomas V. *Our Idea of God: An Introduction to Philosophical Theology.* Downers Grove, IL: IVP Academic, 1991.

Murphy, Mark. "The Natural Law Tradition in Ethics." *Stanford Encyclopedia of Philosophy* (Winter 2011 ed.), ed. Edward N. Zalta. http://plato.stanford.edu/archives/win2011/entries/natural-law-ethics/.

Murphy, Nancey. "Nonreductive Physicalism: Philosophical Issues." In Warren S. Brown, Nancey Murphy, and H. Newton Maloney, eds., *Whatever Happened to the Soul? Scientific and Theological Portraits of Human Nature.* Minneapolis, MN: Fortress Press (1998): 127–48.

Nagel, Thomas. "What Is It Like to Be a Bat?" *Philosophical Review* 83 (1974): 435–50.

Perrett, Roy. "Karma and the Problem of Suffering." *Sophia* 24, no. 1 (April 1985): 4–10.

Pinnock, Clark. *Most Moved Mover: A Theology of God's Openness*. Grand Rapids, MI: Baker, 2001.

Plantinga, Alvin. *God, Freedom, and Evil*. New York: Harper and Row, 1974.

———. "Materialism and Christian Belief." In Peter van Inwagen and Dean Zimmerman, eds., *Persons: Human and Divine*. Oxford: Clarendon Press, 2007, 99–141.

———. "On Ockham's Way Out." *Faith and Philosophy* 3, no. 3 (July 1986): 235–69.

———. *Warranted Christian Belief*. New York: Oxford University Press, 2000.

Plato. "Phaedo." In *Five Dialogues*, trans. G.M.A. Grube. Indianapolis, IN: Hackett, 1981, 93–155.

Polkinghorne, John. *Science and Theology: An Introduction*. Minneapolis, MN: Fortress Press, 1998.

Putnam, Hilary. "Psychological Predicates." In W.H. Capitan and D.D. Merrill, eds., *Art, Mind, and Religion*. Pittsburgh, PA: University of Pittsburgh Press, 1967, 37–48.

Robb, David, and John Heil. "Mental Causation." In *Stanford Encyclopedia of Philosophy* (Spring 2014 ed.), ed. Edward N. Zalta. http://plato.stanford .edu/archives/spr2014/entries/mental-causation/.

Rowe, William. *Philosophy of Religion: An Introduction*, 2nd ed. Belmont, CA: Wadsworth, 1993.

———. "The Problem of Evil and Some Varieties of Atheism." *American Philosophical Quarterly* 16, no. 4 (October, 1979): 335–41.

Savitt, Steven. "Being and Becoming in Modern Physics." In *Stanford Encyclopedia of Philosophy* (Fall 2017 ed.), ed. Edward N. Zalta. https://plato .stanford.edu/archives/fall2017/entries/spacetime-bebecome/.

Schellenberg, John. *Divine Hiddenness and Human Reason*. Ithaca, NY: Cornell University Press, 1993.

———. "What Divine Hiddenness Reveals; or, How Weak Theistic Evidence Is Strong Atheistic Proof." In *The Secular Web*. http://www.infidels.org /library/modern/john_schellenberg/hidden.html.

———. *Wisdom to Doubt: A Justification of Religious Skepticism*. Ithaca, NY, and London: Cornell University Press, 2007.

Searle, John. *Mind: A Brief Introduction*. Oxford: Oxford University Press, 2004.

——. *Minds, Brains, and Science*. Cambridge, MA: Harvard University Press, 1984.

Shoemaker, Sydney. *Self-Knowledge and Self-Identity*. Ithaca, NY: Cornell University Press, 1963.

Singer, Peter. "Famine, Affluence, and Morality." *Philosophy and Public Affairs* 1, no. 1 (1972): 229–43.

Skinner, B. F. *Beyond Freedom and Dignity*. Indianapolis: Hackett, 1971.

Smart, J. J. C. "Sensations and Brain Processes." *Philosophical Review* 68 (1959): 141–56.

Stark, Rodney. *Discovering God: A New Look at the Origins of the Great Religions*. New York: Harper Collins, 2007.

Stevenson, Ian. *Twenty Cases Suggestive of Reincarnation*, 2nd ed. Charlottesville: University Press of Virginia, 1974.

——. "Birthmarks and Birth Defects Corresponding to Wounds on Deceased Persons: 1993." In Kelly, ed., *Science, the Self, and Survival after Death*, 263–78.

——. "Reincarnation: Field Studies and Theoretical Issues." In Kelly, ed., *Science, the Self, and Survival after Death*, 201–27.

——. "Some New Cases Suggestive of Reincarnation: The Case of Ampan Petcherat: 1973." In Kelly, ed., *Science, the Self, and Survival after Death*, 229–50.

Swinburne, Richard. *The Coherence of Theism*. Oxford: Oxford University Press, 1977.

——. *The Existence of God*, rev. ed. Oxford: Clarendon Press, 1991.

——. *Providence and the Problem of Evil*. Oxford: Clarendon Press, 1998.

——. "What Difference Does God Make to Morality?" In Robert K. Garcia and Nathan L. King, eds., *Is Goodness without God Good Enough?* New York: Rowman and Littlefield, 2009, 151–55.

Tegmark, Max. "Parallel Universes." *Scientific American* (May 2003): 41–51.

Thomson, Judith Jarvis. *The Realm of Rights*. Cambridge, MA: Harvard University Press, 1990.

Tooley, Michael. *Time, Tense, and Causation*. Oxford: Oxford University Press, 1997.

Underhill, Evelyn. *Mysticism: The Nature and Development of Spiritual Consciousness*. Oxford: Oneworld Publications, 1999; first published 1910.

Unger, Peter. *Living High and Letting Die: Our Illusion of Innocence*. Oxford: Oxford University Press, 1996.

Upaniṣads, trans. Patrick Olivelle. Oxford: Oxford University Press, 1996.

van Lawick-Goodall, Hugo and Jane. *Innocent Killers*. Boston, MA: Houghton Mifflin, 1970.

van Inwagen, Peter. *An Essay on Free Will*. Oxford: Clarendon Press, 1983.

———. "Genesis and Evolution." In *God, Knowledge, and Mystery: Essays in Philosophical Theology*. Ithaca, NY: Cornell University Press, 1995: 128–62.

———. *Metaphysics*. Boulder: Westview Press, 1993.

Wainwright, William. *Philosophy of Religion*. Belmont, CA: Wadsworth, 1988.

Ward, Keith. "The Evil God Challenge: A Response." *Think* 14, no. 40 (Summer 2015): 43–49.

Warren, Henry Clarke. *Buddhism in Translations: Passages Selected from the Buddhist Sacred Books and Translated from the Original Pâli into English*. Cambridge, MA: Harvard University Press, 1896. http://www.sacred-texts.com/bud/bits/bit-2.htm.

Webb, Mark. "Religious Experience." In *Stanford Encyclopedia of Philosophy* (Winter 2011 ed.), ed. Edward N. Zalta. http://plato.stanford.edu/archives/win2011/entries/religious-experience/.

Weil, Simone. *Waiting for God*. New York: Harper, 1951.

Wesley, John. "The General Deliverance" (Sermon 60). In Albert C. Outler, ed., *The Works of John Wesley*, vol. 2. Nashville, TN: Abingdon Press, 1985, 436–50.

White, Roger. "Fine-Tuning and Multiple Universes." *Noûs* 34, no. 2 (2000): 260–76.

Widerker, David. "Frankfurt's Attack on the Principle of Alternative Possibilities." *Philosophical Review* 104 (1995): 247–61.

Wielenberg, Erik J. "Omnipotence Again." *Faith and Philosophy* 17, no. 1 (January, 2000): 26–47.

Wiggins, David. *Identity and Spatio-Temporal Continuity*. Oxford: Basil Blackwell, 1967.

Wolterstorff, Nicholas. *Justice in Love*. Grand Rapids, MI: Eerdmans, 2011.

———. *Justice: Rights and Wrongs*. Princeton, NJ, and Oxford: Princeton University Press, 2008.

Yandell, Keith, and Harold Netland. *Buddhism: A Christian Exploration and Appraisal*. Downers Grove, IL: IVP Academic, 2009.

Zimmerman, Dean. "The Privileged Present: Defending an 'A-Theory' of Time." In Theodore Sider, John Hawthorne, and Dean Zimmerman, eds.,

Contemporary Debates in Metaphysics. Hoboken, NJ: Blackwell, 2008, 211–25.

INDEX

and naturalism, 62–66, 204,
210–11
and soul-making theodicy, 55
naturalism, 3–4
arguments for, 4–8
natural law theory, of ethics, 127–29,
137–45
objections to, 145–50
natural nonbelief, 123
necessary being, 3, 15–17, 19
necessary falsehood, 16–17
necessary moral truths, 131–33
necessary truths, 2, 16
as related to middle knowledge,
171
neuro-computer, 32–33, 157, 160
non-reductive physicalism, 193–94,
205–6
normative relativism, 128
no-see-um inference, 102, 106
numerical identity, 234

objective truth, 38, 82
omnipresence, 257n.4
omniscience, 2, 152, 179–80
open theism, 176–79
epistemic and truth-value types,
178
Origen, 155
overrider response, to the problem
of evil, 47
overriding reasons thesis, 39, 42–43,
79–85

pairing problem, 219–21
perfectly morally good, 1
Perrett, Roy, 242
person, defining, 233
Peter (apostle), 98, 101
phenomena of suffering, 62–63,
210–11
Plantinga, Alvin, 218, 220
Plato, 191
Polkinghorne, John, 28
possible prophet objection, 163

principle of conservation of energy,
217
principle of credulity, 11, 12
principle of simplicity, 5, 74, 209,
198
doubts about, 263n.18
principle of sufficient reason, 19
prior probability, 73
probabilistic law, 36, 61, 214
problem of cruel and wicked punishments, 246–47
problem of evil, 45–46
proportionality problem, 245–46
proximate cause, 14
psychological continuity theory, of
personal identity, 236–39
punishment theodicy, 51

qualia, 199, 202, 204
qualitative identity, 234
quantum vacuum, 258n.6

reasonable non-belief (or non-theism), 7, 89, 109, 119–21
in relation to skeptical theism,
101–4
reductive physicalism, 64, 191–92
problems for, 199–204
reincarnation, 225
support for, 227–30
religious experience, 9–10
Rowe, William, 45, 57–58

same-body view, of personal identity, 234–35
same-brain theory, of personal identity, 235–36
same-soul theory, of personal identity, 239
Schellenberg, John, 7, 89–91, 109,
118–22
scientism, 259n.30
Seacord, Beth, 225, 246
Searl, John, 64, 200, 202
secondary cause, 156–57

C. Stephen Layman
is professor emeritus of philosophy at Seattle Pacific University.
He is the author of five books, including *The Shape of the Good*
(University of Notre Dame Press, 1994) and most recently
Philosophical Approaches to Atonement, Incarnation, and the Trinity.

CPSIA information can be obtained
at www.ICGtesting.com
Printed in the USA
LVHW050430140122
708426LV00020B/2204

9 780268 202064